AZAN ON THE MOON

CENTRAL EURASIA IN CONTEXT SERIES
Douglas Northrop, Editor

AZAN ON THE MOON

ENTANGLING MODERNITY
ALONG TAJIKISTAN'S
PAMIR HIGHWAY

TILL MOSTOWLANSKY

UNIVERSITY OF PITTSBURGH PRESS

Small portions of chapter 1 and 5 appeared in earlier form in "The Road Not Taken: Enabling and Limiting Mobility in the Eastern Pamirs," *Internationales Asienforum / International Quarterly for Asian Studies* 45, nos. 1–2 (2014): 153–70.

Small portions of chapter 2 appeared in earlier form in "Paving the Way: Isma'ili Genealogy and Mobility along Tajikistan's Pamir Highway," *Journal of Persianate Studies* 4 (2011): 171–88, and in "Making Kyrgyz Spaces: Local History as Spatial Practice in Murghab (Tajikistan)," *Central Asian Survey* 31, no. 3 (2012): 251–64.

Small portions of chapter 3 appeared in earlier form in "Humanitarianism Across Mountain Valleys: 'Shia Aid' and Development Encounters in Northern Pakistan and Eastern Tajikistan," in *Mapping Transition in the Pamirs: Changing Human-Environmental Landscapes*, edited by Hermann Kreutzmann and Teiji Watanabe (Dordrecht: Springer, 2016), 229–44.

Small portions of chapter 5 appeared in earlier form in "'The State Starts from the Family': Peace and Harmony in Tajikistan's Eastern Pamirs," *Central Asian Survey* 32, no. 4 (2013): 462–74.

Cover art: Photomontage incorporating photos by Bernd Hrdy
Cover design by Alex Wolfe

For Brook and the paradise birds of Murghab.

CONTENTS

ACKNOWLEDGMENTS

At one point during my fieldwork in Tajikistan, a baby boy died in the family with whom I was living. Shortly after the sad incident, his mother explained to me that children of a young age were *nariste*—sinless and pure—beings. She told me that she believed her son had been transformed into a colorful bird and was now winging his way through paradise. In commemoration of him, I dedicate this book to all *nariste* who play, shout, and cry along the Pamir Highway and make the region a lively place of beauty.

This book is the product of a long-lasting engagement with people who live in or feel connected to places in Tajikistan's Gorno-Badakhshan Autonomous Region. Without their willingness to interact, their openness, support, and courage, this study would not have been possible. In order to protect their identities, I cannot thank them individually. Instead I would like to express my gratitude with a collective "thank you" in Kyrgyz, Shughni, Tajik, Russian, and Dari: *Yrakhmat! Qulogh! Rakhmat! Spasibo! Tashakor!*

This book started to take shape at the University of Bern, where I am deeply indebted to Karénina (Nina) Kollmar-Paulenz, and from a distance at the University of Manchester, where Madeleine Reeves, with her deep anthropological understanding of Central Asia, has been a constant source of inspiration and motivation. I have profited hugely from both Nina's and Madeleine's expertise and cannot thank them enough for their support. Throughout this project Magnus Marsden, previously at SOAS in London and now at the University of Sussex, provided me with guidance, important feedback, crucial institutional support, and fascinating insights into the anthropology of Afghanistan, Pakistan, and Tajikistan.

At the University of Bern, I am grateful to the Faculty of Humanities, the UniBern Research Foundation, and the Burgergemeinde Bern, which supported my fieldwork financially, and to several people who have critically addressed parts of this study in research colloquia, namely, Susanne Leuenberger, Sébastien Mayor, Frank Neubert, Seline Reinhardt, Jens Schlieter, and Sarah Werren. I have furthermore profited from frequent discussions and fruitful collaboration with Andrea Rota, with whom I had the pleasure of sharing an office in Bern.

Numerous people supported me during my research in Central Asia. In Khorog, I particularly thank Davlat, Khurshed, Mohigul, Nabot, Sash, and Shams; in Dushanbe, Bakhtiyor, Gulnora, Gulzira, and Joao; and in Osh, Mital Aka and his family. In Bishkek, I received support from the American University of Central Asia, in particular from the Social Research Center and the Central Asian Studies Institute, which granted me two visiting research fellowships, the first from February to August 2010 and the second from July to December 2013. In Bishkek, I furthermore thank Danyiar, Aizat, and Kolya. I would also like to express my gratitude to Diana Ibañez-Tirado and Aliaa Remtilla for their inspiring comments on my work and their hospitality in Tajikistan and the United Kingdom.

Special thanks go to Bernd Hrdy who, apart from contributing his images to this book, has also been a great friend and travel companion; to Markus Hauser, who contributed to my cartographic understanding of the region with his Pamir Archive; and to Hermann Kreutzmann and Tobias Kraudzun, who provided valuable advice and literature early on in this project.

At different stages of this book I have profited from my colleagues' feedback, critical readings, and other input. In this respect, I would like to express my gratitude to Sergei Abashin, Brian Donahoe, Zohra Ismail-Beben, Botakoz Kassymbekova, Julie McBrien, Robert Middleton, Patryk Reid, and David Straub. I am also indebted to Peter Kracht and Douglas Northrop, who took me on board the University of Pittsburgh Press Central Eurasia in Context Series, to Alex Wolfe, who guided me through the publication process and designed the cover, and to Michelle Filippini, who helped polish the manuscript.

As I went about finalizing this book, the Asia Research Institute (ARI) at the National University of Singapore provided me with the perfect environment to focus on revisions, and my colleagues at the ARI showed a great deal of interest in my work and care for my well-being. Their support has been crucial and I would like to express my sincere gratitude to them.

Finally, I would like to thank my parents, Vera Mostowlansky and Urs Lehmann, who have been there for me through it all, from beginning to end, and my wife, Brook Bolander, who, with her bright intellect and infinite support, has brought a never-ending parade of ideas, things, and people to my life and this book.

NOTE ON PEOPLE, PLACES, AND LANGUAGES

The names given for all my interlocutors who appear in this book are pseudonyms. I have, however, used real names for well-known public figures. The names of places are real, too. Where they exist, I used the English version of place names. In all other cases, I applied versions that are officially used in the respective local contexts.

The way I address my anonymized interlocutors in this book corresponds to the concrete interactional contexts that I encountered during my fieldwork. In an environment in which several languages meet (Kyrgyz, Pamir languages, Russian, Tajik), there was not one clearly defined way to address people of different ages, gender, and ethnicities. The use of first names was common in conversations about third persons. As a result, I use first names to refer to most of my interlocutors. Yet when addressing a person directly I attempted to employ the correct pronouns for elder people (*siz* in Kyrgyz, *vy* in Russian, *shumo* in Tajik) and for those younger than myself (*sen* in Kyrgyz, *ty* in Russian, *tu* in Tajik). An exception is Kudaibergen, an elderly man whom I usually called *Ata*, which means "Father" in Kyrgyz.

Many quotations have been translated directly from recorded conversations. With the permission of my interlocutors, I made extensive use of my recording device. In this regard, I had the chance to record conversations during events such as memorial feasts, road trips, and family dinners. Switching between different languages in the course of one conversation is a common phenomenon along the Pamir Highway, where a speaker's language preference can change depending on first language, ethnicity, topic, education, political orientation, and language of his or her interlocutor. Interviews and records of everyday interaction reflect this linguistic complexity, which is why a single quote from my field data might exhibit the influence of several languages that have become part of a local linguistic repertoire. What might sometimes appear like a random mishmash of different languages to the observer—for example, when a Russian noun is followed by a Kyrgyz verb and complemented by an explanation in a Pamir language—is actually part of everyday normalcy along the highway.

In English translations I provide words from the source languages in parentheses (or brackets in those cases where I have inserted the words into direct quotations) whenever I consider them helpful for the understanding of those readers who know the respective language or when the meaning is ambiguous. All final translations in this book are my own. However, Aizat Aisarakunova from Bishkek patiently supported me with longer transcriptions and translations from Kyrgyz and Russian. In addition, friends in Khorog sometimes helped me with the evaluation of material in Tajik and Shughni.

The transliteration of Kyrgyz, Russian, and Tajik words largely follows the American Library Association and Library of Congress (ALA-LC). Romanization tables for Slavic alphabets. In the case of Kyrgyz, I applied the following changes to the ALA-LC standard: ж = j; ө = ö; y = ü; ң=ng. Since there is no standardized writing system (and therefore no standardized system of transliteration) for Pamir languages, I transliterated words in Shughni according to the ALA-LC system for Tajik. For the transliteration of authors' names and book titles I was guided by the source language.

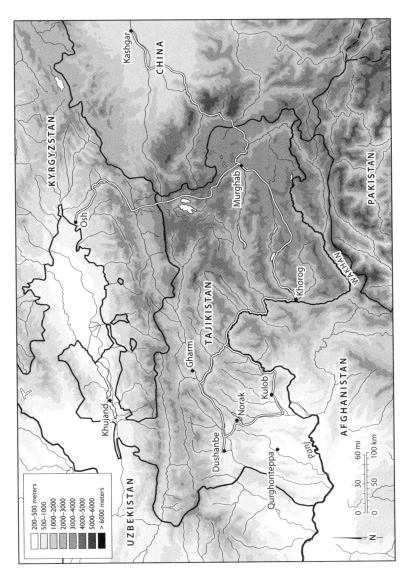

MAP 1. Tajikistan

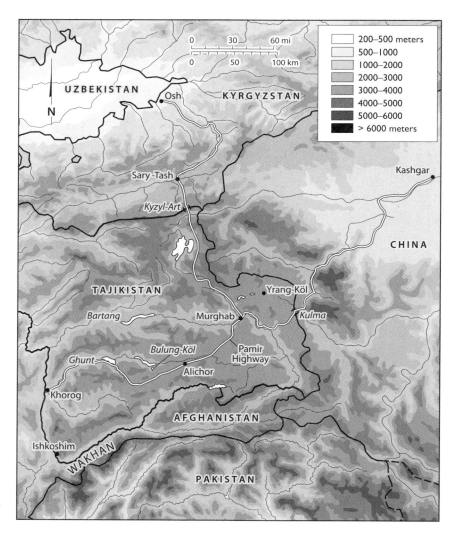

MAP 2. The Pamir Highway

THE MOON AND THE HIGHWAY

"What is this music?" From the street the melodious sound of the muezzin was heard. Rather surprised, the Egyptians tried to restrain their laughter and said, "That is not music, it's the *azan*. Like the church bells it calls the true believers to prayer." . . . [Neil] Armstrong's reply to this explanation was like a bolt out of the blue: "This voice. I heard it when I was first walking on the moon. It made my flesh crawl! In the beginning it seemed noisy, but over time listening to this voice made me feel good." Complete silence ensued in the hall. . . . Then Armstrong said: "Oh Allah, I didn't find you on earth but on the moon! . . . I stepped on the moon without a prayer, but now I'm going to pray. You can call me a Muslim now."

Nauka i fakty 2004, 5

In 2010, during a stay in Murghab, Tajikistan's easternmost district, my host and friend Nursultan gave me a stack of booklets on Islam. The passage above comes from one of these booklets, entitled *Science and Facts Give Evidence: "There is no God but God and Muhammad is his messenger."* The story of the alleged conversion of Neil Armstrong, American astronaut and first man to walk on the moon, at a conference in Egypt is popular throughout the region. On the one hand, the story's reference is emotionally close to the way people in Murghab and other settlements along the Pamir Highway experience the landscape they inhabit: as an arid and rocky high plateau that is sometimes called "the moon" (*ai, luna*) and often considered marginal and not quite part of this world by outsiders. In this regard, the *azan*—the Islamic call to prayer—literally stands for contemporary public expressions of Islam in Murghab. On the other hand, modern science (*sovremennaia nauka*) and technology as depicted in the booklet not only provide legitimacy for religious ideas but are generally an essential part of everyday debates in the region.

P.1. A stretch of the Pamir Highway in the district of Murghab. Photograph
© Bernd Hrdy, 2008.

To be or not to be "modern" (*muosir, sovremennyi, zamonavī, zaman-bap*) is a fundamental question in Murghab. While often considered an "out-of-the-way place" (Tsing 1993, 27), Murghab is in fact a place on the highway. A close look at the booklet *Science and Facts Give Evidence* demonstrates not only the attempt to legitimize Islam from a scientific point of view but also shows that people's lives along this highway are informed by both ancient and more recent trajectories of globalization. Originally developed in Russia and Turkey, the Russian-language booklet was printed in Kyrgyzstan's capital, Bishkek. From there traders transported it on the Pamir Highway (Pamirskii trakt) via Osh in the Ferghana Valley to Murghab.

Its stories are no less globalized than the booklet's physical origins. Almost all of them are narratives of the scientific foundations of Islam that are popular and widespread in the broader Muslim world. And most of them describe how scientists and explorers, the wise men of the modern day, use experiments, technology, and keen observation to prove that Islam is right and true. In return, religion leads to the perfection of such scientific assumptions, particularly through its all-encompassing emotional component. This is what Nursultan and I discussed after I had studied the booklet: because people tended to forget about the relation-

P.2. Entering the district of Murghab from the direction of Khorog. Photograph © Bernd Hrdy, 2008.

ship between these different spheres, he told me, his homeland had fallen into decay and despair.

Nursultan's homeland, Murghab, is part of Tajikistan's Gorno-Badakhshan Autonomous Region and borders Afghanistan, Kyrgyzstan, and China. Murghab has an ethnically (and confessionally) mixed Muslim population, most of which lives along the main artery, the Pamir Highway. The Pamir Highway connects the city of Osh in southern Kyrgyzstan with the town of Khorog in Tajikistan and dates back to the early 1930s, when the Soviets aimed to integrate the border region into the larger framework of the Union under Stalin. Starting in 1935, automobile traffic accelerated the speed of connectivity between Osh and Khorog. At the same time, it also transformed the social and physical landscapes of Murghab, the Pamir Highway's high-altitude transit district. As a result, in the course of the twentieth century Murghab was turned from an alleged no-man's land into an assemblage of roadside communities.

Unlike inhabitants of other regions of Gorno-Badakhshan and Tajikistan more generally, people in Murghab were not subjected to comparable large-scale forced resettlement in the Soviet era.[1] Migration and the transformation of demography and physical topography were often unintended side effects of Soviet road construction but are now remembered rather nostalgically for having stimulated job opportunities and prosperity. Born into a region of Soviet modernization projects and what is left of them, many people along the Pamir Highway have integrated debates on how to interpret these narratives of change into their everyday lives. Who belongs to the "realm of the modern" (*sovremennost'*) and who sticks to what is considered "old" (*kadim*) is a matter of constant negotiation. Far from being limited to spoken and written words, dichotomies of old and new, backwardness and progress, are embodied and expressed in everyday interaction, resulting in ever-provisional "projects" of modernity. Pursuing this observation, the guiding questions of this monograph are: How do people along the Pamir Highway negotiate, incorporate, modify, and reject different "projects" of modernity? How do they relate these "projects" to their own marginality? And what can this tell us about people's positionality in Tajikistan and the broader region?[2]

I argue that answers to these questions are important for understanding how people along the highway order their world and bring categories of identity and difference into existence. At the same time these answers help show why self-representation and the ways inhabitants of the region position themselves as communities often differ fundamentally from patterns of description that are ascribed to them by outsiders.

This book is based on ethnographic data that I gathered as a fellow inhabitant and traveler in and between various places along the Pamir Highway between 2008 and 2015. It aims to provide alternative perspectives on Tajikistan from the standpoints of people who live in places that are usually referred to in terms of remoteness, disconnectedness, and marginality. In doing so, it is meant to address the ways these rubrics are challenged by local notions of the world.

TRAVELING INTO THIN AIR

In 2007, while working for a development project and living in Tajiki-stan's capital Dushanbe, I made many friends who traced their origins back to the mountain valleys in the east of the country. The moun-tains my friends referred to as their homeland, the Pamirs, are located in the Gorno-Badakhshan Autonomous Region (GBAO)[1] and span the borderlands where Afghanistan, Kyrgyzstan, and China meet. Gorno-Badakhshan is often perceived as an isolated backwater from a Dushanbe point of view, and the topos of remoteness frames depictions of GBAO. Descriptions of the Pamirs range from orientalist views of the region as a wild, romantic, spiritual place to a deserted mountain area that is in-habited by bellicose people.[2] While usually referred to as "far away" (*dur*) by people in Dushanbe, development reports and studies often label the Pamirs "extremely isolated" (Breu and Hurni 2003, 6) or "extremely pe-ripheral" (Vanselow 2011, 32). Discourses of natural beauty, spirituality, and danger, both in the sense of human aggression and natural disasters, derive from such notions of remoteness.

Many of my friends in Dushanbe, with or without origins in the Pamirs, associate the mountainous region with purity and health, speak-ing of hot springs, pilgrimage sites, and fresh mountain air, but also with destruction, referring to bad roads, landslides, and civil war. And yet only a very few people from western Tajikistan have actually been to the Pamirs, and even those who feel a genealogical connection to Gorno-Badakhshan often have an ambivalent attitude toward the region. For them it is not only their "homeland" or "motherland" (*vatan*), but also

I.1. A road maintenance outpost between Murghab and Osh. Photograph ©
Bernd Hrdy, 2009.

represents, on the one hand, a safe refuge and, on the other, boredom, and
it constitutes a place that often has to be left for a better life in Dushanbe
or abroad.

A trip from Dushanbe to Khorog, the capital of Gorno-Badakhshan,
can take anywhere from one hour to several days. When the weather is
good, a lucky, or privileged, minority of travelers can secure seats on a
small passenger plane. All others have to rely on private ground transport that is organized by drivers who regularly commute between the
two places. If the final destination is located even farther to the east in
the district of Murghab, travel time increases from one to several additional days, depending on season, weather, road conditions, and vehicle.
Many people in the eastern parts of Gorno-Badakhshan therefore orient
themselves toward the city of Osh in southern Kyrgyzstan which, even
when the road is in bad shape, can usually be reached within a day or
two.

From a Khorogi point of view, the image of the stretch of road to Osh
in southern Kyrgyzstan, which traverses the district of Murghab, is often
that of a deserted, wild, and unhealthy land. High altitude (above 4,000
meters), the lack of oxygen, the tendency of strange dreams to occur, and
rumors of unpleasant ghosts make the place undesirable to visit. And just

as I did not find many people in Dushanbe who had been to the "remote" Pamirs, during my fieldwork I also did not meet many from Khorog who had been to the even more "remote" Murghab. While some had stopped in Murghab's district center (also called Murghab) on the way to Osh, hardly anyone could remember more than Kyrgyz herders with their herds of yaks and flocks of sheep and a handful of scattered settlements where life could only be imagined as unbearably difficult. A conversation I had in 2009 with a young scholar from Khorog who had just completed a degree in political science at a university in Great Britain emphasizes the extent to which Murghab is subject to cultural and geographic fragmentation within Gorno-Badakhshan. Indeed, after having read Edward Said's book *Orientalism* while he was in Great Britain, he stated that people in Murghab were "our oriental others."[3]

The "double remoteness" of the settlements along the road between Khorog and Osh is also reflected in the literature on Murghab, which paints a picture of an archaic wasteland that is inhabited by Kyrgyz cattle breeders.[4] Thus, when I decided to pursue my first period of fieldwork for my doctoral dissertation on the communities along Tajikistan's Pamir Highway in the summer of 2008, I had little more to rely on than the stereotyped image of a rough and impoverished land far away from everyone and everything. This lack of knowledge on Murghab defined my initial fieldwork preparations. None of my urban friends in Dushanbe and few people in Khorog could really give me any advice on how to plan an enterprise like this, let alone provide me with contacts in Murghab with whom I could potentially stay. Advice ranged from buying a military jeep for transportation to bringing my own food and piles of special clothes to help me ward off the Arctic cold the Pamirs are infamous for in the flatlands. Only when I became friends with border guards from Khorog and their Murghabi fellow soldiers did things become easier. I bought a white secondhand four-wheel-drive Lada Niva at the bazaar in Dushanbe and a satellite phone for emergencies, and I was given the address of a friend of a friend in Murghab.

THE HIGHWAY AS FIELD

My fieldwork actually began when I climbed into my newly purchased car and left behind the last houses of Khorog in the summer of 2008, accompanied by a close friend, the Austrian photographer Bernd Hrdy. Nowadays, the only way to reach Murghab from the flatlands and lower mountain areas is the road that stretches out from Khorog to Osh in southern Kyrgyzstan. The road, informally known as the Pamir Highway (*Pamirskii trakt*), is part of highway M41, which leads from Termiz in southern Uzbekistan via Tajikistan to Kara-Balta, a town a few kilometers west of Kyrgyzstan's capital, Bishkek.

For many travelers, the town of Murghab, with its approximately seven thousand inhabitants, is just a stopover along this dusty, high-altitude stretch of road. However, for people who live along this stretch, Murghab is the road's center and is inextricably linked with its history, geography, and administration. From this vantage point, Murghab is transformed from a peripheral settlement along the road into the link that connects Khorog and Osh and therefore becomes central itself. Located on the plateau high above the road's termini, Murghab offers its inhabitants at least two directions in which to turn: toward Osh and toward Khorog. This feature, in combination with the fact that Murghabis have gotten used to living along this difficult and often mutable stretch of road, reinforces the agency they can exert on the road and turns the Pamir Highway into a place that they shape.

When Bernd and I set off for Murghab in my white Lada Niva, we came across countless remnants of what once belonged to the Soviet road infrastructure, including deserted gas stations, checkpoints, shelters for truck drivers, sanatoriums, and, suggestive of the present and future of the region, a terminal for China trade. The communities that had been established to maintain this infrastructure, to build and sustain the road, are still linked together. In the effort to maintain an open way through the Pamirs' mountain valleys and the high plateau of Murghab, transportation relations were established that have outlasted the Soviet empire that created them. Yet only after visits to many settlements along the road was I able to see that strong kin, friendship, and professional connections had also been established between and within these communities.

With the town of Murghab as the highway's center, many of the road's outposts originate from, relate to, or depend on the settlement. On the first trip to Murghab in 2008, my car broke down in close proximity to such an outpost. Damage to the gearbox had stranded us on one of the mountain passes between Khorog and Murghab and was proof of my complete ignorance of Russian cars at that time.[5] As I soon found out, the bazaar traders in Dushanbe had realized I was a novice and sold me a Niva that was stuffed with cheap Chinese parts. Fortunately, a military vehicle eventually towed us late that night to Mamazair, an outpost for road construction workers, from where I was able to call the family whose

I.2. A car repair workshop along the Pamir Highway. Photograph © Bernd Hrdy, 2008.

contact details I had been given in Dushanbe. As it turned out we had to spend a day in Mamazair before support and spare parts could be brought from the district center. This gave me an initial impression of life in a road-maintenance outpost and encouraged me to visit many more such places where road workers live with their families.

Our arrival in Murghab the next day was not as I had imagined it prior to departure. Being towed to my field site was not only embarrassing but also established my initial role and identity in my new home and neighborhood—that of a rather hapless foreigner in need of guidance. Nursultan, the man behind the contact address, helped us out of Mamazair that first day, and it would not be the last time he would come to my rescue when I got stuck in the middle of nowhere. He, and later on his wife Gulira, became close friends in Murghab.

In contrast to my initial embarrassment and dependence on the first people I met, there were also positive effects that came with my inability to pretend I was local. My vehicular breakdowns, which occurred on a regular basis and in almost every part of the district, made me a rather well-known figure in and around Murghab. On numerous occasions strangers would approach me and ask, "Aren't you the guy whose white Niva with Dushanbe number plates broke down in my village some time ago?" Thus the breakdowns were not only a source of embarrassment—

they also opened doors and gave me the opportunity to make new contacts and interview people.

The day of our arrival from Mamazair was the beginning of a slow integration process into Nursultan and Gulira's family. While I have lived with several other families along the Pamir Highway for extended periods of time since that first visit in 2008, Nursultan and Gulira gave me a home I could always go back to. In addition, their large circle of family members and friends allowed me to extend my network of people from the town of Murghab to various other places along the road.

This book is based on the ethnographic data I began to gather during that first trip and continued to gather over the course of more than fifteen months of fieldwork conducted from 2008 to 2015. Except for the last fieldwork period in 2013 and a shorter follow-up visit in 2015, I lived in Murghab as a single man. At the beginning of my research in Tajikistan, I was twenty-seven years old and thus considered a man on the far edge of marriageable age. Being unmarried and "around thirty" is atypical for men in Murghab; it usually raises suspicions and is seen as suggestive of problems. In my case, within Nursultan and Gulira's family it gave me a status best described as "older brother-and-uncle" (*aka*), no longer the "son" (*bala*) I had been considered in my previous fieldwork experiences in Kyrgyzstan.[6] On the one hand, this change of social status led to an initial distance from family members. On the other hand, it lent a certain gravitas to my research and granted me the authority to enter into discussions with elders. While I had been regarded a "boy" (*jash bala*) during previous fieldwork in Kyrgyzstan, I was now a peer to many of the family members and the odd *aka* to the children in the house and neighborhood.

At the beginning of my fieldwork, I gave priority to conducting open interviews to learn more about people's lives in the region, a perspective that had rarely been explored from an anthropological point of view. Furthermore, I participated in official and private events such as weddings, national celebrations, life-cycle rituals, election campaigns, funerals, Friday prayers, and memorial days. In addition, I met with district officials to discuss their opinions on my research topic and questions and to gather statistical information. After a while people started to recognize me and would sometimes approach me of their own accord.

During my first stay in Murghab in 2008, I concentrated my interviewing and participant-observation efforts on the town. As my research progressed I soon began to look beyond the district center. In the course of collecting life stories and narratives of mobility and tracing family networks and transnational connections, it became clear that concentrating exclusively on the town would not do justice to the way people perceive and situate themselves in the world. The Pamir Highway as a cross-border link between the cities of Osh in southern Kyrgyzstan and Khorog at the Tajikistan-Afghanistan border still determines many aspects of life in Murghab, as do the villages and road maintenance outposts between these two cities. This is why, after my first visit, I began to accompany people along the Pamir Highway and beyond as a fellow traveler and interlocutor. In doing so, I also tried to do justice to the broader meaning that the highway has for the people who live on and along it. As a result, I visited and stayed with people along the road, met their old companions from the army and work, and observed how they maintained kin relations, established new friendships, pursued economic opportunities, and became different people in different places.

On the one hand, people along the Pamir Highway make use of the road as travelers on a pathway. At the same time, many of them have also long been involved in making and maintaining the highway as a place in the course of constant construction and repair work.[7] Thus, in addition to people's mobility on and along the road, the highway, in its historical and present materiality, fosters the "cementing" of social relations (Harvey 2010). As a territorializing entity, the Pamir Highway also gives us, like many others roads, insights into "modern state formation" (Harvey and Knox 2008, 80) and highlights the importance of the material base that goes hand in hand with cultural change.[8] Hence, following Matei Candea (2007, 181), this book is an attempt to conceive of Tajikistan's Pamir Highway as a "window into complexity" that allows us to view a panoply of sociality but which can never be a "holistic entity to be explained."

NAVIGATING THROUGH THE FIELD

The people with whom I interacted in the field are different in age, gender, language, ethnicity, religion, and profession. Baktygül, for instance, is an elderly Kyrgyz woman who used to be employed as a teacher and childcare worker in the Soviet Union and later became a leading figure in the field of herbal healing in Murghab. As a "heroine mother" (*mat'-geroinia*) of ten, she spends her time commuting between various places in Murghab, Osh, Khorog, and Dushanbe, following in the tracks of her children. Holiknazar, on the other hand, is a middle-aged Pamiri man whose family is spread out between Murghab, the mountain valley of Bartang, and Osh, where his wife is from. His life spans all these places. In contrast,

Kamal usually stays in Murghab because he is a busy and perpetually overworked government official; in his own words, "Somebody has to keep working up here." Yet he sends his wife to sanatoriums in Kyrgyzstan for treatments and his children to Dushanbe to study.

This short description of some of the people whose lives I shared between 2008 and 2015 and with many of whom I still keep in touch via e-mail, Facebook, WhatsApp, or phone illustrates the multiple points of orientation that are of great importance to people along the Pamir Highway. Such multiplicity naturally includes linguistic complexity, a result of the fact that people along the Pamir Highway maintain communication with one another and with individuals from a wide range of places both within and outside of Gorno-Badakhshan.

To live along the Pamir Highway means to be multilingual. Statistical data from the local government (*ökmöt*) in Murghab from 2015 list approximately twelve thousand of the district's fifteen thousand inhabitants as ethnic Kyrgyz, thereby implying that they speak Kyrgyz, a Turkic language of the Kipchak branch, as a first language. The remaining three thousand people are ambiguously labeled "Tajik," a term that refers to their ethnic categorization in official documents but hides the fact that at home the vast majority of these people do not speak Tajik, a southwestern Iranian language, but a range of Pamir languages that are not mutually intelligible to Tajik speakers.[9]

The question of language in Gorno-Badakhshan has been highly politicized since the early days of Soviet rule. In order to ensure, at least pro forma, a coherent Tajik Soviet Socialist Republic based on a majority of Tajik speakers, Soviet planners showed little appreciation for the distinct Pamir languages that are dominant throughout the region and across the borders in Afghanistan and China (Bergne 2007, 62). Despite the fact that Soviet ethnographers observed the emergence of a common Pamiri (*pomirī*) identity among speakers of Pamir languages as early as 1935 (Hirsch 2005, 279), Pamir languages received no official status beyond the right of usage and therefore do not qualify for either a standardized script or recognition as a language of instruction in schools (Straub 2014, 177).[10] Moreover, in the Soviet Union, many inhabitants of Gorno-Badakhshan developed a particular affinity for Russian, which used to be the dominant language of education in the region. As a result, with Tajik now the official national language, Russian still used for technical and international (*mezhdunarodnyi*) communication, and Kyrgyz and various Pamir languages spoken at home and in public, people along the Pamir

Highway often navigate among half a dozen languages in their everyday lives.[11]

Not surprisingly, the region's multilingualism presented a challenge to me as I conducted fieldwork along the Pamir Highway. Fortunately, the major languages represented in Murghab for the most part coincide with language training and practical experience that I received prior to 2008 in the course of my studies and field research across Central Asia. Thus I started my fieldwork with a working knowledge of Kyrgyz, Russian, and Tajik, and could add to this by studying Shughni, a Pamir language of southeastern Iranian origin, while in the field.

What brings together the main actors of this book in more general terms is their close attachment to Murghab as a region and to the Pamir Highway as a social landscape. The "social" in this landscape is visible through the connections they have established among themselves and with other individuals and particular places. One of my main aspirations in the course of my fieldwork was to be able to follow these connections, which are primarily ordered and organized along the road. In quantitative terms I traveled more than ten thousand kilometers along the Osh-Khorog road between 2008 and 2015. This figure includes trips in trucks, in shared taxis, and in my own car.

My mobility along the Pamir Highway, which is regarded as part of a sensitive border region, occasionally raised the concern of Tajikistan's secret service. The KGB, as the agency is still colloquially called, sometimes considered my movements suspicious. Even though I had permission from the Academy of Sciences in Dushanbe to conduct research in Murghab, my activities appeared strange to the agents. Talking to villagers, participating in life-cycle rituals, and spending my time in cars for the sake of being on the road did not meet the officials' expectations of proper research. As a lone foreign man, I did not match the image of the scholars who had come from Moscow and Leningrad to do research in Gorno-Badakhshan during the Soviet period. Back then, scientists traveled to the region in group expeditions and conducted research on flora and fauna rather than on roadside communities. And with a long history of espionage in the border region of Tajikistan, Afghanistan, and China in the nineteenth and twentieth centuries, I did not blame the authorities for keeping an eye on me.[12]

Conflict, aside from the problems with authorities, was a central theme during my time in the field. Yet it was not conflict on an individual, interpersonal level that evoked anxiety but notions of war on a broader scale.

From the beginning of my work along the Pamir Highway in 2008, the conflict in Afghanistan had been present in people's minds. In addition, in 2009 other violent events appeared on the agenda. By then the armed conflict in Tajikistan's Rasht Valley had begun and led to rumors of political dissolution and fears of the return of the civil war that had brought turmoil to the country in the 1990s.[13] At the same time, the Uyghur riots in the neighboring Chinese province of Xinjiang brought debates about violence and death to Murghab.[14] This was not only fostered by the geographic proximity of Xinjiang but also by the fact that many people in Murghab have relatives on the other side of the border in China. Another tragic and violent event during my fieldwork was the unrest in Osh, which began shortly after Kyrgyzstan had been politically destabilized in the spring of 2010.[15] In the aftermath of a coup d'état, ethnicized violence broke out in the city and caused immigrants from Murghab to temporarily or permanently flee back to the Pamirs. In this regard, the latter part of my fieldwork was informed by feelings of instability and insecurity that affected not only people along the highway but myself as well.[16]

With Osh set ablaze, my friends in the city scattered to the four winds. Some moved back to Murghab. Others left for Bishkek or even more distant places in Russia and Kazakhstan. Among these friends were Kyrgyz, Russians, Tajiks, and Uzbeks. But it was not only the dissolution of a sense of community that led to a change of attitude in Murghab toward southern Kyrgyzstan. When in the summer of 2010 there were no deliveries from the looted bazaar in Osh, confidence in the city as a major economic point of reference was shaken. To be sure, traders quickly found ways to reorganize commercial routes, and shortages of fruit and vegetables were limited to a brief period of time. Yet a sense of being surrounded by unrest increased during this period. In addition, in 2012 fighting between government forces and local militia broke out in Khorog and lasted for several days.[17] In Murghab, this further contributed to the feeling of being surrounded by violence. At the same time, Murghab constituted a kind of safe haven in a region of conflict. Indeed, the argument commonly voiced by people from Murghab had proven right in a sense: Murghab was "pure" (*taza*) and unaffected by immediate violence in troubled times because it was—like the moon—"far away" (*alys*).

RECORDING MODERNITY

Murghab's geographical remoteness puts a distance between people along the Pamir Highway and places of conflict in the surrounding flatlands.

Yet they are clearly not isolated; they are, on the contrary, closely connected to other places and actors, both within and outside the region. These connections become visible through, for instance, development projects in the region, China trade, the presence of transnational religious movements, drug and ruby trafficking, international trophy hunting, labor migration, and the presence of government agencies. Despite these ties beyond the Pamir Highway, Murghab has largely remained absent from research agendas and its position is still, as Willem van Schendel (2002, 651) has put it, that of an "area of no concern" in the margins of the nation-state.[18]

In the course of my fieldwork, people along the Pamir Highway frequently referred to their homeland's ambiguous status within Tajikistan, and "encounters across difference" (Tsing 2005, 3) with government officials, foreigners, and fellow citizens from the western parts of the country triggered heated debates. As a consequence, my interlocutors raised questions such as "Who are they and who are we?" "Who is more developed?" and "Who is modern and who is not?"

For example, in the early stages of my research in 2009 I spent a lot of time at a friend's house in Murghab that was quite different from any other building in the neighborhood: an antenna on the roof signaled the existence of a radio station inside the house. Years ago a development organization from Australia or New Zealand—no one really remembered—had installed radio stations all over Gorno-Badakhshan in order to achieve better communication in case of natural disaster. These radio stations have now gone out of fashion, as various companies have begun to establish mobile networks throughout the region. At that time, however, these solar-powered radio stations had a special status as a means of communication to far-distant villages. On the rather flat and sparsely populated high plateau of Murghab, few people really worry about disaster; even when earthquakes shook the desert they would often go unremarked upon. Thus, people usually turned to the disaster prevention network when they wanted to ask their relatives in the village what to bring from the bazaar, how grandmother was doing, and if they had finally found the errant yak. This subsequently turned houses with radio stations into places of high social density. People would come and go, share tea and bread, and exchange the latest news.

In addition to being a mere tool for local communication, these radio stations also encompassed aspects of global connection. No traveling was required to go beyond Gorno-Badakhshan—simply by switching the frequency people could hear voices from other countries and regions. Listening to what other people talked about to each other in everyday conversation, from Russia to Africa, turned the radio station into a small window on the world. Due to its capacity to transmit news and information in real time, the internationally sponsored radio station brought fragments of other parts of the world into the Murghabi house. In my presence, people listened to "strange" (*kyzyk*) and "incomprehensible" (*neponiatnye*) languages on the radio. They were also puzzled by Afghan radio operators who would sing love songs over the radio all day. Visitors to the house wondered why the guys in the neighboring country "had gone crazy again" (*s uma soshli*). In subsequent discussions, one common argument was that Afghans were still enmeshed in "savagery" (*dikost'*), hence there was no need to wonder about their absurdities. In other words, being "modern" distinguished the listeners from Afghans and they could thus not understand Afghan behavior anymore.[19]

People along the Pamir Highway frequently discussed such topics with reference to temporality and by drawing qualitative distinctions between themselves and those on the other side of the border, notably through the concepts of *kadim* and *sovremennyi*. *Kadim* primarily means "old" or "ancient," while the term *sovremennyi* is a Russian word that means "contemporary," "up to date" and, in a broader sense, "modern." These terms and respective synonyms and periphrases crop up frequently in my interview recordings and protocols from participant observation. In these data, debates about the role of "the old" and "the contemporary" (and their embodiments) predominate and surface in reference to such diverse spheres as gender, politics, morality, ethnicity, and religion.

Many of the interviews I conducted during my fieldwork were not simple dialogues between me and an interlocutor but conversations among three or more people. This setting resulted from the fact that houses along the Pamir Highway usually include only one heated room, where family members, guests, and sometimes coworkers assemble and chat. Thus, some meetings that had initially been planned as one-on-one interviews turned into long informal talks about everyday life in the region. Occasionally, the busiest of people would also take me on walks and visits to neighbors, allowing me to record their conversations. In such situations, the topics of discussion were not under my control and I took on the role of observer, interjecting a question for clarification once in a while.

My ethnographic data also point to the importance of the material foundations of modernity, ranging from infrastructure and technology to clothing. In this regard, Bruno Latour's (2007, 68) call to "follow the actors in their weaving through things" was of particular relevance in the course of my fieldwork. In a region where a road, the Pamir Highway, informs decisions relating to "progress" and "backwardness," infrastructural artifacts and objects moving along the highway become active participants that often influence people's course of action. Against this backdrop, this book builds on Göran Therborn's (2003) argument that modernity is not multiple but diversely "entangled." With reference to the concepts of "shared" and "connected" histories, such an approach seeks to avoid a priori categorical definitions of different "modernities" such as, for instance, Western, Islamic, and Soviet.[20] Instead, and with reference to Shalini Randeria, Martin Fuchs, and Antje Linkenbach (2004), this book's focus lies on the processual character of modernity in the sense of local "projects" that are continuously in the making in the course of people's everyday lives and are subject to ordering, evaluation, and hierarchization.

STRUCTURE OF THE BOOK

This study is organized around two core parts. The first part focuses both on the Pamir Highway as a place in and of itself and on more discrete places along the road. In this regard, I trace historical links between present-day encounters in Murghab, Tajikistan's easternmost district, and the Soviet Union's efforts to modernize and integrate its Afghan and Chinese borderlands into the larger framework of the Union from the 1930s onward. I furthermore show how modernity, initially an imposed and ideologically enforced category, permeated the region in the course of road construction and provisioning, creating a sense of privilege and distinction vis-à-vis the surrounding flatlands. In the second part of this book, I look at three contemporary sites of engagement along the highway in which modernity is key: identity, Islam, and the state. While highlighting each of these different sites in separate chapters I show that they are closely intertwined by means of local "projects" of modernity through which people along the road situate themselves amid marginalization, political processes, religious reform, and economic change.

In chapter 1, I introduce the interconnection between the road and modernity. Using examples from my ethnography on the road I show how these tie in with Göran Therborn's (2003) take on modernity as a particular "time conception" that can be simultaneously directed toward the past and the future. Multiple meanings of modernity become, for instance, visible in the context of current Chinese road construction, through which the government of Tajikistan has attempted to promote repeated processes of modernization in the region. I argue that people along the Pamir Highway also perceive these attempts as a threatening attribution of backwardness to the Soviet period, which they, in contrast, generally recollect as a time of progress and prosperity.

In chapter 2, I focus on the people who have spent their lives constructing and maintaining the Pamir Highway and have thereby contributed to transformation and place making in the district of Murghab. In this regard, I show that their care and concern for the road derives not only from its role as an existential supply line but also from having lived with and on the highway. Thus, on the one hand, I look at the affective qualities of infrastructure. On the other hand, I also show how this infrastructure has facilitated the unintended construction of new landscapes in Murghab, as reflected in the emergence of local histories and places of pilgrimage.

In chapter 3, I foreground identity as a site of engagement along the Pamir Highway. Analyzing the use of time as well as debates about TV shows and movies, personal hygiene, and ethnically coded customary practices, I show that people living in places along the road navigate through a multiplicity of identities in their everyday lives. At the same time, I argue that despite the high degree of internal differentiation within in the region, the people uphold a shared sense of distinction—based on the rubric of modernity—from places beyond the highway.

In chapter 4, I explore the role of Islam in the district of Murghab. Taking seriously people's stance toward religion as a force that has the potential to perfect modernity and is therefore not in contradiction to it, I look at various attempts to reform Islam on the highway. In this regard, I show that such reforms are organized along particular trajectories that are informed by sectarian difference and political change. For instance, while Kyrgyz *daavatchy*s, representing the Tablighi Jama'at, a globally active movement for faith renewal, have become sidelined in the course of Tajikistan's war on terror, Shia Ismaili institutions carrying out projects of development and religious reform are now firmly rooted in the region and widely perceived as part of statecraft.

In chapter 5, I look at the salience of marginality and the state along the Pamir Highway, focusing on the introduction of laws, trade, and imaginaries of ideal political rule. In this respect, I show that the region's marginality is the outcome of political processes in the course of which people along the road have become "illegible" to the state. I also maintain that recent road construction and the opening of the Kulma link to China further contribute to notions of marginality in the region due to people's exclusion from major trade endeavors. Finally, I explore oscillating visions of ideal political rule against the backdrop of such exclusionary practices, on the one hand, and violent conflicts in the surrounding valleys and flatlands on the other.

PART I

MODERN PLACES

CHAPTER 1

MODERNITY
AND THE ROAD

APPROACHING MODERNITY

Nursultan has spent a large part of his life in the army. Back in the Soviet era, he opted for a professional military career and was educated in a military academy in Russia. When civil war broke out in Tajikistan in 1992, he was thankful for having made that choice. By becoming a border guard (*pogranichnik*), back then a highly popular profession in the Pamirs, Nursultan followed in the footsteps of his father, who had also served at the Afghan border. Surrounded by Afghanistan, Kyrgyzstan, and China, Gorno-Badakhshan is a border island that had been an outpost of the empire for decades. Since early Soviet times, securing the Central Asian border was a function of Soviet nation building and the implementation of modernization policies (Shaw 2011, 333), and professional army careers were common among men along the Pamir Highway. Later, during Tajikistan's civil war in the 1990s, the Russian army provided well-paid and prestigious jobs for the region's men. The stories of those times are still alive, often recounted during evenings when nostalgia for bygone days is stimulated by a drink or two. On one such occasion, Nursultan, sober himself, artfully narrated army stories from the late 1980s to a group of drunken friends. A story, told in his house in the presence of many guests, went as follows:

> Especially with young recruits it was very easy to see where they came from. You have to imagine, we had all sorts of people there: Russians, blond Balts, Kazakhs, Kyrgyz, Tatars, Tajiks. . . . But of all the Central

Asians, the Turkmen have always been the dumbest. They were pure villagers [*kishlachnye*] from places where time hasn't moved forward at all. They didn't even know a word of Russian when they joined. But the army made them learn the language. . . . Now, I tell you this: one day a handsome blond Lithuanian officer called some Turkmen guys and said in Russian, "Bring me a bucket of sparks!" Of course, the Turkmen didn't understand a word and started running around with a bucket looking for sparks [*Nursultan imitates disoriented people running around*]. I can tell you, of all these guys in the army, people from the Pamirs were the most modern [*sovremennye*], right after the Slavs and the Balts.

Nursultan's story was followed by a discussion about the most and least developed people of the former Soviet Union. While ethnic groups of European origin were all ranked at a high level of development and labeled with terms such as "modern" (*sovremennyi*), "civilized" (*tsivilizovannyi*), and "cultivated" (*kul'turnyi*), most Central Asians were classed as "uncivilized" (*netsivilizovannyi*) and "underdeveloped" (*slaborazvityi*). All guests agreed, however, that the ethnic groups of the Pamirs were first among the Central Asians.

When the group of guests dissolved and the cleanup began, I asked Nursultan about the use of the term "modern" in the Pamirs, as I had heard townspeople distinguishing themselves from villagers through the use of precisely this word. Nursultan agreed that people in the district town (*tsentr*) were "modern" in contrast to people from far-distant villages such as Shaymak and Toktamysh at the Tajik-Chinese-Afghan border. "But this is not something we say to each other here," Nursultan added with slight embarrassment. "We are all equal. And these villagers are more modern than, for instance, people in Afghanistan."

Nursultan's example shows that modernity is a concept that can be used to distinguish and hierarchize people within time and space. When Nursultan labeled Turkmen "villagers," he was not only referring to their rural origins but also to a particular social space which they are presumed to inhabit. In Nursultan's understanding, a *kishlachnyi*, a villager, can be somebody who lives in a city but has a lifestyle that is characteristic of a rural environment, coded by, for instance, education, clothing, and behavior in public. This notion explains why people from the Pamirs often label themselves "modern" despite living far from larger cities. Indeed, they consider their lives in the lunar highway landscape and at the border different from those in the surrounding flatlands.

For Nursultan, modernity is also an evaluative category that can lead to embarrassment when scrutinized and used in the wrong context. It is furthermore a relational category that is applied when people meet and is used to evaluate their actions and modes of being. Nursultan mentioned the knowledge of languages (which is tied to the level of education) as a defining feature of modernity. Knowing Russian not only means knowing the former administrative language along the Pamir Highway but also symbolizes broader involvement in the Soviet project of modernization (Kirmse 2013; McBrien 2009). Far from the mere status of a "colonial" or "imposed" language, Russian has been diversely interwoven into local languages (Mostowlansky 2017)—it dominates vocabularies of technology and higher education (Bahry 2016), and it indexes the ability to interact beyond local, national, and regional (i.e., Central Asian) boundaries.

Driving Cars and Swaddling Babies

In the course of my fieldwork, I frequently traveled back and forth between Khorog and Murghab. Summer trips on the Pamir Highway are usually easy in comparison to the tiring winter journeys when cars invariably get stuck in the snow. This is why Alisher, who frequently drove me and several other passengers up to Murghab, was driving a Mitsubishi Pajero as his summer car when I traveled with him for the first time in July 2009. A Mitsubishi Pajero is a Japanese four-wheel-drive vehicle that manifests a particular kind of modernity on the highway. Although the Pajero was designed for a rough environment in "the furthest corners of the world" according to its official promotional material (Mitsubishi 2011, 3), Alisher considered it a "soft car" (*miagkaia mashina*), with low fuel consumption in summer but frequent breakdowns in snowy winters. Alisher contrasted the shortcomings of the Pajero, a car of foreign origin (*inomarka*), with the durability and stamina of cars from the Soviet Union or Russia, which he referred to as "our cars" (*moshini mo*). For instance, Alisher considered the UAZ, a Russian military jeep with a Soviet past, to be the right car for the Pamir Highway because "it was built for roads like this." The example of cars that Alisher associated with specific places of origin and visions of modern technology illustrates how he sought to define their genealogies. While cars and roads that originated during Soviet times work perfectly well together year-round, they are famous for wasting resources. Alternatively, cars that originate from "the West" (*zapad*), which includes Japan, can provide comfort and save money on fuel but are, in return, not designed for the local roads, especially in winter.

FIGURE 1.1. A sign in Khorog that reads, "The borders of our homeland protect all of our people." Photograph © Bernd Hrdy, 2008.

For Alisher, the effects of such coexistence went beyond the realm of narrative, demonstrating that the entanglement of different "projects" of modernity can have actual material consequences: foreign cars offer comfortable summer trips with fewer expenses and thus more net income. On the other hand, Alisher's Russian military jeep secured his income as a driver in winter, too.

Processes of entanglement are linked to encounters across difference. In the course of such encounters, people along the highway integrate, assimilate, and reject particular fragments deriving from various "projects" of modernity. Thus, interaction is central in situating modernity along the Pamir Highway more generally. The immediate continuation of my first journey with Alisher offers a good illustration of this. While on the way from Khorog to Murghab in the summer of 2009, we discovered that he already knew my Murghabi host, Nursultan. In fact, they had known each other since childhood, as both had grown up in the Murghab of the 1970s and 1980s. When Alisher realized that he would be driving me to Nursultan's house, he became quite excited at the idea of meeting his old friend again.

Alisher and Nursultan used to be good friends, they told me later, but geographical distance and family life had caused their paths to diverge. So the brief, silent atmosphere at the beginning of Alisher's visit to Nursultan's house was not surprising. However, an emotionally charged conversation started when Alisher spotted the cradle (*beshik*) in which Nursultan's newborn baby boy was sleeping. The infant was tightly swaddled and woke up crying at exactly the moment Alisher entered the living room. After a few seconds of silence, Alisher started a conversation with Nursultan in Russian—the only language they have ever shared, as Alisher's first language is Shughni while Nursultan speaks Kyrgyz.

> Alisher: He cries because you've tied him to the cradle [*imitating the process of tying the baby up forcefully*]. Don't you know that this is bad for the baby? You know what they teach us in the Imam's programs? They tell us to give them freedom [*svoboda*]. They should be able to move freely.
>
> Nursultan: I don't know. I believe freedom now would be bad for him. He would be nervous and uncontrolled in the future.
>
> Alisher: I've got two girls. We let them move around freely when they were babies. Now they're doing well in school, again thanks to the Imam.
>
> Nursultan: Maybe, but it's not our thing up here. We're different. There's less development around here.
>
> Alisher: But there are local Ismailis, I mean, the Imam tries to reach out to every corner of Badakhshan. And he's from the European civilization.

As the conversation went on, Nursultan and Alisher could not agree on the correct treatment of the child in the cradle.[1] Alisher later told me that this had to do with differing degrees of "development of civilization" (*razvitiia tsivilizatsii*); he strongly attributed his own lifestyle to "modernity" (*sovremennost'*). While both men had spent similar childhoods in Murghab in the 1970s and 1980s, their lives and the ways they now made sense of the world had—much to their own surprise—somehow diverged.

For Alisher, who moved to Khorog a long time ago, the man he referred to as "the Imam" has brought many changes to the region since the early 1990s. "The Imam" was the Aga Khan IV, who is the social and spiritual leader of the Nizari Ismailis, a branch of Shia Islam whose members are spread over several continents.[2] The imam's "programs" mentioned in the conversation are development projects sponsored by institutions of the Aga Khan Development Network (AKDN). In the context of Gorno-Badakhshan, where a vast majority of the more than 200,000 inhabitants (2010) identify as Ismailis, these development projects play an ambivalent role in everyday life.[3] They claim to include and serve all

FIGURE 1.2. A monument in Murghab commemorating World War II and a
welcome sign for the Aga Khan. Photograph © Bernd Hrdy, 2008.

inhabitants of the region, yet they simultaneously strengthen a sense of
common belonging and identity among Ismailis.

While there are pockets of Sunni Muslims in the western parts of
Gorno-Badakhshan, according to 2015 data from the local government
(*ökmöt*), the majority of people in the district of Murghab are Kyrgyz (approximately twelve thousand), who almost exclusively identify as Sunnis,
while a minority (approximately three thousand) are speakers of various
Pamir languages who are Ismaili. Against this backdrop, the encounter
between Nursultan and Alisher makes manifest the complexity of categories that come into play when they both refer to contrasting notions of
place (Murghab versus Khorog), religious identity (Sunni versus Ismaili)
and development (local versus European). In this interactional setting,
Nursultan and Alisher employ the concept of modernity to order and hierarchize these contrasting notions. At the same time, they use modernity to support and legitimize their own standpoints.

Grasping Entanglement

The two ethnographic vignettes presented suggest the salience of temporal, spatial, and material dimensions of modernity. At the same time,
they highlight the plurality of modernity. Shmuel Eisenstadt (2000), one

of the most influential recent theorists of modernity, coined the concept of "multiple modernities" in order to frame this plurality. In his work, Eisenstadt emphasizes that modernity is not coterminous with "Westernization." In his attempt to describe alternate forms of modernity, Eisenstadt established Weberian ideal type categories for different "modernities" on a broad civilizational scale, including "Western," "socialist," "Islamic," and so forth. Johann Arnason (2000) follows Eisenstadt's outlook on the post-Soviet space, emphasizing the legacy of a distinct Soviet modernity ("the Soviet model").

In her recent work on Islam and modernity in Kyrgyzstan, Julie McBrien (2008, 2009) shows that Eisenstadt's framework supports the argument that modernity plays a central role in "non-Western" contexts, thus tying in with a large body of literature in critical theory on modernity in anthropology and the social sciences more generally.[4] Following Eisenstadt's notion of "multiple modernities," she argues that we must "recognize Central Asia as modern, as having long been modern, in order to understand its religious landscape, but that we must connect the region to the broader history of modernity in order to enhance our notions of this contentious analytical concept" (2008, 16). McBrien (2008, 26) also convincingly claims that viewing Central Asia, with the help of Eisenstadt's concept, as a region that had long been involved in a particular Soviet notion of modernity "not only overcomes the determinism of modernization theory, but provides a broad enough working schema to allow for the Soviet experience as a modern one."

For this study of modernity along the Pamir Highway, Eisenstadt's work poses two challenges. First, in his "multiple modernities" framework, "the West" remains the implicit conceptual mother of modernity, always lurking somewhere beneath the surface. One could argue that such an approach is in fact still informed by a cold war discourse that constructed a distinct realm of socialism.[5] In this ideologically shaped discourse, socialist countries were always ranked second behind "the West" and were located just ahead of third world countries. In this respect Sharad Chari and Katherine Verdery (2009, 29) call for a liberation of "the Cold War from the ghetto of Soviet area studies and postcolonial thought from the ghetto of Third World and colonial studies." Second, Eisenstadt's work triggers the question of the extent to which a multiplicity of and circulations between ideal types are possible. In his multiple modernities framework, it remains unclear how different modernities relate to each other, how they intersect, interact, conflict, and coincide.

In his critique of "post–Second World War North Atlanticist 'modernization' theory," which builds on Eisenstadt, Göran Therborn (2003) develops responses to these two challenges and suggests that the "globality of modernity" may be approached as not simply "multiple" in the sense of different concepts existing side by side or being part of a process of diffusion but as nonlinear and "entangled." Looking at modernity situated in time and space, he advocates a temporal, yet nonlinear, understanding of modernity.[6] In this sense, modernity does not designate a particular chronological period or particular institutional forms. As a consequence, very different "periods of modernity, followed by de-modernization or re-traditionalization," can be observed (2003, 294). In this vein, Therborn defines modernity "as a culture, an epoch, a society, a social sphere having a particular *time orientation*" (italics in original). From his perspective, modernity is "a time conception looking forward to this worldly future, open, novel, reachable or constructable, a conception seeing the present as a possible preparation for a future, and the past either as something to leave behind or as a heap of ruins, pieces of which might be used for building a new future" (2003, 294). By following Therborn in his approach, I suggest, we might get a clearer picture of how deeply ingrained global connections are in everyday life in Central Asia, of where to locate power relations, and of how to understand when margins become central and centers marginal. By speaking of "entangling" modernity I refer to the processual character of social encounters involving modernity and express my interest in interrelations rather than coexistence.[7]

In the context of the anthropological study of globalization, which is crucial to any understanding of modernity, Anna Tsing (2005, 3) suggests looking at different forms of interrelations as "encounters across difference," situated within "zones of awkward engagement, where words mean something different across a divide even as people agree to speak" (2005, xi). If we look at places along the Pamir Highway as being part of such a "zone," Nursultan and Alisher's baby encounter is one across difference, as are many more, including Afghan traders who swap Western humanitarian aid for rubies in Murghab, Chinese truck drivers speeding along the highway, and a Swiss ethnographer meeting road construction workers in the pursuit of "learning the Pamirs" (*Pamir okuu*). Tsing calls the vicissitudes within such encounters "friction." Considering it neither a synonym for resistance nor contradictory to hegemony, Tsing defines friction as "inflect[ing] historical trajectories, enabling, excluding and particularizing" (2005, 6). To this effect, friction serves as an entrance to the ethnographic account of global connections in which the universal particularizes and the particular aspires to the universal.

Recalling Nursultan and Alisher's encounter presented earlier in this chapter, it becomes clear that modernity can be inherently contradictory, uniting, competing, dividing, and transforming. At the same time, it suggests that modernity along the Pamir Highway is rooted in the materiality of road infrastructure, development projects, cars, border posts, and cradles, or the absence of them.[8] If we follow Brian Larkin (2013, 328) in his definition of infrastructures as "built networks that facilitate the flow of goods, people, or ideas and allow for their exchange over space," then the road takes on a central role in making Murghab part of such a network. To people along the highway the infrastructures of modernity with and through which they live are also inherently unpredictable and unstable due to erosion, natural disaster, and changing trajectories of political intervention.[9] Being denied access to a larger network might result in loss, while the promise of new forms of connectivity raises hopes, fears, and expectations. Madeleine Reeves (2016, 3) highlights the salience of such meeting points between materiality and sociality and suggests looking at the "simultaneity of the social and the material in the coming-into-being of infrastructural forms." The following section is dedicated to the exploration of the possibility of perceiving historical and contemporary processes along the Pamir Highway through this lens, navigating through different material, spatial, and temporal dimensions.

ON THE ROAD

When people talk about the Pamir Highway in the district of Murghab, they rarely make more than a subtle reference to "the road" (*doroga, jol, roh*). In fact, "the road" has become such a basic precondition for people's lives in the region that there is little need to emphasize its importance in linking together most aspects of the everyday. At the same time, "the road" nonetheless crops up here and there in conversations, where it is often mentioned in descriptions of not only human movement across the region but also movement of technology, ideas, and innovations.

In the summer of 2010 I traveled to a number of pilgrimage sites with Nursultan and several of his friends. On our visit to places where Kyrgyz martyrs (*sheiit*) had died and still emanate spiritual blessings (*bereke*), we were accompanied by Kudaibergen Ata, a former government employee with a wealth of knowledge about local history and an expert when it comes to locating the unmarked and often unnoticeable sites. When we reached Lake Bulungköl, a small lake several kilometers off the paved road, Kudaibergen Ata and Nursultan started a conversation about the origins of the lake. As it turned out, in earlier times there used to be a town where the lake is now. The town was inundated by the lake because the inhabitants were not willing to treat a wandering *oluia*, a man close to God, respectfully. Only one elderly lady invited the *oluia* to her house as "God's guest" (*Kudai konok*) and was subsequently spared by the flood. As a result of welcoming the *oluia*, she had developed the ability to walk on water.

Kudaibergen Ata and Nursultan agreed that skills like the one given to the elderly lady by the *oluia* have not been preserved. During the Soviet period, state agencies turned the lake into a fishpond and, to supplement the small number of existing indigenous species, stocked it with breeds introduced from abroad.[10] The new fish flourished and eventually made it to other bodies of water in the region. The fishpond has since become famous for its tasty fish. Yet as a consequence, its religious significance was ultimately overshadowed by gourmet interests. The following conversation between Nursultan and Kudaibergen Ata, which took place during our trip to the lake, shows what role the road played in this shift of meaning.

> Nursultan: I heard that fish and spawn were brought here. Completely different fish were brought here, right?
>
> Kudaibergen Ata: Yes, they were brought in by plane to Osh first and then on the road to here. . . . There were many of them. One day I was called to the office. We had to set them free at 9 in the morning. Worms were brought as well. When we set them [the worms] free they went into the sand. . . . Then people said these worms would spread very quickly and they would become food for the fish in the lake.

Sitting at the lakeside for a while, Kamal, who was also with us that day, remembered the distribution of Siberian fish in the Pamirs in all its details. While first specifically referring to the stocking of Lake Bulungköl with 37,000 gibel carp in 1967 (Savvaitova and Petr 1999, 180), he later told me how tons of fish had been brought by truck from Osh and released in a number of lakes in the region.

These examples show how technological and biological innovations entered Murghab via the road throughout the second half of the twentieth century. The transformation of landscapes, going hand in hand with cultural change, was a common Soviet practice that was meant, as Emma Widdis (2003, 3) put it, to minimize "the vast distances that separated centre from periphery" and to create an "integrated social body."[11] Moving fish to mountain lakes in the Pamirs was part of such a strategy, as were the construction of the highway itself and the establishment of settlements with job opportunities along the road. Michel Foucault's (1984, 252) statement that "space is fundamental in any exercise of power" reflects Soviet attempts to integrate, "develop," and control the eastern Pamirs through transformation that included the reorganization of the landscape and its social formations.

Modernity, and Yet Another One

Doreen Massey (2005, 107) looks at space as a sphere of "dynamic simultaneity" that is "constantly connected by new arrivals" and "waiting to be determined . . . by the construction of new relations."[12] From such a perspective we might envisage the Pamir Highway not just as an end product and artifact, but also as standing for a multiplicity of temporal, material, and spatial trajectories that intersect in Gorno-Badakhshan. Historical accounts point to the region as a crossroads of trade routes and meeting point of people and political entities.[13] Such encounters range from, among others, the ancient and medieval Silk Road, with Marco Polo purportedly having crossed the Pamirs in the thirteenth century (Ricci 1931, 61) to Alexander the Great's military conquests, wars against Chinese armies, and the Great Game between the Russian and British Empires in the nineteenth century. People along the Pamir Highway refer to and situate themselves amid such historical genealogies. For instance, local scholars produce works on the history of Murghab that are widely debated and linked to political processes in the region (see chapter 2).[14] At the same time, Chinese road construction, the opening of the Tajikistan-China border, and the recently enforced revivalist rhetoric of China's Silk Road Economic Belt, also known as the "One Belt, One Road" (*yidai yilu*) strategy, have found their way into everyday conversations. In the course of such conversations people along the Pamir Highway frequently express anxiety, anger, disappointment, and hope regarding these ongoing spatial transformations.[15]

When debating local history, people along the highway often distinguish between different strands of time that do not necessarily correspond to standard periodizations found in historical literature.[16] In this regard, they commonly talk about the time from the nineteenth century to 1917 as "the time of Nikolai," deriving from Tsar Nikolai II. The period prior to that is called "the time of Manas" (*Manas maal*) in Kyrgyz, referring to the Kyrgyz epic hero Manas, "ancient time" (*kadim maal, qadim*) in Kyrgyz, Shughni, and Tajik, or "long ago" (*davno, davno*) in Russian. For the period after 1917 there are the terms "Soviet time" (*Sovet maal*) and "in the Union" (*Soiuzda*) in Kyrgyz, "in the time of the Union" (*pri Soiuze*) in Russian, and "during the Union" (*vaqti Shuravī*) in Tajik. At times my interlocutors also distinguished between different periods within the Soviet era that they ordered according to the leading political figures at a given time—for instance, Stalin, Khrushchev, and Andropov. In addition, they referred to the time since 1991 as "Tajikistan" and to the time of the civil war between 1992 and 1997 as "the mess" (*bardak*) in Russian and "war" (*voina, sogush, jang*) in Russian, Kyrgyz, Shughni, and Tajik. Events to come they situated either in the "future" (*kelechek, oyanda, budushchee*) in Kyrgyz, Shughni, Tajik, and Russian, or in the "afterlife" (*akyret, okhirat*) in Kyrgyz, Shughni, and Tajik.

It is important to emphasize that these periods of time are not fixed entities and that people employ them in ways that go beyond set temporal boundaries or linear time lines. For instance, "the time of Nikolai" can reach back into a precolonial past, while "ancient times" might also refer to the early Soviet Union of the 1920s or a future to come. Yet there are specific limits to the application of the terms. In conversations and interviews in Murghab, my interlocutors frequently used "ancient time" (*kadim maal, qadim*) for events and practices prior to the 1930s and envisioned for the future but rarely for the period in between.

People along the Pamir Highway attribute major forms of transformation with regard to politics, culture, economy, mobility, and materiality to the 1930s. In this regard, my interlocutors emphasized the following events that signaled the starting point of "modernity" (*sovremennost'*) in Gorno-Badakhshan: In the spring of 1931 the Council of People's Commissars of the Soviet Union granted permission to construct a paved road from Osh to Murghab and Khorog.[17] Pamirstroi, the governmental body that managed the road, supervised the ambitious construction process, and parts of the road were opened on 7 November 1933, the sixteenth anniversary of the 1917 October Revolution (Popov 1935, 21). Shortly thereafter, in the spring of 1935, regular automobile traffic between Osh and Khorog commenced (Kreutzmann 2009, 15). As a result, the Pamir Highway provided Soviet authorities with a vital supply line, stretching 730 kilometers from Osh in southern Kyrgyzstan to Khorog at the Afghan border, allowing them to cut previous social and economic ties with Afghanistan and China. In 1934 they created a "border zone"

FIGURE 1.3. A high-altitude stretch of the Pamir Highway between Murghab and Osh. Photograph © Till Mostowlansky, 2015.

(*pogranichnaia zona*) in Gorno-Badakhshan in which border troops, and later the KGB, monitored citizens' movements as well as social and economic activities. It appears that after a period of small-scale resistance, a heavily militarized border regime was in place by the end of the 1930s, preventing the region's inhabitants from maintaining previous connections across the border.[18]

Today people along the Pamir Highway characterize the construction of the road and the disappearance of previously existing routes, practices, and geographical orientations as having gone hand in hand with the abandonment of the "ancient" and the "old." Throughout the twentieth century, the Soviet state cloaked these dramatic economic, social, cultural, and material changes in the rhetoric of "development" and "progress" (*razvitie, taraqqiyot*).[19] Nowadays, many people along the road view this transformation as both an achievement and a loss.

The Soviet state had established and cared for the Pamir Highway as the most important supply route leading into the border zone of Gorno-Badakhshan. The previously triumphant rhetoric surrounding the highway connecting Osh and Khorog has now vanished. Yet other actors have entered the stage and promise new forms of connectivity and "modernization." For instance, in 2004 the governments of Tajikistan and China opened a 93-kilometer stretch of road between Murghab and the Chinese border. The so-called Kulma road, named after the mountain pass marking the border, now connects the Pamir Highway to the Chinese road network and beyond.[20] In official speeches the two countries have emphasized the importance of a close economic relationship. At the same time, people in Murghab also described the opening of the Kulma road as a frightening dismantling of a previously closed and stable border and expressed anxiety over convergence with a formerly hostile and presently expansionist China.

In media statements and public speeches, Tajikistani government officials discuss the Kulma link and the remaking of the road leading from China via Murghab and Khorog to Dushanbe in terms of progress to come and the promise of a prosperous future. A good example of this came in the form of a public letter of gratitude from Alimamad Niyozmamadov, the then governor of Gorno-Badakhshan, to the representative of the local Murghabi government, which was printed on the front page of the regional Kyrgyz-Russian newspaper *Sary Kol* in June 2004.

> The Murghab–Kulma motorway has been built and put into operation for the people of Gorno-Badakhshan, but especially for the inhabitants of your district [Murghab]. This was made possible through the joint efforts of the leaders of the two brother nations, and the will and the feat of strength of the workers and engineers of the organization "Badakhshan-roh," who worked under incredibly difficult climatic and environmental conditions.
>
> The prime minister of the Republic of Tajikistan, the honorable Mr. Okil Gaibullaevich Okilov, participated in the opening ceremony of the Kulma checkpoint, and mentioned there that this event was not only of high political and international importance, but also of strategic significance. Henceforth and forever Gorno-Badakhshan has left its geographical isolation behind.

In his letter, Niyozmamadov invoked the image of emerging ties with China and the connection to a transnational network of roads, including the Karakoram Highway in Pakistan, as the end of Gorno-Badakhshan's isolation.[21] He furthermore stated that the road to the Kulma pass was a "road of life" (*doroga zhizni*)[22] for people in Murghab that would lead Tajikistan to "prosperity" (*protsvetanie*) and "development" (*razvitie*).

Niyozmamadov's letter celebrating the opening of the road was a skillful presentation of the state's achievements in the region and an explanation of the road's advantages to the people who live alongside it. In creating an overland link to China, the government in Dushanbe attempted to repeat the introduction of modernity. The construction of the Pamir Highway between Osh and Khorog in the 1930s had served as a springboard for modernity and the abandonment of the "old" in the Soviet context. Yet linking Murghab with China in 2004 meant not only a repetition of modernization but also what one could call the reinscription of backwardness to the period prior to this. Shaped by acts of statecraft (Jansen 2015) and the materiality of infrastructure (Humphrey 2005; Sneath 2009), modernity was presented as a condition to come; at the same time, it was still perceived locally as a past condition that was poised to return.[23]

Pathways to the State

In Soviet and more recent representations of statehood in Gorno-Badakhshan, roads play an important role. In the cases presented above, political actors invoke the image of the end of the region's backwardness and the introduction of modernity. In this sense, roads serve as a tool in the attempt to present an image of the region as part of a powerful state "whose ends are those of a unified society" (Thompson 2008, 321). However, this is only one side of the story. Even in the course of the radical transformations that have been introduced to the region over the past century, it is not just ideology and economic power that have mattered. In this regard, Penny Harvey (2005, 126) makes the important point that "roads inevitably lead us to 'the state,' but indirectly." While the state is omnipresent in the process of constructing, legitimizing and, at times, neglecting roads, the concrete materiality of the state-effects of roads is often unintended, disrupted, and "circuitous." In this sense roads, and infrastructure more generally, serve as examples of how "politics is materialized in the mundane" (Reeves 2014b, 241). Simultaneously, they invite us to look at how people live with them, what they do with them, and how they might employ them in ways that differ from their intended purposes and functions.

The aforementioned processes of transformation surrounding Lake Bulungköl and the relocation and spread of fish during Soviet times serve as an example of this inherent multidimensionality of infrastructure. On the one hand, the Soviets attempted to "develop," control, and make economically viable the allegedly "empty" border region by means of the road. As a part of this attempt, the lake's shift from a site of religious significance to a fishpond ties in neatly with the general rhetoric of modern-

ization in the secularist Soviet teleology.[24] Yet as I passed by the lake with
Nursultan and his friends on that summer day in 2010, we were actually
visiting pilgrimage sites (*mazar*) that we accessed via the road. Many of
these sites had developed in close proximity to the road—not before but
during the Soviet period. The Pamir Highway has therefore not merely
fundamentally reshaped the region as planned and intended. Rather, as
Penny Harvey and Hannah Knox (2015, 5) put it, intentions projected
onto the road (and other infrastructural systems) "always run up against
[their] intrinsic multiplicity and the strength of the existing relational
fields into which they are inserted."

The multidimensional status of the Pamir Highway as a touchstone
for different political and economic powers and a place of often positive
centrality in people's everyday lives puts into perspective the pessimistic view of roads that dominant space theorists have promoted. In his
study of the Kakavijë–Gjirokastër highway connecting southern Albania
with northern Greece, Dimitris Dalakoglou (2010, 133) argues that critical discourses on roads in the influential works of Henri Lefebvre, Marc
Augé, and David Harvey suggest a rather one-sided frame for the study
of motorways.[25] For instance, in his work *The Production of Space*, Henri Lefebvre (1991, 165) laid the groundwork for a somewhat pessimistic
perception of paved roads as symbols of domination.[26] Using figurative
language to emphasize the concept of dominant space as the "realization
of a master's project," Lefebvre (1991, 165) describes the effect of contemporary road construction as that of a knife cutting apart space: "In order
to dominate space, technology introduces a new form into a pre-existing
space—generally a rectilinear or rectangular form such as a meshwork or
chequerwork. A motorway brutalizes the countryside and the land, slic-
ing through space like a great knife. Dominated space is usually closed,
sterilized, emptied out."

The notion of a lack of sociality as an inherent quality of roads is also
put forward by Marc Augé (2008, 64), who defines roads as "non-places,"
a term negatively associated with alienation and the absence of the social.
In his study *Non-Places: An Introduction to Supermodernity*, he argues
that, as "the real non-places of supermodernity" (77–78), motorways involve people in a highly regulated domain that leads away from human
interaction to interaction with institutions. Lefebvre's and Augé's pessimistic notions of the road as a symbol of alienating modernization processes reflect specific concepts of modernity that are defined by loss and
destruction.

This kind of analytical take on infrastructures, including roads, raises several concerns for an anthropological study of the Pamir Highway: the binary opposition of road and humans as defined by the absence or presence of sociality is challenged by the constant performance of social acts in the course of journeys on the highway, everyday lives along it, and the human interaction with the highway in the form of maintenance and construction.[27] By approaching the Pamir Highway from a multidimensional perspective, this study aims to go beyond what James Scott (1998, 347) calls the "high modernist optic" of "resolute singularity" in which roads are mono-functional. This requires, as Penny Harvey (2005, 131) has observed, a conceptualization of the highway and its adjacent border region as a site of "fantasy and projection for politicians, planners and local people." It is on this site that the "temporal and spatial coordinates" of the state are being reconfigured (Harvey 2010, 32) in the process of making governance possible over a vast and extended territory.[28] At the same time, the road is not just the materialization of an abstract and distant state on the local level, standing for competing regimes and visions of modernity. It is, moreover, the site where the state is constantly being performed at different points in time (Rasanayagam, Beyer, and Reeves 2014, 11).

CHAPTER 2

MAKING MURGHAB

MEMORIES OF CONSTRUCTION

At the very beginning of my fieldwork, on a summer day in 2008, Murghabi friends put me in touch with Nuraly, an elderly Kyrgyz man who was supposed to be "knowledgeable about local history" (*tarikh bilgen adam*). Later that day, I went down to the bazaar to look for his mud-brick house in one of the narrow alleys. A short while later I found myself in Nuraly's living room, sitting on the floor, drinking tea and chatting to a man who had lived through most of the twentieth century in Murghab. While I was initially interested in Nuraly's family history and genealogy, I soon noticed that he kept mentioning "the road" (*jol*) as a central reference point in his biography.

Nuraly depicted the road as a source of life and opportunity, as a nurturing force that was essential to the region. Nuraly is retired now but used to work for various road construction agencies that were active in Murghab during the Soviet period. This is why many events in his life are closely connected to paving the way from Osh to Khorog. Like many elderly people in Murghab, Nuraly experienced the Soviet "fight for the road" (*bor'ba za dorogu*), starting in the 1930s, as an undertaking that permanently transformed the region.

Nuraly told me during our first meeting that his grandfather had migrated to Murghab when it was not yet a clearly defined settlement. It was in "the time of Nikolai" when Nuraly's grandfather left his village close to the city of Osh and moved to the Pamirs in search of a "peaceful place" (*tynch jer*) to live. Nuraly explained that at this time—the period at the turn of the nineteenth to the twentieth century when the Russian tsar

Nikolai was in power—the surrounding flatlands were regions of "unrest" (*tynch bolgon emes*). "That's why my forefather came to the mountains, to a peaceful place," Nuraly said as he rooted through his closet for a book he wanted to show me.

The book that Nuraly wanted me to see was red and heavy. The front page was marked with the Soviet hammer and sickle insignia in gold relief and the similarly radiant title *The Motor Highway Osh-Khorog*, 1974 (*Avtomagistral' Osh–Khorog* 1974). When Nuraly opened the book and let me read the first couple of pages, it became clear that he wanted me to get to know his many friends and relatives who had participated in the construction of the highway. The road that linked his birthplace to the Soviet world beyond the Pamirs was strongly connected to people, and the aim of the book was, as indicated by its subtitle *Accomplishments and People* (*Dela i liudi*), to remember those who had contributed to this endeavor.

The carefully designed red book was published by the All-Union Ministry of Transport Construction in 1974 in the city of Osh, which at that time was part of the Kirghiz Soviet Socialist Republic. In the short preface, an anonymous author summarizes the history of the construction of the Pamir Highway from 1931 to 1974, points out the introduction of recent technological innovations such as avalanche protection galleries, and praises the labor of the countless road construction workers. Moreover, the author emphasizes road construction in the Pamirs as an important part of economic, scientific, and political advancement. In this context, the materialization of a concrete geographical interconnection between the Kirghiz and Tajik "brother republics" (*bratskie respubliki*) is especially highlighted. Furthermore, the author argues that the highway provides "the opportunity to fully make use of the high mountain pastures of the Alai Valley, as well as to scientifically study the natural richness of the 'Roof of the World.'" In order to accomplish economic goals and to facilitate scientific research, forces of nature had to be defeated. "Under difficult climatic and hydrogeological conditions" a road project had been established, the author argues, which not only supported the achievement of specific economic and scientific goals but which also had obvious impacts on the lives of the local population. Standing on a par with other monumental infrastructure projects such as dams, power stations, and factories that were built all over the Soviet Union,[1] the construction of the highway up to the Pamirs, the "Roof of the World," transformed physical and social landscapes: "In the course of construction of

FIGURE 2.1. The statue of Lenin in Murghab. Photograph © Till Mostowlan-sky, 2015.

the Osh–Khorog highway, a cadre of heads of road-construction sections and the construction department No. 898 have emerged from local ethnic groups [*iz mestnikh natsional'nostei*]. Many construction workers have been decorated with orders and medals of the Union of Soviet Socialist Republics for selfless labor while constructing the highway, and for guaranteeing continuous and year-round transport connections between the two brother republics" (Avtomagistral' Osh-Khorog 1974, no page number). The rest of the book is mainly dedicated to the visual depiction of members of these local cadres, including people from towns and settlements along the road. The book describes the construction of the Pamir Highway as a joint Soviet initiative that resulted in the establishment of a modernized landscape. This landscape of paved roads, multistory buildings, statues of Lenin, heavy construction equipment, and electrified villages is presented as complementary to the beauty of nature.

The red book that Nuraly proudly showed me as proof of his own and his friends' careers suggests an idealistic notion of Soviet modernity in which a tamed nature is in balance with reorganized modern space. Such a notion of the construction of the Pamir Highway ties in with other depictions of the Soviet "fight for the road." For example, a collection of essays about road construction in Kyrgyzstan and Gorno-Badakhshan that was published in 1935 provides an insight into the early process of paving the way from Osh to Khorog. In the preface, the editor defines "the fight for the road" as an essential part of establishing socialism in the "periphery" (*okraina*) of the country: "Recent years have struck a final crippling blow to the roadlessness[2] of Kirgiziia. We now have highways instead of mountain paths in many districts. Instead of the camel and the ox, the Soviet automobile now speeds along on these roads. And instead of isolated districts there is now one connected and unified economic whole where there used to be inaccessible periphery until recently" (Slavinskii 1935, 3).

The image of places along the Pamir Highway as only recently having been modernized is salient throughout Soviet depictions of road construction. For instance, in the booklet *The Road of Friendship* (*Doroga druzhby*), the author D. Dzhumaev (1984) juxtaposes a remote and poor Gorno-Badakhshan before the 1930s to the subsequent period in which the highway stands as a symbol of Soviet progress, heroism, conscience, and enthusiasm. In this regard, Dzhumaev depicts the Pamir Highway as a symbol of Soviet connectivity alongside which people have "electricity and a Moscow–Pamir television connection, their own PhDs, and one of the highest literacy rates in the world." Thus "the region [Gorno-Badakhshan] needed [the road] like air, like bread" (Dzhumaev 1984, no page number). From the early days of traffic on the Pamir Highway in 1933, this connectivity was closely linked to the mobility of people to and from different parts of the Soviet Union. As Dzhumaev states, the first four men who drove their cars on the road were the German Gerner, the Ukrainian Povazhnii, the Kyrgyz Tarychev, and the Uzbek Umurzakov.

Nuraly, the former road construction worker (*jolchu*), likewise remembered the process of paving the road as a multiethnic enterprise. However, in contrast to the Soviet literature that puts an emphasis on equality along the "road of friendship," he also remembered the hierarchical aspects of the endeavor. Nuraly told me that it was people from ethnic groups that did not originate in the Pamirs who were active in teaching the techniques that were needed to trigger change: "There were many Russians. Russians worked on the road. Each organization had at least three to five Russian families. Then there were Tatars who came from Russia, Tatarstan, Kazan, and Ufa. There were many of them. They were the managers and supervisors. Russians taught us everything."

Subsequently, Soviet knowledge transfer to the Pamirs, as a region that had been considered "peripheral," was realized not only in the realm of road construction. Other fields such as education, the organization of living space, and food, as well as fashion and clothing, underwent similar transformation processes in the course of Soviet rule. Such changes were well documented in local newspapers and party announcements but are nowadays most visibly remembered in family photo albums, a thorough examination of which is often part of a guest's duty. During my exploration of dozens of family photo albums in settlements along the Pamir Highway, I found that the impact of what "Russians taught us," as Nuraly put it, also materializes in the way people represent themselves in pictures and in the things that characterize this new knowledge and often serve as unnoticed background settings: female road construction workers with shovels; skirts and ties in mixed school classes; bottles of imported vodka on a wedding table; border posts along the borders with Afghanistan and China.

Caring for the Road

"The fight for the road" in the Pamirs has not only been painstakingly described as a triumphant victory but also as a bone-grinding battle against the forces of nature and human weakness. Both challenges to successful road construction are eventually surmounted, with the road being domesticated and controlled, yet they keep coming back in attempts to threaten the established order. T. Popov's (1935) description of the construction of the Pamir Highway sketches pictures of demoralized and suffering workforces paving the way from Osh to Khorog, never quite sure that they could finish the project. Only when parts of the Pamir Highway were finally opened in 1933, after several years of frustration, did Gorno-Badakhshan finally overcome its role as a "deserted" and "inaccessible periphery," as seen from a Soviet perspective. As a result of this breakthrough and in order to "make way for the Soviet automobile," the Pamirs had "parted their peaks through the will of the Party and the working class" (Popov 1935, 21). Similarly, in his work on transport development in Soviet Tajikistan, Sadullo Nazrulloev (1979, 95) interprets the early construction of the Pamir Highway as "vivid testimony to the Party's care [zabota] for the oppressed and backward [otstalye] peoples of Tsarist Russia."

While Soviet authorities cared for the construction of the road, they were less considerate of people's geographical orientations, kin networks, and economic connectivity. Cross-border ties with Afghanistan and China had been strong before the construction of the Pamir Highway,[3] Murghab's transformation from a Russian army outpost into a district town, and the militarization of the border in the 1930s.[4] Today, people in Murghab remember the city of Kashgar in present-day Xinjiang (China) as having been a much closer and better-known destination for the exchange of livestock than Osh in the Ferghana Valley. Back in 2009, some of my elder interlocutors could still recall their parents telling them stories of their travels by horse and camel to Kashgar. These trips purportedly lasted no more than five days and were therefore much shorter than the journey to Osh, which took at least one week in summer and fifteen days in winter.

The construction of the Pamir Highway went hand in hand with the Soviet strategy of keeping the Central Asian frontier, including Gorno-Badakhshan's borders with Afghanistan and China, "under lock and key" (Shaw 2011, 332). As Charles Shaw (2011, 332) argues, this strategy was inspired by the idea of "separating the sacred socialist world from the profanity of capitalism" and establishing a contrast to "the loose flows of people, goods and money under the tsar." As a consequence, Gorno-Badakhshan and, subsequently, the people along the highway were incorporated into the category of "border societies" that could be found all over the Soviet Union. In an attempt to prevent inhabitants of such "border societies" from feeling oppressed, the Soviet state tried to create "friendship and trust" (Shaw 2011, 331). For the inhabitants of Gorno-Badakhshan, closing the borders meant that they were cut off from economic opportunities, and emotional ties with relatives across the border were severed. The Pamir Highway played an important role in enacting state-directed "care" and infusing the radically transforming border region with a sense of homogeneity that eventually made it part of a "loyal and secure frontier" (Kassymbekova 2011, 362).

People along the highway recall the hardships and drawbacks of establishing the road connection between Osh and Khorog in much less exuberant and more nuanced terms than those that are found in official representations. My elder interlocutors in particular, who were directly involved in the construction and supply industry, still have detailed memories of the difficulties and unpredictable swings from clear and passable roads to complete isolation. From the road workers' point of view, snowfall and the lack of technology played a crucial role—and continue to do so to the present day. Many of them emphasized that the road was periodically closed between the 1930s and the 1960s. Only sometime after 1965 was there sufficient technology, including bulldozers, snowplows, and motorized graders available throughout the year. According to these

FIGURE 2.2. Trucks with humanitarian aid for the Pamirs stuck in snow at Taldyk Pass in Kyrgyzstan. Photograph © Robert Middleton, 1995.

memories, sometime around the mid-1960s the army provided additional personnel and technology in order to ensure constant road maintenance, supposedly on direct orders from Moscow.

People along the Pamir Highway, as well as in other parts of Gorno-Badakhshan, refer to this period from the 1960s on as marked by "Moscow provisioning" (*Moskovskoe obespechenie*).[5] As Madeleine Reeves (2014c, 114) points out, "Moscow provisioning" denotes Soviet attempts to create "centers in the periphery" in strategically selected places all over the Union. These efforts included proffering access to high-quality consumer goods, educational opportunities, and higher salaries and pensions (*nadbavki*), as well as affording privileged mobility within the Soviet Union. At the same time, to be under "Moscow provisioning" not only meant to be materially well resourced but also to have a "certain kind of cultural and aesthetic connection" to the center (Reeves 2014c, 114). As a result, Reeves argues, *Moskovskoe obespechenie* was as much about incorporation and enclosure as it was about provisioning. Despite the end of "Moscow provisioning" more than a quarter of a century ago, particular elements of this arrangement have remained to the present day: the now generally low salaries and pensions are still better than in the flatlands, educational institutions in Tajikistan have quotas for students from high-altitude regions, and along the road there is a sense of readiness for life in Moscow and other urban centers.

Against this backdrop, the historical and contemporary significance of the Pamir Highway as the only major way for humans and goods to reach and leave Murghab can hardly be overestimated. And indeed, numerous road construction workers were on duty in the Soviet era to try to stay one step ahead of the asphalt's tendency to disintegrate. As Kamal, a Murghabi official in his fifties, told me during one of the many afternoons we spent discussing the region in his office, "Back then the main thing was that goods arrived on time." The road "was built for that," and its role was to prevent a "blockade" (*blokada*) of a socioeconomic field that the highway itself had created.

The improvement of the road in the course of Soviet rule corresponds to the general feeling of development and stability that many people along the Pamir Highway locate between the late 1960s and the breakup of the Union in 1991. As a veteran of Soviet road construction, Nuraly especially misses this period. Sometimes he longs for the network of people, supply stations, and the bustling atmosphere of truck stops (*avtobaza*). "It was good between 1970 and 1990," he said, but "starting in 1991 everyone was given to a separate republic. . . . Now the road isn't so good anymore. . . . The Kyrgyz say they control their own part and Tajikistan controls its own. . . . In the past cars worked day and night; between two hundred and two hundred and fifty cars passed every day. Now there is little movement; now businessmen come from Osh and they leave. Now technology is used for Kulma and the China road that goes to Khorog. That's fine, but in comparison to earlier times there's little technology here." Nuraly's reference to the existence of "little technology" is aimed at the current lack of political will that, were it to exist, could pool resources in order to fight against the dissolution of the highway between Murghab and the border with Kyrgyzstan. He also mentioned the absence of bulldozers and snowplows, thereby drawing attention to the fact that the road is, as he called it, in constant need of "maintenance" (*karmoo*). As an important precondition for the conduct of most everyday practices in the settlements along the road, the Pamir Highway has to be constantly reconstructed.

Fighting and caring for the highway's materiality, both lifesaving and threatening, implies an existential interdependency between people and the road that invites analytical reasoning beyond a simple life–matter binary. Being in a constant state of dissolution and far from inert, the highway is, as Jane Bennett (2010) puts it, made of "vibrant matter" that is in need of care and maintenance. People along the Pamir Highway not only highlight the road's economic significance but also their emotional connections to it. By making it a lived, essential part of their biographies, they also emphasize the affective qualities of their relationship with a road that stands for promise and loss, provisioning and hardship.[6]

MOVING AND SETTLING

Throughout my fieldwork from 2008 to 2015, although the new Kulma road link between Tajikistan and China existed, its use was restricted to traders who entered China with a visa that they had obtained in Dushanbe. As a result, people from the district of Murghab focused their travel activities on the stretch of road between Khorog and Osh, which is exclusively served by private four-wheel-drive vehicles. Depending on the size of the vehicle, at the time of my research a seat in a usually crammed car cost the equivalent of $20–$30 each way, a pretty penny when you compare it to local wages. Passengers in such cars are usually traders, university students, or people with close relatives in Osh.

In March 2010 I had to travel to Osh and then to proceed to Bishkek. Due to harsh weather conditions, Nursultan advised me to travel early, so we started to look for a car going to Osh in the following days. The fact that the road could become impassible at any time made drivers think twice before risking a very tiring and potentially futile journey through the cold mountain desert and across high, snow-covered passes. When we finally found a driver who planned to leave for Osh with some relatives in his rusty Russian UAZ jeep the next day, I was glad to be offered the last remaining place—in the storage compartment behind the backseat of the vehicle.

Despite the cold and discomfort, this vantage point proved to be an ideal spot to observe the passengers and their interactions, which became increasingly tense due to difficulties on the journey. Besides the middle-aged driver Mital and his friend Tajikbai, all remaining passengers were female. There were Atyrgül, a young student of computer science, and Güljan, an elderly woman who frequently traveled between Osh and Murghab as a trader. In addition, there was a mother with her daughter who needed medical treatment in Osh, as well as a girl from Murghab who had recently married into a family in a village in Kyrgyzstan's part of the Ferghana Valley.

When we set off in the early morning, everyone was confident that we could cover the four hundred kilometers in one day and would arrive

FIGURE 2.3. Drivers waiting at Kyzyl-Art Pass for their vehicles to be checked for drugs. Photograph © Robert Middleton, 1995.

in Osh by nighttime. However, it turned out that nobody had bothered to clear the snow from the road. The difficult conditions on the snow-covered highway meant that we used more gas than expected, and by the time we reached the Tajikistani border post at Kyzyl-Art, the gas tank was empty. Still hung over from the night before, the driver had forgotten to bring an extra jerry can of gasoline, as is the standard practice. With the combined misery of having to face incompetent government agencies that failed to maintain the road, an absentminded driver, harsh weather conditions, various roadblocks, and bad and expensive food, my fellow passengers started to complain. Gradually their anger turned into caustic sarcasm, which they directed at whomever they held responsible for the situation. The women in the car called the driver a "pederast" (*pederas*), which was meant as a general derogatory term to punish Mital for forgetting the extra gas can, and they called young Tajik border guards "retards" (*tormoz*). Appreciation was expressed only for families of "road foremen" (*dormaster*),[7] who live at road supply stations along the highway and who support travelers by providing water, food, and small portions of gasoline.

By the end, we had spent several days on the road. The most difficult stretch was located between Murghab and the first settlements in Kyrgyzstan. This is not surprising, as it is precisely that part of the road that has largely lost its economic and ideological significance in recent years. Interesting neither to the government of Tajikistan nor to that of Kyrgyzstan, in winter the road often remains blocked by snow.

In the course of the women's discussions in Mital's car it became clear that not only changing national interests and incompetent state institutions were responsible for the decay. Indeed, Güljan raised the issue of a more general underlying crisis, which she attributed to a lack of morality and determination. In her opinion, independence had undone the achievements of the Soviet Union, and this crisis was embodied by drivers who drink when they should not; by young uneducated border guards who do not know how to read and write but know how to squeeze bribes out of people; by road construction workers who steal diesel fuel that is earmarked for snowplows; and by Kyrgyzstan's authorities, who have no intention of easing the suffering of people along the Pamir Highway by clearing the short but vital *Alaika* segment from the border to Sary Tash. All this contributes to an image of the road link from Murghab to the Tajikistan-Kyrgyzstan border as having been deserted. It evokes the feeling of a slowly fading supply route that has served as a well-funded and reliable point of reference over the past decades but which is now disappearing in favor of routes leading toward unfamiliar Chinese towns in Xinjiang.

Tajikistan's and Kyrgyzstan's rather lukewarm commitments to maintaining the road from Murghab to Osh emphasize the lack of economic interest in the region. At the same time, for people along the Pamir Highway who feel attached to southern Kyrgyzstan through family, work, or simply habit, the neglected stretch of road is the materialization of the end of the Soviet Union, which considered the region and its people a vital place within a broader geopolitical context. In this regard, an analysis of the Pamir Highway as vibrant matter, both dissolving and newly constructed, not only reflects attitudes toward the road itself but also sheds light on changing meanings of modernity in places along the way.

Sultonsho: Migration to Modernity

Sultonsho was fixing a white Tangem when I met him for the first time in a place called PATU. The acronym PATU stands for the Russian Pamirskoe Avtotransportnoe Upravlenie (Pamir Auto-Transport Directorate) and designates a group of whitewashed houses assembled around a large courtyard at the western end of the town of Murghab. During the Soviet period, PATU used to function as a truck stop. Back then, state-employed mechanics fixed cars in PATU, and their family members offered food and shelter to drivers. Its inhabitants describe PATU as a "happy" and "busy" place at that time. Now, few truck drivers end up in PATU, even though the mechanics' specialized knowledge is still appreciated. This was also the case when I met Sultonsho, who was lying under a Tangem that had suffered damage on a trip from Khorog.

Tangems are Chinese minibuses that are slowly replacing Soviet cars in Tajikistan. Due to its fuel efficiency, the Tangem has become popular in the Pamirs in recent years, though it is hardly the type of car that is most suitable to the bumpy highway. That fact, along with its miniature seats and lack of cargo space, provokes jokes about the Tangem all over the region. Sultonsho's ironic remarks from the car pit about the "luxurious" appeal of the Tangem and our subsequent shared laughs were the beginning of a friendship. Every time I have gone back to Gorno-Badakhshan since 2008, I have learned more about Sultonsho's extended family network within and beyond Murghab.

Sultonsho is in his forties. Just after he was born in a village in the upper Ghunt Valley in the 1970s, his family moved to Murghab, where his father found work as a car mechanic. Sultonsho's father describes life in the lower parts of the Pamirs as difficult at that time. "There wasn't much land, there were a lot of children in the family, and the village was growing in general. That's why I decided to take the job in Murghab," explained Sultonsho's father during one of my visits to PATU. He emphasized that moving from the Ghunt Valley to Murghab meant a change from a village community of Bartangi-speaking Ismailis to a place shaped by the presence of different linguistic, ethnic, and religious groups.[8]

Founded as a Russian military fort (*Post pamirskii*) at the end of the nineteenth century (Bliss 2006, 73), Murghab has a lengthy history of migration, having provided income-generating opportunities to Bartangi, Kyrgyz, and Wakhi early on (Kreutzmann 2015, 88). Yet from the 1930s onward, the construction of the Pamir Highway, with its newly created settlements, including Murghab as an important road supply station, began to contribute to the reshaping of Gorno-Badakhshan through the introduction of what Botakoz Kassymbekova (2011, 350) has called "territory in formation." Sultonsho and his father told me that their move to Murghab within this transformed territory involved a fundamental change of cultural environment. In addition, it signified an ecological and climatic movement from an agricultural mountain village (*qishloq*) to a high-altitude desert (*pustina*). Sultonsho explained this process of change to me in terms of a binary opposition: "While people in the village remained as they were, we took on different jobs and developed a different lifestyle. We became modern [*zamonavī*] and are very modern [*khele zamonavī*] now. Pamiris [*pomirī*] in Murghab were well educated. They were teachers, mechanics, drivers, party members, road construction workers, and border guards." As Sultonsho's words suggest, the process of having become modern through new forms of belonging is tied to particular events of migration.[9] However, as his remembrance of family history also shows, this is far from being a linear process and has resulted in multidimensional notions of time and belonging. For instance, Sultonsho was born in the Ghunt Valley, yet for him and his family Bartang is at least as important a point of reference. Bartang is a river valley just north of Ghunt and belongs to the district of Rushon. The majority of Bartangis who now live in the upper Ghunt Valley migrated there at the beginning of the twentieth century. Sultonsho's uncle, Faruh, who still lives in a village in Ghunt, called the period that followed migration "after Sarez" (*ba'di Sarez*), referring to an earthquake that hit at the beginning of the twentieth century and is still widely discussed in Murghab as a dramatic event in the history of the eastern Pamirs. In 1911, the earthquake led to the formation of a gigantic natural dam in Bartang (Abdullaev and Akbarzadeh 2002, 187). When part of the narrow valley started to fill up with water and turned into a lake, many Bartangis lost their property and land. The lack of land is also what Faruh defines as the main reason for migration. While pastures in Bartang were disappearing, there was still some land left in the high-altitude areas of Ghunt.

For Sultonsho and his family, Bartang is not only a real place with living relatives but also a place that harbors many memories and has its own historical time. This became clear to me on numerous occasions while talking to Bartangis, but it really struck home during a walk with Sultonsho through the small bazaar of Murghab. It was a freezing winter day, but when the intense mountain sun came out of hiding we stopped at the entrance of the bazaar, from where one can view the town stretching out all along the mountain slope. After a while Sultonsho said, "Every single person in Murghab has some home place outside the town. But this town is still the place where most of us have grown up. It's our 'homeland' [*rodina*] now." Back home in PATU, I tried to find out more about Sultonsho's other place of belonging:

> Till: You talked about other places Murghabi people come from earlier at the bazaar.

Sultonsho: Yes. I mean, since we come from Bartang, there are Ishkashi-
mis, Shughni people, and of course Kyrgyz who used to live in different
places according to their family descent. I think Murghab itself wasn't
an important pasture in earlier times.

Till: And you still go and visit Bartang?

Sultonsho: Yes, of course. From time to time if work allows me. Bartang is
a pure, serene place. Wherever you go, people will invite you to their
homes and feed you with meat. My wife and I, we couldn't eat for a
week after our last visit.

Sultonsho went on to tell me about his ancestors' migrations. At some
unspecified time in the past (*davno, davno*), Sultonsho's ancestors supposedly migrated from Iran to Bartang. According to his father's memories,
the Iranian ancestors were part of the religious elite—a status that the
family still maintains today. Even now Sultonsho's living relatives include
Ismaili *khalifa*s and *domullo*s, professions that often entail access to super-
natural powers.

Till: Iran is far away from Bartang. Why did they come to the Pamirs? And
how did they come?

Sultonsho: I don't know exactly why they came to Bartang, but I suppose
they were guided. In our family, it is said that they traveled here [by
flying] on tree trunks.

Till: Amazing. I hadn't thought about that option.

Sultonsho: Yes, at that time, it was a very common thing for *domullo*s. I
can't imagine it myself, but this was really in ancient times [*v drevnosti*].

Till: You mean that this skill doesn't exist anymore?

Sultonsho: No, of course not. People are modern [*sovremennye*] now. We
don't have such skills and would only abuse them [if we had them].

While recollecting his family history embedded in a broader regional
context, Sultonsho emphasized an opposition between "modern" and "old"
in regard to spatial and temporal organization. He referred to Murghab as
a modern homeland and multiethnic place, in contrast to Bartang, which
he described as more homogenous, serene, and traditional.

As a place of modernity with its distinct lifestyles and interconnections,
Murghab is not an exceptional phenomenon. Such places can be found
all over the former Soviet Union and were, just like settlements along the
Pamir Highway, often meant to support specific infrastructural projects.
Another prominent example in Tajikistan is the dam town of Norak in

the western part of the country. Norak was built in the 1960s in order to provide shelter for engineers, workers, and families who were involved in the construction and maintenance of the dam and hydroelectric station (Abdullaev and Akbarzadeh 2002, 156). As Madeleine Reeves (2014c, 114) reveals through the example of Shurab, a mining town in the Ferghana Valley that is administered by Tajikistan, such formerly privileged and provisioned places of modernity became "center[s] in the periphery"—that is, examples of "Moscow multiplying outwards and creating a direct and specific link to particular, chosen settlements that existed as urban 'pools' largely independent of the surrounding landscape." With respect to Murghab, it was not only one single settlement that became a center in the periphery but the whole landscape along the Pamir Highway. Rather than being a distinct settlement and an island of modernity, the town of Murghab is part of a network of such places that are held together by as-phalt. Thus, abandoning the road connection between Murghab and the border with Kyrgyzstan has meant destabilizing and physically cutting off a part of this network.

Having spent his whole life in Murghab, and PATU more specifically, Sultonsho is attached to the stretch of modernity that road construction has brought to Murghab, not least because it has provided him and his family with a way to make a living in the face of the land shortage in the upper Ghunt Valley. At the same time, Sultonsho locates the downsides of modernity in rationalization and the forgetting of ancient cultural skills. As a product of the Soviet planning landscape, Sultonsho defines Murgh-ab as a place of opportunities for which a price had to be paid. The current decay of the Pamir Highway poses a challenge to the idea of Murghab as a place of opportunity. Thus, migration toward a modern lifestyle, and the partial loss of it, have led to a "double-layered" form of nostalgia that emerges from both temporal (ancient, Soviet) and spatial (Bartang, Iran, Murghab) conditions.[10]

Gulira: Challenges to Morality

Although she is also in her early forties and therefore of the same genera-tion as Sultonsho, Gulira has rather different genealogical and biograph-ical points of reference. She spent her childhood at the opposite end of the Pamir Highway in the region of Osh and comes from a Kyrgyz family that included Sunni mullahs and other religious specialists in pre-Soviet times. Her supposedly rich ancestors fled from the Ferghana Valley to

Murghab, as she recalled, when local resistance against Bolshevik rule in the 1920s forced them to leave their home village near Batken.

In my conversations with Gulira and her husband Nursultan during my fieldwork in Murghab, the remembrance of history came across as an important part of everyday life. Both would recall their family histories and the history of Murghab, and visualize the geographic locations of their relatives who are scattered across Tajikistan, Kyrgyzstan, and China. While Gulira was interested in imagining how their relatives and fellow Kyrgyz were living across the border in China and Afghanistan, which were out of her reach, she always considered Murghab a special and privileged place. The fact that her ancestors had fled to Murghab, where turmoil and violence were less fierce than in other parts of Central Asia in early Soviet times, made her proud that her family did not participate in banditry. The Soviet-influenced image of *basmachis*—local resistance fighters against the Red Army—as rapacious robbers and religious fanatics is still persistent in Murghab.[11] For Gulira, the Ferghana Valley as a place of historical and present-day banditry strongly contrasts with the image of the eastern Pamirs as a realm where a calmer, clearer, and potentially purer way of life prevails. This does not, however, imply that Gulira conceptualizes people's morality as merely influenced by the environment and geographical space. Even in a serene place like Murghab, Gulira argues, people can become corrupt and decadent. While sitting at the stove in her and Nursultan's house, as we often did in the winter of 2010, she told me her version of Murghabi history and how it related to people's contemporary lifestyles. Occasionally she would order her children to pour some butter (*mai*) into the stove in order to calm the "talking fire" (*ot süilöit*) and then reflect on the fate of ancient settlements in the region.

Many centuries before the Russian conquest of the Pamirs, mining towns had been established in the region of Murghab. Some of these mining towns were explored by archaeologists in the course of the twentieth century (Bubnova 2005, 198), and the results of this academic work have found their way into local narratives. People along the Pamir Highway often link specific historical knowledge about gold-, silver-, and ruby-mining towns with very real anxieties about social and moral decay in Murghab. Close to Yrang-Köl, for instance, in a village at the Chinese border just east of Murghab, the population of a gold-mining town had, according to Gulira, suffered an unfortunate fate due to its moral corrup-

Figure 2.4. The moldered façade of the airport in Murghab. Photograph ©
Till Mostowlansky, 2010.

tion. Gold and the accompanying uncontrolled accumulation of wealth
had led to the establishment of settlements where "sin" (*grekh*, *künöö*)
was predominant.

> Gulira: Sin (*grekh*) was there in ancient times, too. Look at Yrang-Köl . . .
> this is what usually happens when people get rich [*bai*] and greedy
> [*zhadnyi*]. There used to be gold in Yrang-Köl and people went look-
> ing for it.
>
> Till: When was that?
>
> Gulira: It was a long time ago [*davno, davno*]. It was in ancient times
> [*kadim chakta*]. When they got rich through gold, they also got cor-
> rupt. People sinned, slept with each other without being married [*nike
> bolgon emes*], they drank, had parties [*vecherinka*] all the time. People
> turned into homosexuals [*aial aial menen, erkek erkek menen*]. And
> when God had enough of it, he opened the ground and the gold village
> disappeared. It's now a big grave close to the Chinese border.

For Gulira, Murghab today is in the same state of moral decrepitude as
the mining settlement at Yrang-Köl. Thus she sees the forgetting of morality and cultural skills as neither solely a feature of the past (the decay of
Yrang-Köl) nor of the present (the decay of Murghab). It therefore cannot

FIGURE 2.5. A sign made of stone in Murghab spelling out "Happy unity."
Photograph © Till Mostowlansky, 2010.

exclusively be attributed to modernity but rather constitutes a potentially universal process.

Gulira spent some of her childhood in the Ferghana Valley, but soon the family moved back to Murghab, where her father was employed as a scientist. Natural science research institutions were relatively prominent in the Pamirs at that time due to the mountains' specific high-altitude context. Going to a Russian school and being surrounded by academics, Gulira had the great wish to one day become a scientist, too. However, the breakup of the Soviet Union thwarted her plans, and the beginning of the civil war in 1992 brought a strange and rough environment to Murghab that was soon dominated by drug traffickers and soldiers.

Gulira remembers the years of perestroika just prior to this as an extremely happy time, as "bliss" (*kaif*) that was influenced by the global sounds of the 1980s. Back then Gulira used to go to a club called Jashtyk ("Youth"), where she danced to the music of Modern Talking, Boney M, and the Russian band NaNa. But then, with little in the way of economic prospects, the future of Tajikistan uncertain, and far too many foreign soldiers around, Gulira married Nursultan, a young local Kyrgyz officer of Murghabi origin and member of the Russian army who was stationed at border posts and roadblocks in the region.[12]

Even though the Soviet Union was already fading back then, the presence of the Russian army managed to preserve the remnants of the past for some time. The army provided jobs in the region, and there were still enough foreigners around to simulate the multiethnic environment of the former empire. According to Gulira, the final step of the "mess" (*bardak*) came later, when Russians began to leave in droves at the beginning of the new millennium. Still sitting at the stove in her Murghabi home, Gulira described the change of environment in educational terms: "I liked the way they taught ethics [*etika*] in school at that time. I don't think the Russians who influenced us here taught us bad things. Of course, they had their bad habits, such as drinking alcohol. But in comparison to us Muslims they understood what leading an ethical life is about." The current lack of ethics has resulted in a "messy generation" (*pokolenie bardak*), of which Gulira counts her little son a member. Gulira believes that this generation can be found all over the former Soviet Union. In Moscow, the Russian members of the "messy generation" showed their lack of values by killing Tajik and Kyrgyz labor migrants, just as young boys in Murghab were behaving like uneducated "hooligans" (*khuligany*).

Gulira's example shows that modernity can be a past and present condition at the same time. The parallels between moral decay in ancient mining towns and present-day Murghab suggest that there is only a fine line between modernity, decay, and the reinscription of backwardness. For her, modernity is a condition that existed in the past and which includes the potential of disappearance as well as the hope of revival. In this regard, the generally positive aspects that Gulira ascribed to late Soviet modernity contrast with Sultonsho's understanding of modernity as cultural loss.[13] The common threads that bind together this polyphony of meanings in space and time are the physical presence of the highway itself and the experience of migration along and beyond it. Accordingly, it is the road as a shared place and life on it as a shared history that provide the basis for selected moments of communality.

PLACE MAKING AND LOCAL HISTORY

The production of knowledge about the past plays an important role in everyday life along the Pamir Highway, and history is a matter of mundane conversations, political speeches, and scholarly analysis. People in the district of Murghab often debate the past with reference to different national, transnational, local, religious, and ethnic histories. At the same time, they also challenge these, thereby creating new, alternative, and overlapping spaces of engagement. In order to understand these process-es, I look at local history as a practice bridging abstract discourse on space and the making of places in Murghab.[14] Against this backdrop, we might think of the production of knowledge about history along the Pamir Highway as a place-making practice that does not just frame the past but also serves to ensure a sense of continuity and cohesion pointing toward the future.

People in Murghab have developed a variety of strategies to counter-balance the effects of living in the contemporary nation-state framework of Tajikistan, which leaves little room for those who are not clearly defined as ethnic Tajiks. In the course of my fieldwork, representatives of the cen-tral government (*hukumat*) in the capital Dushanbe have both enforced and addressed such processes of fragmentation in their interactions with people along the highway. The following example from my ethnograph-ic data indicates the extent of interconnection between references to the past, political positioning, ethnicity, and place making.

The visit of Tajikistan's president Emomali Rahmon in 2010 was a spe-cial event for most people in Murghab. It was occasioned by the fact that the national Day of Unity (Rūzi Vahdat), commemorating the peace trea-ty that officially ended the civil war in Tajikistan on 27 June 1997,[15] was celebrated in Gorno-Badakhshan. In his speeches exalting the country's unity, Rahmon often seeks ways to call for regional and ethnic cohesion. When his helicopter approached the desert plain just outside the town, the waiting crowd in Murghab knew that they could expect a speech that was aimed at preventing the dissolution of common national and local identities—as had just happened earlier that month in southern Kyrgyz-stan. While the ethnicized violence between Kyrgyz and Uzbeks in Osh in June 2010 had caused feelings of unease in many places with multieth-nic populations, it had quite directly affected Murghab through the influx of refugees and a blocked supply route from the Ferghana Valley.

It was a cold and windy summer day on the open plain east of the town. Seemingly weak and breathless, perhaps because of the high altitude, President Rahmon found that his words in Tajik tended to disappear in the noisy desert wind. In addition, while people in Murghab are decidedly multilingual, their knowledge of the president's language is limited, and many people in the audience were unable to understand him. Subsequent translations and interpretations into Russian and Kyrgyz, however, soon turned the president's speech into Murghabi common talk. Although ru-mor had it that the rarefied high-altitude air had given Rahmon such a hard time that he felt the need to abbreviate his speech and even to reject local hospitality, expressed in the form of an invitation to lunch, many of my Murghabi friends found his words quite intelligent and convincing.

In his speech, Rahmon did not directly refer to the ethnicized conflict that had taken place in Osh just two weeks earlier. However, his words were clearly chosen to nip potential friction between different local actors in the bud. Rahmon acknowledged that Murghab was a region with a predominantly Kyrgyz population. But he also emphasized that Murghab was an integral part of "the state" (*davlat*) of Tajikistan. Drawing on Kyrgyz epic narratives, the president then explained why the people of Murghab should have faith in and obey the central government. Rahmon based his main argument on an interpretation of the Manas epic, whose main character is a national hero in Kyrgyzstan and popular among Kyrgyz communities in other countries. President Rahmon's interpretation can be summarized as follows: In a historical time long ago, the Kyrgyz national hero Manas was alive and contributed to a mutual understanding between Kyrgyz and Tajiks by creating family ties. In his search for a suitable wife, Manas became interested in Kanykei, who was the daughter of Temir Khan—a Tajik, as indicated in various versions of the epic.[16] Eventually, the Kyrgyz hero married the Tajik khan's daughter. This was a good reason to maintain peace between the two ethnic groups.

The use of an epic narrative as a call for peace and cooperation appealed to people in Murghab, who saw it as an elegant and even flattering move. The metaphor of marriage between the two ethnic groups, forever intertwined and related by blood, left a strong impact on many members of the audience, and far exceeded the Soviet call for "friendship of peoples" (*druzhba narodov*). After the president had thanked the people of Murghab for surviving in such harsh conditions and for continuing to fly the flag of Tajikistan in the eastern Pamirs, he got back in his helicopter, allegedly glad to escape the befogging lack of oxygen. Only then did the potentially conflicting nature of Rahmon's rhetoric start to stir confusing emotions among some of my Tajik friends living in Murghab. They started asking themselves if they found being the wife of a Kyrgyz such an attractive image.

To invoke Manas, a Kyrgyz epic that plays an important role in nation building in Kyrgyzstan, was a daring act.[17] The Kanykei story may have simply aimed to touch the hearts of the majority of people in Murghab. In drawing on this epic, however, Rahmon's speech clearly demonstrated that he considered the Kyrgyz of Murghab to be the dominant ethnic group in the region. By referring to Manas, President Rahmon ethnicized Murghab as a Kyrgyz place into which Tajiks had married. Yet even though he quite clearly depicted Murghab as essentially Kyrgyz, Rahmon also stands for a forcefully centralizing government whose administration, in the attempt to "fix" ethnicity and territory (Moore 2005, 153–83), has become increasingly bound to the national tools of Tajik statehood. In this context, the production of knowledge about the past in Murghab constitutes a form of place making that both counterbalances and reflects existing power relations.

Murghab as a Kyrgyz Place

People in Murghab reflect upon local history in the district in various ways. My observations underscore the importance of both the spoken and the written word, and of the links between them, for the ways people situate themselves in the history of the region. In the course of my fieldwork I encountered five locally published books that were regularly used and referred to in everyday interaction. Following Karin Barber (2007, 3), I treat these texts as "social facts" and as tools that are embedded in social practices and "are used to do things." The selection of these five books is not accidental. All of them were given to me as presents by people from various backgrounds who often wanted me to regard these written sources as complementary to, and sometimes even as more authoritative than, their own oral narratives. The gifting and use of these books, themselves "forms of action" (Barber 2007, 3), are therefore embedded in a sequence of interactions between my interlocutors and myself or among people of Murghab themselves. In the course of these interactions my interlocutors often suggested that the correct history of places along the Pamir Highway was part of the "history of Sarykol" (*Sarykol tarykhy*), a region which goes far beyond the territory of Murghab. This accurate history, they argued, could be found in these books or in the references they cite.

The five works were written or edited exclusively by local male scholars and journalists,[18] and were published between 2002 and 2007. They include, in chronological order, Bekjol Taipov's *Short Sketches of the History of Sarykol* and Mitalip Jumabaev and Sultan Parmanov's work *Kairyks of Sarykol* (both published in 2002);[19] Saparbaev and Temirkulov's *The Pamir Kyrgyz* (2003); Abdikarim Chokoev's *The Legacies of My Land, or the Return to a Past Life* (2007); and Tadzhidinov and Parmanov's *Legends of Sarykol* (2007). With the exception of *Legends of Sarykol*, which was written in Russian, all of the books were published in Kyrgyz and address a Kyrgyz audience, using terms and toponyms such as "the Pamir Kyrgyz," "my land," and "Sarykol." Due to electricity shortages and the lack of technology in Murghab, all of these works were printed in either Osh or Khorog. All of them are self-published books, which is why the number of copies is difficult to determine. However, many adults in Murghab know of the existence of these books, whose authors are prominent personalities in the region.

A chronological approach to the works shows that the first two books—by Taipov and Jumabaev and Parmanov—were published in 2002, on the occasion of the seventieth anniversary of Murghab's existence as a district and administrative unit of the Tajik Soviet Socialist Republic and subsequently the Republic of Tajikistan (Jomhurii Tojikiston). Taipov's *Short Sketches of the History of Sarykol* opens with pictures of President Emomali Rahmon and the then governor of Gorno-Badakhshan, Alimamad Niyozmamadov. In combination with the preface by Idris Shodzhanov, then a local government representative, this makes Taipov's work an officially sanctioned history book that claims scholarly and political authority. The use of the term "Sarykol" in the title suggests a Kyrgyz territory that extends well beyond Murghab and the national borders of Tajikistan, embracing large areas in adjacent western China and northeastern Afghanistan as well (Taipov 2002, 9). Even though the author acknowledges the fact that historically Kyrgyz have long lived together with Tajiks, Sarykol is presented as a Kyrgyz space of nomads (*köchmön*) and livestock breeders. To be sure, Taipov mentions the historical presence of local Tajiks in the sense of a people who speak a Pamir language called Sariqoli,[20] but this mention of Sariqoli Tajiks (Olson 1998, 300) is simply inevitable because their name—Sariqoli—is clearly cognate with the place-name Sarykol. Overall, the book presents Murghab as a Kyrgyz place through historiography yet aligns itself with the government of Tajikistan. On the one hand, the author praises the current president of Tajikistan as the man who brought peace to the country (Taipov 2002, 11); on the other hand, he directly and exclusively addresses a Kyrgyz audience through the use of the pronouns "we" (*biz*) and "ours" (*-biz*). With sentences such as "our ancestors used to be a nomadic people" (*ata babalarybyz köchmön kalk bolup*), Taipov (2002, 9) defines the historical inhabitants of Sarykol as nomads who were organized in distinctively Kyrgyz kinship groups (*uruu*).

Similar tendencies can be observed in the *Kairyks of Sarykol*. Here, the journalist and editor Sultan Parmanov introduces a collection of "poetry from a high land" (*biiik jerdegi poeziya*) as coming from a "Kyrgyz place" (*kyrgyzdyn jeri*) (Jumabaev and Parmanov 2002, 3). The book contains a poem that emphasizes Kyrgyz-Tajik friendship (*dostuk*) in Murghab and in Badakhshan, which is depicted as their common homeland (35). Nonetheless, the overall depiction of Sarykol is that of a Kyrgyz "homeland" (*meken*) in the "high mountains" (*biiik too*). For instance, in his poem "My Land Sarykol" (*Jerim Sarykol*), Alymkul Aknazarov writes, "I am a Kyrgyz, my land is Sarykol, which my ancestor selected" (*Men kyrgyzmyn, jerim Sarykol, ata babam tandagan*) (81).

A Bag of Light

President Rahmon's aforementioned speech on the consanguinity of the Tajik and Kyrgyz peoples, based on the epic marriage of Manas and Kanykei, relates to a broader historiographical use of epic narratives to legitimize various claims on territory. Examples of how the Manas epic is used to foster visions of Murghab as Kyrgyz land are abundant in Taipov's work, particularly in the author's explanations of Sarykol toponyms (*Sarykol toponimi*). The simple references to close relatives of Manas or to kinship groups that have allegedly lived in the region of Sarykol for an indefinite period of time are enough to stake claims to Sarykol as a Kyrgyz territory, claims that are subsequently believed to be historically legitimate (Taipov 2002, 23).

Toponyms are a favorite tool for the appropriation of places in all the works I have analyzed and provide an example of the close intertwining of local history and everyday debates. This is illustrated by the controversy over the name Murghab itself. Tajikistani officials, and Tajik and Persian speakers more generally, agree that the word *murghob*, as it is spelled in Tajik, means "river of ducks" or "river of birds": *murgh* means "bird," *ob* means "water," and *murghobi* is the Tajik word for duck. However, the Kyrgyz version of the origin of the toponym differs considerably. As stated in the *Legends of Sarykol*, the Kyrgyz word *nurkap*, "a bag of light," is the authentic name of present-day Murghab: "Nurkap (bag with rays of light): This is the name of the area where present-day Murghab is located. There is always sunshine there. That is why they called the place 'a bag with rays of light' [*nurdun kaby*], or Nurkap" (Tadzhidinov and Parmanov 2007, 25).

In *The Legacies of My Land, or the Return to a Past Life*, Abdikarim Chokoev consistently uses the name Nurkap to refer to Murghab. In constructing Sarykol as a Kyrgyz place, Chokoev also underlines the importance of Islam. Indeed, throughout the book, Chokoev portrays Sarykol as a region of religious importance. Because he views Sunni Kyrgyz pilgrimage sites (*mazars*) and the historical existence of *eshan*s, a distinct class of Sunni Kyrgyz religious specialists, as central to the region's religious significance, Chokoev defines Sarykol as a Sunni place where other denominations are of secondary importance.

In the introductory section on the Kyrgyz people (*Kyrgyz eli*), Chokoev looks at the history of Sarykol alongside major events in the conjectural history of the Kyrgyz as an ethnic group. Accordingly, he portrays "the people of Sarykol" (*Sarykolduktar*) as livestock breeders who lived in "Kyrgyz houses" (*Kyrgyz üi*)—that is, yurts (Chokoev 2007, 12). He then proceeds to discuss Sarykol as land (*Sarykol jeri*) that he considers essentially Kyrgyz. Thus he writes, "Sary Kol has been a Kyrgyz land from time immemorial" (14).

In contrast to the other four publications on local history and culture, Chokoev's book provides a detailed account of the places he considers part of Sarykol. His definition of a Kyrgyz land clearly goes beyond the borders of Tajikistan and includes villages and towns in China and Afghanistan. However, when it comes to the representation of people and concrete historical descriptions, Chokoev largely sticks to the boundaries of the present district of Murghab. Here, Chokoev analyzes toponyms and their etymologies and attributes the emergence of specific pilgrimage sites to events in the past. Reports of lives and visits of *eshan*s and mullahs (*moldo*) who have been to the region are regarded as important accounts of the history and people of Alichor, a small settlement west of the district center. As in the case of Murghab and Nurkap, Chokoev contends that the current name Alichor is a corrupted form of much older versions of the Kyrgyz phrase *eldin choru*, "the people's callus," which over time was transformed into *Alinin chölü*, "the desert of Ali" (p. 90).

Appropriating Sarykol with Development Funds

As noted above, Taipov's *Short Sketches of the History of Sarykol* and Jumabaev and Parmanov's *Kairyks of Sarykol* were published on the occasion of the seventieth anniversary of Murghab's recognition as an administrative district; Chokoev's *The Legacies of My Land, or the Return to a Past Life* appeared for the seventy-fifth anniversary. These three works are thus officially sanctioned by the government. In contrast, Saparbaev and Temirkulov's *The Pamir Kyrgyz* and Tadzhidinov and Parmanov's *Legends of Sarykol* received support from international donors. The publication of *The Pamir Kyrgyz* was sponsored by the French NGO Agency for Technical Cooperation and Development (ACTED) and the state-run Swiss Agency for Development and Cooperation (SDC). Similarly, *Legends of Sarykol* received support from ACTED and SDC, as well as from The Christensen Fund (TCF), a U.S.-based NGO.

The involvement of international donors in the promotion of local history and culture shows that the practice of local studies in Murghab is linked to organizations that are present on the international development scene. It furthermore suggests an intermingling of local visions of history and culture with the agendas of development agencies. While such agencies had a variety of sometimes divergent aspirations at the time of my fieldwork in Murghab, in the case of the SDC and ACTED they sought to support "the vulnerable inhabitants" and to strengthen "decentralization." Thus, an emphasis on "the local" as well as efforts to counter "marginalization" provide the backdrop for particular forms of place making ("Pamir High Mountain Integrated Project" 2014).

Moreover, The Christensen Fund shaped local studies in Kyrgyzstan and (to a lesser extent) in Tajikistan through the funding of research organizations, projects, and publications (Mostowlansky 2011a, 297). In this regard, a part of The Christensen Fund's Central Asia and Turkey program was meant to embrace "the core issues of re-establishing connections to the land, traditional ways of life, identity and culture" ("Central Asia and Turkey" 2014). In Central Asia, it was the fund's aspiration to "emphasize the importance of diverse spiritual and cultural values as a barrier to fundamentalism; and aspire to get young people engaged and excited about their cultural heritage and traditional knowledge." As for Murghab, The Christensen Fund envisioned strengthening the "reciprocal relationships between cultures, livelihoods and ecology." This mission required a specific definition of culture and tradition. The Christensen Fund's orientation toward "tradition" and "cultural heritage" as detached from the Soviet experience and pointing toward a pre-Soviet past made it compatible with ethnicizing publications such as *Legends of Sarykol*.

Debate on the Road

Writing down, publishing, distributing, reading, and renarrating the results of local studies comprise an important dimension of place making along the Pamir Highway, and people's references to the past are often embedded in debates. The products of such everyday interactions are far from being stable and fixed. As a consequence, we face "entangled landscapes" (Moore 2005, 22) which are, as Madeleine Reeves (2011a, 314) mentions, "the always-provisional *outcome* of heterogeneous trajectories, of people, things and ideas." The question of how we can make sense of and navigate through such inherent heterogeneity in the case of Murghab leads back to President Rahmon's Unity Day Speech that I mentioned earlier. A year after the speech was given, it still played a role in everyday encounters and served as a nexus where claims about local history, ethnicity, and the nation-state come together in mundane debates.

It was August 2011, a year after the speech, when I had to wait for several days in Osh to find a car going to Murghab. Finally, at one of the city's truck stops I met Döölöt, who was planning to drive to Murghab in his Russian UAZ jeep and agreed to take me with him. As he was not exactly sure when he would set out, I spent most of my time waiting at the *Alai baza*, an assemblage of houses on the roadside from where most passenger cars leave for the Pamirs.[21] At the *Alai baza* I also met my fellow Kyrgyz travelers Jailoobai and Timur, who wanted to return to Murghab after a summer visit to Osh. As it turned out, both men were interested in the history of Murghab and the genealogies (*sanjyra*) of their families. Jailoobai was a Kyrgyz elder, an *aksakal*, and a retired school teacher. Timur was still a university student who often spent the summer months in the pastures herding yaks. It soon became apparent that Jailoobai and Timur had very different visions of Murghabi history and ethnicity, and while they were sitting together with me in Döölöt's UAZ an argument commenced. When we stopped at a teahouse on the way to the Tajikistani border for a late dinner, other travelers got involved in the debate, too. While the *aksakal* Jailoobai argued that Murghab had always been distinctively Kyrgyz, Timur insisted that President Rahmon's speech about Manas the year before stressed the historically close relationship between Tajiks and Kyrgyz. This interpretation suggested that Murghab had always been both a Kyrgyz and a Tajik region.

> Jailoobai [*reacting to the argument that Kyrgyz and Tajiks have both been present in Murghab since ancient times*]: This isn't true. Except for the Pamiris who came to Murghab to build the road, there haven't been any. And that has happened recently.
>
> Timur: But as the president said, the relationship dates back to Manas.
>
> Jailoobai: My grandparents used to call Murghab "Nurkap." It's Kyrgyz. And so it is written in the books about Sarykol . . . and in other historical writings about us.

Timur: I haven't heard of Nurkap from my parents. . . .
Jailoobai: Maybe they're too young. Even Khorog used to be Kyrgyz, they
say. It was pronounced differently back then—Khörög or something.

As the debate went on, our fellow travelers started to contribute and to
position themselves regarding the issue of whether Murghab had historically been mixed (*aralash*) or distinctively Kyrgyz. They linked the president's speech to the results of local studies on history and tried to make
sense of the historical situatedness of Murghabi territory. In this regard,
"Kyrgyzizing" the toponym Murghab meant claiming that the word was
a corruption of a name that had originally been Kyrgyz. As Jailoobai's argument shows, the Kyrgyz pronunciation of a place-name that is conven-
tionally considered Tajik constitutes another way of asserting historical
ownership.

Visiting *Mazars*

The use of toponyms and their history is one strand of place making in
Murghab. Linking specific sites in the region to religious and ethnic belonging is another. In this regard, pilgrimage sites (*mazars*) are of particular importance. *Mazars* have various functions along the highway and are
spread over large parts of the Murghabi landscape. While Kyrgyz in the
region often talk about *mazars* as essentially Kyrgyz and Sunni, Pamiris
tend to locate Ismaili pilgrimage sites (*mazor, oston*) in the southwestern
and western Pamirs, outside the area that people define as Sarykol.[22] Sultonsho, for instance, once told me with reference to the *mazar* in Madiyan, which includes hot springs and a bathhouse, that the Kyrgyz go there
to bathe and pray. In contrast, he and his friends go to Madiyan to bathe
only: "For us [Ismailis] it is just about the healing effect. But the Kyrgyz
believe that a holy man [*shahid*] was killed up there and they buried him
close to the hot springs. You know what one of my neighbors said when
the Kyrgyz prayed there once? 'Holy man? What? It's just a thief, a *basmachi*, who is buried here!'"

The distribution of Kyrgyz pilgrimage sites in the eastern Pamirs
and Ismaili *mazors* and *ostons* in the southwestern and western parts of
Gorno-Badakhshan reinforces the image of the Kyrgyz as the indigenous
population of Murghab. For the Kyrgyz along the highway, a *mazar* is
closely connected to spiritual blessings (*bereke*) and the performance of
pilgrimage to a tomb (*zyiarat*).[23] *Bereke* emanate from the martyr's grave,
whose violent death is usually presumed to be the origin of the historical

FIGURE 2.6. The *mazar* Ak-Balyk between Murghab and Alichor. Photograph © Till Mostowlansky, 2008.

development of a particular *mazar*.[24] Visiting a *mazar* in Murghab therefore not only means performing specific rituals such as "saying prayers"
(*dua* or *pata kyluu*), but also remembering a historical person and a historical event. The martyrs (*sheiit*) of Murghab represent sacrifices from
a broad range of historical periods. Pilgrimage sites I visited included
graves of martyrs who died at the hands of Mongol soldiers, Qing war-
riors, and even Red Army officers in the 1920s. According to my interlocutors, these martyrs were all men and women who had fallen in defense of
Islam at very different times over a wide swath of history. Yet despite this
vast diachronic outlook, people exclusively remembered them as Kyrgyz
and Sunni. Thus, besides healing and the bestowal of *bereke*, a further
important aspect of *mazar*s is their function as territorial markers. In
combination with historical narratives about these sites, visiting *mazar*s
not only evokes the remembrance of pious ancestors but also reaffirms
the notion of Murghab—and of Sarykol—as a land of the Kyrgyz.

After years of field research and trips to many places in Murghab, I
still find it difficult to establish a definitive number of existing *mazar*s
in the region. Every time we planned to visit a *mazar* between 2008 and
2015, my friends thought of a new pilgrimage site that I had not yet seen.
Thus, step by step I began to form the image of Murghabi territory as

paved with *mazar*s that had sprung up at different periods of time, even into the Soviet era. In the summer of 2011, I had the chance to visit half a dozen *mazar*s with Kudaibergen Ata, Nursultan, and other friends. (I briefly referred to this trip in chapter 1 while discussing the transfer of Soviet fish on the Pamir Highway.)

The *mazar* journey with Kudaibergen Ata is an example of the merging of local studies, oral narratives, and physical movement as contributing to place making in Murghab. When we went off to the mountains in my white Lada Niva on that rainy summer day, Kudaibergen Ata was looking forward to visiting a number of pilgrimage sites to which he had not had access in recent years because of their remoteness. For me, this was a good opportunity to see more of the area surrounding Alichor, the settlement to the west of the district center that Abdikarim Chokoev (2007, 90–93) describes in detail in his book on Sarykol. And indeed, Kudaibergen Ata had taken Chokoev's book with him on the trip. As a result, our pilgrimage not only turned out to be a tour de force through pastures and across mountain brooks but also one through the detailed architecture of Chokoev's historical work. The longer we talked about the pilgrimage sites of the region, the clearer it became that Kudaibergen Ata's knowledge differed considerably from the information that Chokoev provided. Yet that did not stop Kudaibergen Ata from sometimes referring to Chokoev's book as an authoritative source of information. To be with Kudaibergen Ata while having Chokoev's study by our side was like being accompanied by two elders engaged in dialogue. While they often disagreed, they also agreed on the fact that even the oldest graves at the pilgrimage sites were of Kyrgyz origin. They applied the same historical explanations when it came to wars and the rulers involved in them but disagreed on the exact events that led to the martyrs' deaths. At the same time, it was clear that they had all been virtuous Kyrgyz men and women who had died for their faith and in defense of Islam and their people. When I asked Kudaibergen Ata who actually visited *mazar*s and the martyrs' graves in the region to receive *bereke*, he replied as follows:

> Kudaibergen Ata: Everybody visits *mazar*s. Kyrgyz people have their own *mazar*s. For example, the Pamiris go to their own *mazar*s [in the western Pamirs]. They have many of them.
>
> Till: And where exactly do people go?
>
> Kudaibergen Ata: As we are talking about the Kyrgyz . . . and Kyrgyz live in Murghab . . . I'm telling you about the *mazar*s to which Kyrgyz

people go. Kyrgyz people live in kinship groups [*uruu*]. Each *uruu* has its own *mazar*. And that is where they usually go.

The notion of Murghab as a Kyrgyz place is, on the one hand, carved into the landscape through history and kinship. At the same time, it is also ingrained in human bodies and dreams. As Kudaibergen Ata told me, the *bereke*—the spiritual blessings that emanate from *mazars*—have healing powers and contribute to a happy and healthy life. He and others also referred to the link between an overnight stay at a *mazar* and the occurrence of an *aian*, a message that is delivered while dreaming (*tüsh körüü*) and in which ancestors play a pivotal role. A *mazar* furthermore supports (*koldoit*) the visitor if he or she comes with pure intentions (*nii-ettin tazalygy*) and bodily cleanliness (*dene tazalygy*). The purity of the spiritual world (*rukhii tazalyk*) that people attributed to a *mazar* is explicitly ethnically and religiously coded. To be sure, some of the *mazars* along the Pamir Highway that are located at hot springs entail the shared dimensions of health, well-being, and hygiene. In the Soviet Union, turning to nature for health was commonly propagated as part of an encompassing spiritual, aesthetic, and medical complex.[25] Infrastructure supporting hot springs in Gorno-Badakhshan was usually built in this context. Yet the vast majority of *mazars* that I encountered in Murghab consisted of rocks, trees, or small lakes. For people along the highway these places, which are perceived as distinctly Kyrgyz and Sunni, bear witness to historical and present-day difference in the region.

PART II

SITES OF
ENGAGEMENT

CHAPTER 3

NASHA–VASHA

OURS AND YOURS

PICKING A TIME

Time is a matter of frequent discussion along the Pamir Highway. Whoever enters a private house or an office not only has to wonder whether the typically Chinese wall clock is accurate, but to also reflect on the particular system of time it follows. While in Khorog most clocks are adjusted to the time of the capital Dushanbe, people in the district of Murghab tend to be divided between those who adhere to the official Tajikistani time and those who insist on the existence of a Murghabi time (*Murgab saaty*) or Badakhshani time (*Badakhshan saaty*). Many people in Murghab, located roughly a thousand kilometers east of Dushanbe, set their clocks an hour later than those in the capital. While the insistence on a minor and locally restricted time difference could be regarded as a marginal issue, diverging opinions on the correctness of time have also led to friction between representatives of the government (and those in support of it) and Murghabi clock owners. The supporters of Murghabi time have come up with a number of strategies to justify their insistence on the time difference. Explanations include naturalization ("we need to follow the sun"), geographical location ("nearby Kyrgyzstan has the same time"), history ("the abolished daylight savings time of the Soviet Union"), and religion ("correct prayer time"). In contrast, critics of such attitudes often interpret them as indicative of ignorance (*alar tüshünböit*), stubbornness (*upriamstvo*), or even separatist tendencies. The government official Kamal's encounter with several male village elders, which I witnessed in the summer of 2010 in a settlement close to the town of Murghab, is embedded within such processes of differentiation.

Kamal had asked for a meeting with the village elders in order to solve administrative questions and to announce a change in laws in the region. All participants were Kyrgyz, and they had planned to hold the meeting within the framework of a lunch. However, when Kamal and I arrived in the village at noon, no elders were to be found. They had already had their lunch and were now resting in their houses or had left the village for the pastures. Kamal, whom I considered a stable source of reason and who described himself as seeking "harmony" (*yntymak*),[1] erupted in anger and, even on the way back to Murghab, could not stop complaining about the stupidity and stubbornness of the elders. As a state official and member of the president's People's Democratic Party of Tajikistan (Hizbi Khalqī-Demokratī Tojikiston), he had assumed that everybody would observe the official time zone that the government had established. As it turned out, however, the village elders had knowingly insisted on the use of the unofficial Murghabi time.

After his blaze of anger in the car on the way back to town, the matter of time became increasingly important to Kamal. During many of our subsequent encounters, he mentioned the topic and expressed both embarrassment and indignation. To an official, the rejection of official Dushanbe time not only signified the villagers' disregard for the government but also had very personal implications. As Kamal later mentioned, getting involved in petty conflicts over time would not do the people of Murghab any good. In his vision, Murghab was to become an "international" (*mezhdunarodnyi*) place with international people who would be involved in China trade and act as mediators between Tajikistan, Kyrgyzstan, Afghanistan, and China. In order to realize this vision, Kamal sent his children to Chinese and English classes and saved money for their university studies in the capital.

As the example of Kamal demonstrates, the decision to observe a specific time zone is multidimensional along the Pamir Highway. The use of Murghabi time is interpreted as source of pride, mere stubbornness, or local resistance. Kamal's rejection of it also lays bare his wish to claim an identity for himself as well as for his fellow Murghabis that both goes beyond locality and is aligned with the requirements of the central government. Against this backdrop, we might think along the lines of Katherine Verdery's (1996, 39) argument that "the social construction of time must be seen as a political process."[2] In her analysis of the "etatization" of time in socialist Romania, she focuses on temporal politics in the context of a "struggle over time, as people were subjected to and resisted new temporal organizations." In this regard, insistence on Murghabi time, and resistance to Dushanbe time, can also be seen as identifying with the time system that was introduced in the Soviet Union. What Kamal experienced as "stubbornness" against an "international" outlook, other interlocutors along the highway perceived as legitimate resistance against the new regime. Moreover, such perceptions are mapped in complex ways onto visions of "backward" versus "open," "international," and "modern." The construction of difference between supporters of Murghabi time and central authorities does not mean that such labels are applied unambiguously, with "modern" always mapped onto Dushanbe time and "backward" onto Murghabi time. While state officials might consider the use of Murghabi time stubbornly "backward," many people along the Pamir Highway see the use of a time that differs from official time as a statement against an authority that they consider less modern.

Ajmi's Pun

In 2010, the same year of Kamal's encounter with the reluctant village elders, I was staying in Nursultan and Gulira's house in Murghab when guests from Khorog arrived. As they had to leave again early the next day, an after-dinner discussion in Russian arose about when to wake up the next morning. Soon Nursultan and his guests started to reason about time issues in an increasingly ironic undertone.

> Asadbek: We have to leave very early tomorrow morning. I don't have time at all.
> Nursultan: Then you should leave around 7 a.m.
> Asadbek: We should definitely leave earlier. Let's make it 6 a.m.
> Nursultan [*looking surprised*]: I don't understand. That's too early. Do you mean 6 a.m. Dushanbe time?
> Asadbek: Ah I see, then it's gonna be 6 a.m. according to our [*nasha*] time and 7 a.m. according to your [*vasha*] time.
> Nursultan [*pointing at everybody in the room*]: 7 a.m. according to our common way [*po-nashemu*, here meaning "our common Badakhshani time"]!
> Ajmi [*laughing*]: I hope you didn't tell the president about your opinion on this. There's ONE official time. He wouldn't be pleased about this *Nasha—Vasha* at all.

The conversation shows that the Russian terms for "ours" (*nasha*), "yours" (*vasha*), and "our common way" (*po-nashemu*) were used to distinguish different approaches to time. When Asadbek said "ours," he meant the use of Dushanbe time and contrasted it with "yours" to denote Murghabi time. While Khorog, as the guests' town of origin, mostly functions on Dushanbe time, many people in Murghab prefer the 1-hour time difference.

The negotiation of identity in the conversation was marked by Nursultan's reference to "our way," a phrase intended to insist on a regionally organized agreement on time difference. By "our way," he meant "our common Badakhshani time," which, in Nursultan's opinion, should be reintroduced for the whole of Gorno-Badakhshan. It is furthermore a reference to the distinction between western Tajikistan and the autonomous region of Gorno-Badakshan as an entity with its own peculiarities. Ajmi's pun, a play on the title of the popular Russian television series *Nasha Russia* ("Our Russia"; see below), was a trenchant comment on the president's neglect of the local setting and thus indicates the political dimension of the use of time through the personified image of the state. The president, who is not pleased with the expression of difference, is a metonym for Tajikistan's government and its ambition to exercise control through the introduction of centralized authority.[3] When Ajmi coined the term *Nasha–Vasha* ("Ours–Yours"), she was pointing out the conflicting nature of time categories.[4] The fact that she expressed this through irony and evoked laughs from all people present in the room hints at the negotiation of identity as both playful and grave. Her pun was all the more incisive because, as I will show later in this chapter, the TV series *Nasha Russia* has caused a great deal of private and public debate in Tajikistan that reflects the processual character of identity.

Making Sense of Identity

People along the Pamir Highway are to some extent linked by shared experiences of modernity. At the same time, as the two ethnographic vignettes on time as well as material presented in the previous chapters suggest, places along the highway are also characterized by a high degree of difference. The ways people organize and make sense of these differences are subject to negotiation in everyday life and raise the question of how ethnic, political, and religious diversity is reproduced along the road.[5] Andrew Beatty (2002, 470–71) suggests tackling this question by focusing on why people find "certain ideas and practices compelling and reject or set aside others" and on how they grow up with and "come to embody cultural difference."

The concept of identity, controversial and often blurred, is key to an understanding of difference. In this regard, Martin Sökefeld (2001, 538) notes that it is useful to conceive of identity as "a category of practice and a category of analysis" that is subject to "the duality of essentialist and constructivist readings." In this sense, identity provides a tool to simultaneously convey "the essentialist implications of actors *and* the (de)constructivist stance of social scientists." The "Janus-faced semantic structure" of identity can, according to Sökefeld, help the analyst avoid conflating practice and analysis. Sökefeld (2010, 235–37) furthermore argues that the concept of identity, including both self-identity (i.e., "the identity of the individual self with itself") as well the identity of a group (i.e., "the identity of an individual with other individuals"), is made up of three related terms: multiplicity, difference, and intersectionality. While multiplicity refers to the fact that identity does not exist in the singular but "only as identit*ies*—formed through a plurality of relationships of belonging and otherness," he defines difference as a tool for the distinction of "one person from another person, or one group or category from another one." In combination with multiplicity, difference challenges identity. Against this backdrop, the self can be seen "as a bundle of different possible identifications, particular aspects of which may be put to the fore." Which aspects are put to the fore depends on the specific others against which a particular identity is established. Finally, intersectionality points to the fact that "different identities . . . which characterize an individual are not unrelated among themselves." In contrast, they influence each other and may include "conflict and antagonism, inconsistency and ambivalence." In sum, Sökefeld argues that these three aspects—multiplicity, difference, intersectionality—allow for a fruitful combination of the psychological concept of identity, which is oriented toward the individual, and identity as a concept focused on social or cultural collectives. In this reading, social identity is closely linked to the individual based on a particular combination—that is, a multiplicity—of identities that intersect in shifting ways.

By referring to the encounters of Kamal and the village elders, and of Nursultan, Ajmi, and Asadbek, I suggest looking at identity as entailing forms of self-essentialization that evolve in nonlinear, non-static ways. While such encounters produce binaries and create distinctions, they are also inherently situational and open to change. For instance, the fact that the elders insisted on their habitual use of time and positioned themselves against Kamal does not mean that they would act the same way outside their village. Moreover, Nursultan's reference to common Badakhshani time might make him a supporter of a regional identity in one context, but it does not mean that he would not align with Dushanbe time in another. In his work on Ladakh, Martijn van Beek (2000) refers to this situational aspect of identity, which can be explained by Sökefeld's notion of intersectionality, as a "necessary fiction." While acknowledging the material, political, and often violent presence of identities in everyday life, Van Beek also highlights the frequent need to dissimulate them. This notion is relevant to an understanding of how people along the Pamir Highway position themselves amid a range of different ethnic, local, political, national, and religious identities. These differences might be postponed, hidden, and obscured at certain moments and pronounced to the point of exaggeration in other situations. At the same time, I argue that, despite their fluid and situational character, identities leave their marks on everyday life and help us understand the ways people along the road situate themselves in time and space, including within the broader framework of contemporary Tajikistan.

TV AND AFTER

When I stayed at Nursultan's house in Murghab at an early stage of my research in 2008, I was astonished by the fact that there was no TV set in the living room. For the first time during my life in Tajikistan, I encountered evenings without television. When I asked Nursultan and his wife Gulira why they had no TV, they explained that "bad Russian channels" (*jaman orus kanaldary*) would have a negative influence on the children. In addition, electricity was in short supply in Murghab at that time and technical problems at the local hydroelectric power station left people in the dark several nights a week. As time passed, Nursultan and Gulira's attitude toward the use of television changed due to sad circumstances. During my stay their youngest son, a boy about six months old, died. The loss of the child engulfed his parents in grief. While Nursultan had to go to work, Gulira stayed home with their remaining children but felt increasingly depressed. When the electricity supply in Murghab was reorganized and there was enough electricity in Nursultan's house to run equipment, he quickly decided to buy a TV set in order to distract his wife. Subsequently, I spent many a day watching TV and DVDs with Gulira and her remaining three children. Focusing mainly on movies and series in Russian and Kyrgyz, we soon came across the comedy show *Nasha Russia*, which was being discussed all over the country.

In 2010, public debates on the TV series *Nasha Russia* reached their peak in Tajikistan. The series first stirred outrage among officials, and when the motion picture *Nasha Russia: Balls of Fate* (*Nasha Russia: Iaitsa sud'by*) was released in 2010, it was quickly banned from Tajikistan's cinemas and bazaars.[6] The authorities expressed particular displeasure over the movie's main characters, two allegedly Tajik labor migrants in Russia who are depicted as backward and dumb. Despite the ban, people along the Pamir Highway had little difficulty finding DVD copies of the movie and the series on the region's flourishing black market, and references to the show became part of everyday communication. At that time, a visit to friends' houses in the Pamirs often included watching an episode of *Nasha Russia*. In this regard, debates related to *Nasha Russia* triggered reflection on the differences and similarities between Kyrgyz, Pamiris, and Tajiks and their belonging to different stages of cultural development.

The Russian comedy show *Nasha Russia* had already been on the air since 2006. The show, produced by the Russian TV network TNT, was based on the licensed concept of the UK sitcom *Little Britain*, which had also caused controversy and was described as a "sadistic piece of spite" in UK media (Hari 2005). In *Nasha Russia*, the actors Mikhail Galustian, Sergei Svetlakov, Valerii Magd'iash, and others present a random cross section of Russian society to the audience. Similar to *Little Britain*, this cross section is mainly populated by dim-witted individuals and marginalized groups. The approximately twenty characters in *Nasha Russia* include the viewer Sergei Iur'evich Beliakov, who talks to his TV, and the gay worker Ivan Dulin, who is insanely in love with his boss Mikhalych, as well as two foreign labor migrants, Ravshan and Dzhamshut.

The origin of Ravshan and Dzhamshut, who appeared in seasons 1–4 but vanished in seasons 5 and 6, remains unknown and controversial.[7] The producers of *Nasha Russia* dropped the two characters after an intervention by the author Sambel Garibian and the Union of Armenians in Russia (Soiuz Armian Rossii, SAR). The main producers of *Nasha Russia* are of Armenian origin, and Ravshan and Dzhamshut were thus occasionally presumed to be Armenian. Yet Garibian and the SAR emphasized that they considered the series an insult to both Armenians and Tajiks. Their criticism targeted Russian racism toward Armenians and Tajiks, and they argued that the series could potentially cause disturbance on a broader scale in Russia, Armenia, and Tajikistan ("Armian s tadzhikami" 2010).

The uncertain origin of Ravshan and Dzhamshut and the related confusion appear to be intentional. On a handful of occasions on the show, the two characters are described as coming from a place called Nubarashen. While Nubarashen is a district of Armenia's capital Yerevan, Ravshan and Dzhamshut are never explicitly referred to as being of Armenian origin. In contrast, they are frequently mentioned as "guests from Central Asia" (gosti iz Srednei Azii), but without any more specific mention of nationality or ethnicity. Even though their appearance leaves much room for speculation, Ravshan and Dzhamshut are generally identified as Tajiks, and sometimes as Uzbeks, by Tajikistani audiences on the basis of their appearance and language: they have "big eyes" in contrast to the "narrow eyes" usually attributed to Kyrgyz and Kazakhs, and they speak an artificial, Tajik-like idiom. The story line of episodes involving Ravshan and Dzhamshut follows a similar pattern from the early days of Nasha Russia to the final season in which they appear. The background for all stories is the work environment of the two labor migrants that is also—mirroring an all-too-frequent reality—where they live and spend a lot of their private time. At the beginning of the series, a construction site in Moscow constituted the framework for encounters between cunning Ravshan, silent Dzhamshut, and their quick-tempered Russian superior, who is called Nashalnika in an unidentifiable "pidgin" form of the Russian word for "boss" (nachal'nik). Later, the construction site of the Olympic village for the 2014 Winter Olympics in Sochi in southern Russia was introduced as a new setting for jokes about culturally differing attitudes toward house construction and interior design, misconceptions of language, visits of labor law commissions, and troubles with immigration authorities.

According to critics in Tajikistan, Ravshan and Dzhamshut episodes, as well the feature-length movie, present the presumably Tajik labor migrants as backward and dull.[8] At the same time, a contextualization within the framework of Nasha Russia shows that there is barely an individual or group that is spared by the radical sense of humor that pervades the show. While Ravshan and Dzhamshut are obviously not very smart—for example, they install radiators on the outside wall of a house, reasoning that since the radiators will keep Moscow warm, a warm Moscow will also guarantee a warm house—their Russian boss is hardly more intelligent. With his lack of communication skills and a narrow-minded worldview, Nashalnika fits in well with the other characters on the show, who all ooze with goofiness and exaggeration. It is thus not self-evident that

Nasha Russia, as a TV show that drags members of various milieus in Russia through the mire, should necessarily lead to anger and political implications in a Central Asian republic. Rather, this anger about *Nasha Russia* in Tajikistan, which even led to death threats against Mikhail Galustian, the actor who plays Ravshan, needs to be situated in a context in which, as Lisa Rofel (1994, 701) argues, the "political" and the "popular" intermingle and "are mutually constituted."[9]

"Those Tajiks from Dushanbe"

After having watched an episode of *Nasha Russia* with Gulira on a lazy winter morning in 2010, I noticed the following expression of difference in our subsequent conversation. "Till," she said to me, "these guys don't know a word of Russian because Tajiks from Dushanbe are so uneducated [*negramotnyi*]." While clearly enjoying her voicing of a frequently used local cliché, Gulira suddenly stopped laughing and added, "But you know, I also speak with this accent and you might think I'm the same as them."

At first I was surprised by Gulira's sudden expression of solidarity with the comedy characters and her identification with them. And yet laughing at and feeling pity for Ravshan and Dzhamshut as they stumbled from one embarrassing situation into the next was a common way of watching *Nasha Russia* in the Pamirs at the time of my fieldwork. The construction of difference from supposedly "rural" (*aiyldyk*) Tajiks, who now ruled the capital, got mixed with the feeling of a common Central Asian destiny in Russia. Since everyday racism in Russian cities is not restricted to labor migrants from specific ethnic backgrounds or milieus but is directed at the broader category of Central Asian "blacks" (*chernye*),[10] laughing at Ravshan and Dzhamshut also meant making fun of oneself. It is exactly this discrepancy in moments of "cultural intimacy"[11] with respect to the Tajik nation and attempts at differentiation through feelings of superiority that I often encountered while watching *Nasha Russia* with people along the Pamir Highway.

The TV's overall influence on perceptions of the outside world and the western part of the country is hard to overestimate, particularly in light of the fact that many young women and children have not been outside the region. At the same time, the contents of television programs not only shape people's reflections and attitudes, they are a matter of critical discussion as well. Gulira, for instance, often legitimized her opinions on topics such as religion and politics by saying that she had seen it "on TV" (*po televizoru*). However, many hours of TV and discussions later, I realized that the legitimizing addition "on TV" often referred to the results of debates that took place after TV shows. In this regard, Lila Abu-Lughod (2004, 4) has pointed out the importance of exploring the interrelation of particular TV series and people's everyday lives, particularly the "discussions and commentary on programs that occurred outside of viewing times."[12]

Talking about "those Tajiks from Dushanbe" was sometimes initiated by a *Nasha Russia* episode, but in debates my interlocutors rarely stuck to the program they had just watched. Laughing about Ravshan and Dzhamshut returning to their homeland from Moscow and being celebrated as rich khan-like snobs when in fact they worked as low-class manual laborers in Russia, for instance, not only led to a debate about the double standards of labor migration. It also initiated thoughts on how differences within Tajikistan are reflected in settings of migration. Alikhon, a Pamiri friend in Murghab in his midtwenties who has experienced years of labor migration himself, told me shortly after watching an episode, "When you're in Moscow you clearly see differences between Tajiks and Pamiris. Pamiris are more adapted there, more local, they don't carry documents and don't bribe. The Tajiks from Dushanbe can be distinguished from Russian citizens without any difficulties—they start to bribe immediately and hardly know any Russian." For Alikhon, people along the Pamir Highway are more familiar with a Russian "lifestyle" (*obraz zhizni*) and are therefore better prepared for life in Moscow than western Tajiks. A reason for this lies in the Soviet past, which Alikhon defined as a period of modernization of Gorno-Badakhshan that was linked to Russified school education and "Moscow provisioning." As discussed in chapter 2, Gorno-Badakhshan's privileged status in the Soviet Union and the related "provisioning" imparted a sense of being part of a center in the periphery (Reeves 2014c, 114) and thus prepared for a life in Moscow. At the same time, Alikhon also explained his ability to live a modern lifestyle as an effect of the Ismaili presence in Gorno-Badakhshan. Ismaili institutions have been financing large-scale development projects in Tajikistan since the early 1990s, thereby prolonging an already existing sense of modernity in the region. In contradistinction to Tajiks from western Tajikistan, and marginalized as coming "from the mountains" in Dushanbe, Alikhon liked to speak of himself and his friends from Gorno-Badakhshan in terms of a positive marginality. In her work on south Kalimantan in Indonesia, Anna Tsing (1993, 27) notes that while the "cultural difference of the margins" was a "sign of exclusion from the center," it was also "a tool for destabilizing central authority." As much as the construction of cultural difference from the center can be read as a sign of exclusion in the case of Gorno-Badakhshan, it needs to be emphasized that the feeling of belonging to modernized margins in contrast to a less modernized center also ends up turning the margins into the center. It is then not only marginality that is, as Sarah Green (2005, 5) says, "truly central," but people at the margins who consider themselves more advanced and more civilized than those who live in the center.

Genghis Khan or Videos of the Imam?

Winter passed quickly as we watched *Nasha Russia* in Gulira and Nursultan's home in 2010, and in the summer another series became popular among the members of the family. One morning Nursultan had gone out to the bazaar and returned with a sack of flour and a set of DVDs titled *Genghis Khan*, a Chinese broadcast dubbed in Russian and with Russian subtitles, which served as major family entertainment for the weeks to come. *Genghis Khan* was produced by China Central Television (CCTV) in 2004 and has since been aired in many Asian countries. The plot of the series is based on biographical accounts of the thirteenth-century Mongol ruler and entertains the viewer with a mix of family history and action scenes. For Nursultan and Gulira, *Genghis Khan* became an antidote to the dilemma that Ravshan and Dzhamshut represented. Instead of the bitter irony and suffering of labor migration, *Genghis Khan* provided them with the glory of a historical time in which Central Asia still had a just ruler, "a real khan," as Nursultan put it. The identification with the characters in the series ranged from lifestyle and appearance to genealogy. While the kids in the family were mostly amazed by how much Genghis Khan's family "looked like Kyrgyz," Nursultan and Gulira emphasized the fact that Mongols used to have the same nomadic lifestyle as Kyrgyz and were divided into similar kinship groups. For instance, the name Naiman was once mentioned in an episode, and Nursultan turned to me and said, "Under Genghis Khan's rule there was the descent group [*uruu*] Naiman. I am *Naiman* and therefore my children are. We belong to that time. We come from the Yenisei where the Naiman originated."

The way the members of Nursultan and Gulira's family positioned themselves vis-à-vis *Genghis Khan* points to the broadcast as being emotionally charged and entailing dimensions of embodiment and nostalgia. By distinguishing themselves from Tajiks on the basis of their Turkic descent, language, and physical characteristics, members of the family were referring to categories that have strong resonance among the Kyrgyz of Murghab. On the one hand, being Kyrgyz along the Pamir Highway means speaking Kyrgyz, a Turkic language, and being of Turkic descent, which is marked by kinship and is embodied in "Mongol" physical features. At the same time, it also means showing reverence for political leaders and historical events that symbolize Turkic influence in Central Asia. For instance, when Nursultan referred to and identified with the greatness of the Naiman in *Genghis Khan*, he was not only talking about a distant, long-forgotten past. He also presented this past as having a social presence in the present (Bloch 1977) and as desirable for the future. Thus, the practice of watching and discussing television series along the Pamir Highway sheds light on processes of localization of media content in the course of which a multiplicity of different identities surface and intersect.

Pamiris along the highway, on the other hand, face quite a different dilemma: they are labeled "Tajik" in documents and official discourse, yet feel distinctly Pamiri due to their first language (Pamir languages) and their religion (Ismailism). In this regard, being Pamiri means belonging and yet not properly belonging to the ethnic category "Tajik" (*Tojik*) that is inscribed in their passports and other documents. As mentioned previously, this dilemma dates back to the early days of Soviet rule and Tajik nation building (Bergne 2007; Straub 2014) and has remained highly politicized ever since. Contemporary political processes, in the course of which statehood in Tajikistan has become increasingly tied to Tajik ethnicity (*millat*) and the prototype of a Tajik-speaking Sunni Muslim, have further complicated this relationship.[13]

This threefold dilemma—ethnic, linguistic, and sectarian—situates Pamiris at the margins of the state, not just geographically but also in bureaucratic procedures in which their lived identities are, as Veena Das and Deborah Poole (2004, 8) have put it, often "illegible" to the state. Marginalization within the nation-state furthermore intersects with processes of reform within Pamiri Ismaili communities that started with the breakup of the Soviet Union and the beginning of the civil war in Tajikistan in the 1990s. In Tajikistan, this has included the establishment of different religious, social, and economic institutions that enable local Ismailis to interact with other Ismailis around the world. Jonah Steinberg (2011, 15) describes these attempts at Ismaili expansion as "borderlands into the fold." In Steinberg's interpretation, bringing "disparate and scattered communities . . . into the fold of the imamate" means to "teach the far-flung communities *that they are Isma'ili* and to present them with a standardized version of what that means (in part through the narrative vehicle of an official history). Second, it is tied up with an attempt to teach them the details of *how* to be Isma'ili. And third, it functions to socialize them to *modern* ideals and ideologies through the *medium* of Isma'ilism" (15; italics in the original). Within the global community of Ismailis (Jamat), orientation toward the Aga Khan IV, the current Ismaili spiritual, social, and political leader, is of paramount importance. As the Ismaili imam, the Aga Khan IV embodies the ideal of a Muslim leader who acts as a mediating force between divine and human space and who holds the authority to interpret and explain the truth behind the esoteric utterances of Islamic teachings. Considered the direct descendant of the Prophet Muhammad (through Muhammad's daughter Fatima and her husband Ali), the current and forty-ninth imam legitimizes himself on the basis of genealogy and history. With the imamate as the central institution, Ismailis have created a range of organizations as a means to structure and administer their community, which is scattered over numerous countries throughout Asia, Africa, Europe, and North America.[14] Within this global community, Ismailis living along the Pamir Highway experience a kind of double remoteness that situates them at the margins, both geographically and structurally, of the already marginalized population of Central Asian Ismailis (Mostowlansky 2011b).

The process of standardization and integration into the global Jamat is, on the one hand, organized through institutional frameworks and religious elites. On the other hand, the "cultural work" (Larkin 2008, 2) of media technologies that propagate Ismaili discourse and make the imam's presence material has attained particular importance. Movies, websites, social media groups, books, and music, among other media, belong to this infrastructure of communication, which is frequently, yet not exclusively, financed and directed by Ismaili institutions. In this regard, the recognition of the Aga Khan IV as the forty-ninth Ismaili imam, for instance, is not only realized through interaction between him and his followers during visits, but also on the basis of images and the distribution of DVDs and video files of events and speeches.[15]

During my stays in Khorog in 2009 and 2010, I was given the chance to copy a series of DVDs that had been produced to celebrate the Aga Khan's visits to numerous countries in the course of 2007, his Golden Jubilee year marking fifty years of his imamate. Alikhon, with whom I had previously watched *Nasha Russia* on several occasions, was amazed that I was able to bring some of the Golden Jubilee movies to Murghab because access to them was restricted in Murghab at the time. I noticed that while Alikhon had expressed both joy and disgust when we watched episodes of Ravshan and Dzhamshut, when we watched the Golden Jubilee movies he sat in silent and rapt admiration. We sat with his whole family around my computer and gazed at half a dozen movies that repeated the Aga Khan's receptions, inaugurations, and philosophical speeches in countries all over the world. We finished only after several hours, and Alikhon then told me that these were "the real movies," in contrast to what was shown on TV.

"The real movies," in which the Aga Khan played the starring role, were different from the series we had previously watched in terms of aesthetics and meaning. They evoked a feeling of harmony instead of one of discord. But they also portrayed a range of symbols to which Alikhon attributed the term *sovremennost'* in the sense of "modernity": mobility; smooth landings on perfectly well-maintained airstrips; diplomatic rituals on the global scene; the inauguration of infrastructure projects and educational centers; clean hospitals; and speeches about development and pluralism.

To Alikhon it was clear that "the real movies" constituted a contrast to *Nasha Russia* and its uneducated labor migrants. In a similar way, he considered Pamiris in Moscow different from western Tajiks. As I mentioned with regard to Alikhon's earlier quote, Tajiks could easily be distinguished from Russians on the basis of their appearance and behavior. This, Alikhon emphasized, was not the case with Pamiris, who more closely resembled Russians because of their level of education, their knowledge of progressive Russian civilization, and, not least, an embodied modernity that extends out into intimate spheres such as posture and personal hygiene.

To Stand or Not to Stand

The construction of difference between Pamiris along the Pamir Highway and Tajiks involves ethnic, linguistic, regional, "developmental," and religious identities. These not only intersect in debates on TV programming but are also commonly expressed in other everyday encounters. During my fieldwork, Pamiris frequently labeled themselves "modern" because of their particular Soviet past, which includes other people along the Pamir Highway, too. At the same time, they often emphasized that they were "modern" and "progressive" in the present because they are Ismailis. In the course of discussions with Alikhon, for instance, he emphasized that

Tajiks "such as Ravshan and Dzhamshut" were not "modern" because they come from a cultural environment that got left behind with the Soviet Union. In addition, from his perspective, being Sunni Muslims put another obstacle in the Tajiks' way of becoming "modern," thereby turning the dichotomy "modern vs. backward" into the distinction "Ismaili vs. Sunni" (Marsden 2005, 193–238).[16] When talking about Tajiks from Dushanbe, Pamiris along the Pamir Highway frequently used the Shughni word *chakht*. *Chakht* denotes a person who does not walk straight. In a metaphorical sense, this includes being hunched and crooked as well as following the wrong path, in contrast to the religiously "right path" (*rohi mustaqim*) of the Ismailis. But the construction of religious difference also goes beyond the metaphorical use of words. Its actual embodiment is ingrained in everyday interaction and reaches into private realms that only rarely surface in debates—for instance, into competing concepts of personal hygiene.[17]

The matter of personal hygiene became particularly salient when I traveled from Khorog to Murghab with two Tajik truck drivers in the summer of 2009. The two drivers, who were happy to give me a lift for the novel company they figured I would provide, were both from Dushanbe and worked for a transport company that was involved in China trade. Both Muhiddin and Firuz had already traveled the route from Dushanbe to the Chinese border close to Murghab several times and had established a network of contacts along the road. In addition to places where they could meet their girlfriends (*dukhtar*), they also frequently visited roadhouses along the highway where truck drivers meet, eat, and drink tea. About halfway to Murghab we stopped at one of these roadhouses, which are often located in private courtyards, and left the truck to go have dinner. Before entering the house, however, we joined a group of Pamiris who were urinating a little farther up the road. When we approached the group of men who were standing there relieving themselves, Muhiddin provocatively asked the strangers why they did not squat "like Muslims." As he did not get a reply, Muhiddin stopped a few meters from the group, squatted, and began to urinate. We then went back to the house, and only when we left the roadhouse after dinner did I have the opportunity to ask Muhiddin what his earlier provocation meant.

Muhiddin considered standing while urinating to be a non-Muslim act.[18] To him, such an act was not only unhygienic but also challenged his idea of correct Tajik behavior. When I asked Muhiddin why the issue of differing urinating styles was seen to separate Muslims from non-

Muslims and Tajiks from non-Tajiks, he told me that the group of Pamiri men that we had encountered on the roadside were "like Russians" (*rangi rusho*). The mention of ethnicity as a primary marker indicates what has been noticed for a broader Central Asian context (Pelkmans 2007): ethnicity is frequently used to "code" religious difference. Taking this point further, in Muhiddin's opinion, Pamiri men whose behavior he considered non-Muslim therefore not only violated the requirements of their religion but also those of their ethnicity; while officially labeled Tajiks, these men were behaving in a non-Tajik way.

Subsequent discussions of the topic with Pamiris in Murghab reflected very different opinions on correct hygienic practices. For them, squatting included connotations like "old-fashioned" (in the sense of "backward"), "female," and "something that Sunnis do." In their vision, a modern and progressive male would feel no need to follow regulations that cannot be strictly justified by reason but that are based on tradition—a sentiment that I frequently encountered when Ismailis talked about Sunnis from Dushanbe. Negative perceptions of "backward Tajiks" were passed westward and therefore to the realm of "yours." "Ours" as "more modern" and superior in education and lifestyle, however, was not only organized along ethnic and religious lines but equally according to regional belonging.

Even though Murghabi Kyrgyz are Sunnis like most Tajiks in the western part of the country, Pamiris do not use the same markers of distinction when interacting with them. Rather, they often described the Kyrgyz to me as the ethnic other, as Turkic, as nomadic, and as Genghis Khan's offspring, in contrast to their own Persian genealogy that leads back to Alexander the Great. In the broader context of Tajikistan, past and present shared lives along the Pamir Highway provide common ground for the distinction between modern highway places and the less modern rest of Tajikistan. Within Murghab it is often also the distinction between nomadic and sedentary lifestyles, and between Turkic and Persian descent, that informs discourses on and practices of backwardness and modernity.

THE KYRGYZ WAY

Early on a spring morning in 2009, I was waiting with Alisho in his car next to the main bazaar in Khorog. Alisho, a Pamiri man in his thirties, is a self-employed driver and works on the stretch of road between Khorog and Murghab. I had traveled with him several times before and knew his routines. After he had filled his Lada Niva with just enough passengers to cover fuel expenses and make a small profit, he would pick up vegetables and fruit to bring to his family in Murghab. Then he would drive by a client's house to fill the remaining space in his Niva with cargo. Finally, after a couple of hours of waiting, we would leave Khorog in the jam-packed car and head toward the Ghunt Valley. Since Alisho needed entertainment during the trip, he usually made me sit in the front seat. Soon I was well informed about developments in his family and the latest news from Murghab, where he lived with his wife and children. We were about an hour into the journey when Alisho stopped the car at the roadside and began to cool the radiator with water from a nearby spring. Then, passing by the car, Alisho suddenly noticed that the latch of the rear compartment had broken on the bumpy road. Loudly shouting the Russian swearword *bliad'* ("bitch"),[19] Alisho got a piece of wire from the glove compartment. While provisionally fixing the latch with the wire Alisho said, "We're going to do this the Kyrgyz way [*po-kirgizskii*]."

To do something "the Kyrgyz way" is an expression that is frequently used along the Pamir Highway. It mostly appears in Russian as *po-kirgizskii* or in Kyrgyz as *kyrgyzcha*. Depending on the situation, doing something "the Kyrgyz way" can mean rather different things. On the one hand, "the Kyrgyz way" is spontaneous and flexible and signifies the ability to skillfully adapt to a specific situation. On the other hand, it also means following alternate rules, doing things not quite right, working sloppily, and not being able to plan ahead. People along the highway, both Kyrgyz and non-Kyrgyz, use the term and thereby express irony, pride, and affection, as well as sometimes derogatory views. While Alisho used "the Kyrgyz way" to generally explain a situation of imperfection and improvisation, for many of my Kyrgyz friends *kyrgyzcha* also implied a link to specifically Kyrgyz practices.

When I discussed the wide range of interpretations of "the Kyrgyz way" with Kamal, who was both Kyrgyz and a government official in Murghab, he told me that "this word has a broad meaning":

> For example, some people had a conflict with their neighbors. If it was more of a misunderstanding, then it could be solved between them—according to the Kyrgyz way [*kyrgyzcha jol menen*]. . . . They would come with the request not to go to the police. This word has a broad meaning. And it also has a philosophical side [*filosofskii jagy bar*]. Then it also has an ironic side as a joke [*ironicheskii jagy dagy bar tamasha katary*]. If the issue is solved with the help of customs [*ürp-adat, kaada-salt*], then it is the Kyrgyz way. Here the law [*zakon*] has no influence.

Thus, in Kamal's view, "the Kyrgyz way" first encompasses a legal dimension that allows people to solve particular issues outside "(state) law" (*zakon*). This reading of "the Kyrgyz way" is closely related to notions of Kyrgyz "customs" (*salt*).[20] Kamal furthermore attributed a humorous aspect to "the Kyrgyz way," which resonates with Alisho's use of the expression when fixing the car, and he saw a "philosophical side" to it that, as I demonstrate later, ties in with visions of morality. Finally, Kamal also emphasized a reading of "the Kyrgyz way" that highlights its religious dimension and addresses sectarian concerns:

> It also has a religious meaning [*dinii maanisi*]. For example, all of this is only solved within Sunni Hanafi Islam [*Imam Azam maskhabynda*]. This is the link to religion [*din*]. All of this is related to customs [*ürp-adat, salt*]. Religion is also related to it. And it ends with the Kyrgyz way. For example, it's not a secret that when there are these kinds of moments—when someone goes to the police or the prosecutor—then it can still be agreed upon in the Kyrgyz way. It is solved in the Kyrgyz way and we don't need a fine [*shtraf*] or a criminal procedure. They would agree among themselves. . . . It would be solved in the Kyrgyz way. This is related to national psychology [*uluttuk psikhologiia*].

Kamal's statement emphasizes that "the Kyrgyz way" includes a broad range of fields of social interaction in which people negotiate the meaning of being and behaving Kyrgyz.[21] On the one hand, the interconnection between ethnicity, religion, and custom provides the grounds to restrict "the Kyrgyz way" to those who identify as Kyrgyz. On the other hand, the example of Alisho shows that a non-Kyrgyz person can make use of "the Kyrgyz way" if he or she has the knowledge to do so. In a similar way, I was sometimes acknowledged for doing things "the Kyrgyz way" in the course of my fieldwork. Eating with my hands, getting used to very infrequent showers, participating in Kyrgyz life-cycle rituals, and applying correct seating arrangements in the presence of elders belonged to behavioral patterns that people along the Pamir Highway classified as *kyrgyzcha*. Yet in other instances, they used the term to draw boundaries, to express a distinction between Sunnis and Ismailis, to emphasize ethnicity, and to claim particular places. Furthermore, Soviet cars could be turned into Kyrgyz ones when people tore out the seats to make space for livestock. At the same time, some sought treatment of life-threatening diseases "the Kyrgyz way," especially when "modern" medicine in the hospital had had no effect.

A common theme underlying "the Kyrgyz way" is that of fixing, rectifying, repairing, and healing. Whether it is a car or a person, a conflict or an inappropriate lifestyle, *kyrgyzcha* implies the ability to fix the world with the help of a piece of scrap wire and a set of negotiable rules. This set of rules, for which Kamal used the terms *ürp-adat, kaada-salt*, and *salt* synonymously, offers an alternative to the established manner of handling the world that modernity has brought with it along the Pamir Highway in the form of bureaucratic procedures, (state) laws, and university-trained doctors.[22] In this regard, "the Kyrgyz way's" potential of fixing the shortcomings of modernity is not only a matter of reasoning in the realms of technology, law, and health, but also when it comes to "morality" (*moral'nyi chak*). Through the interconnectedness of Soviet upbringing and "the Kyrgyz way," for instance, the spheres of supposedly "old school" (*kadim chaktan*) customs and modernity become intertwined.

Toward Good Communism

For Baktygül, Soviet education was just right and fit perfectly well with what "the Kyrgyz way" was all about. Baktygül is an elderly Kyrgyz woman and mother of ten. Back in Soviet times she was a pedagogue, and many people in Murghab respect her as a strict teacher who positively influenced their lives. Now Baktygül is retired and practices herbal healing, again a field of work that people in the town and beyond honor as being of vital importance. For Baktygül, "the Kyrgyz way," and therefore *salt*, has gone through a period of decay. While there used to be elders who could uphold and teach "the Kyrgyz way" during the Soviet period, they are now all gone. When discussing the topic with a patient of hers during a session of herbal healing, Baktygül said (in reference to Soviet times):

> *Salt* was strong [*küchtüü*]. For example, if a girl had given birth illegally [*nezakonnyi*], she was moved out of her home with her father and her mother. People told them to go wherever they wanted to but they had to leave because they had spoiled our land. She should have been pure [*taza*]. Now there are many girls who give birth illegally, both unmarried girls [*kyz*] and young married women [*kelin*]. Earlier, men lived with one wife [*aial*]. Now they live with two, three, four, five wives. Imagine, for example, if I had a wife and then I let her go and marry another, and then let her go again and marry another. Now it's become a mess [*bardak*]. It's bad. People don't maintain *salt*. Our Kyrgyz *salt* was so pure and good. Now it isn't anymore.

In Baktygül's view, until recently the presence of elders as guardians had guaranteed the transmission of *salt*.[23] Yet while there are of course still elders in Murghab, they have ceased to behave in a way that could contribute to the upkeep of "the Kyrgyz way." Baktygül locates reasons for this in the current condition of change along the highway, which she juxtaposes to the Soviet Union (*Soiuz*) as a nurturing structure and institutional base in which *salt* could be protected. In contrast, the present-day situation is marked by moral decay and the need for restoration of "the pure Kyrgyz way."

Baktygül's statement is not to be seen as mere nostalgia for the Soviet past. As a matter of fact, people along the Pamir Highway also utter frequent criticism of the Soviet Union, and communism (*kommunizm*) in general, as having oppressed religion (*din*). Thus, rather than longing for the past, they envision a future built on a perfected version of the past. On a different occasion when we were sitting in a discarded UAZ in front of her house, Baktygül told me that I come from a place where there must be "a good form of communism" (*jakhshy kommunizm*) because there is no oppression of religion. Baktygül thought of Switzerland, my country of origin, as communist, just like the Soviet Union, in the sense of a lawful, moral, and well-organized place. However, in contrast to the Soviet Union, she envisaged such an ideal state, merely symbolized by Switzerland, as a place in which religious practice and "the Kyrgyz way" could flourish freely.

Baktygül's wish for the persistence of "the Kyrgyz way" within a positively communist society sheds light on the possibility of shared lives in places along the highway in which difference is part of everyday normalcy. In her study of *salt* in ethnically homogenous Kyrgyz communities in Talas (Kyrgyzstan), Judith Beyer (2009, 22) mentions that her informants presented *salt* as "homeostatic," "being 'in our mentality' [*mentalitet ichinde*]," and "'in our blood' [*kanybyzda*]." She furthermore argues that such an understanding "liberates them from having to reason or justify in each case why something is done in a particular way or why something cannot be done differently." They thus do not have "to reflect about why *salt* is part of their world" because "it already is part of them." This is an important point and resonates with the ways people along the Pamir Highway view "the Kyrgyz way." At the same time, social encounters along the road are always encounters across difference in the course of which people are urged to reflect upon why things are done this way and not differently. Thus while there is a Kyrgyz world on the highway, conceptualized as reflecting a "national psychology" (*uluttuk psikhologiia*), to use Kamal's words, there are others, too, that challenge it.

In his seminal work *Ethnic Groups and Boundaries*, Fredrik Barth (1969, 18) points to the importance of boundary making and interaction in contexts of cultural difference. He argues that in such contexts, interdependence and a "positive bond" across ethnic boundaries derive from complementarity with regard to at least some cultural features. In places on the Pamir Highway, such shared cultural features are constituted by a common, modern past. In a world of good communism, as Baktygül envisaged it, Kyrgyz and Pamiris live side by side and interact but do not mix and remain distinct. This is also exemplified by the fact that there are only about a dozen interethnic marriages along the Pamir Highway, all of which date back to the Soviet period during which interethnic intimacy was encouraged as the embodiment of the "friendship of peoples" (*druzhba narodov*).[24] Against this backdrop, the multidimensionality of "the Kyrgyz way" allows for participation beyond ethnic boundaries while at the same time triggering exclusion of non-Kyrgyz others. "The Kyrgyz way" might be linked to innovation, creativity, humor, and notions of backwardness open to everybody navigating along the Pamir Highway, but its legal and religious aspects also reinforce ethnic boundary making and are thought to revive and flourish in an idealized future past.

CHAPTER 4

MUSLIMS ON THE ROOF OF THE WORLD

HOLY MEN AND TERRORISTS

During a lunch at Alikhon's house in 2013, his mother, a woman in her late fifties, told me that while "we still prayed to the previous imam in Murghab, people abroad were praying to the Imam of our Time [*Imomi zamon*]." She continued: "I saw his picture for the first time in a magazine somebody had brought along in the '80s. We were really late in knowing what was going on outside." Alikhon's mother is a devout Ismaili and, according to her family, has been that way since long before public displays of piety became a legitimate part of everyday life along the highway in the 1990s. While her husband, a retired car mechanic, used to love his drink and joined in praying only "after the Union," she had been performing Ismaili rituals all along. By the "previous imam," she meant Sir Sultan Muhammed Shah Aga Khan III, the current Aga Khan IV's grandfather and predecessor. The Aga Khan III passed away in 1957 but continued to be a central point of reference along the highway as connectivity with places outside the Soviet Union remained fragile.[1] The example of Alikhon's mother challenges the still widespread assumption that the distinction between Soviet and post-Soviet corresponds to the binary nonreligion/religion, interpreting contemporary Islam in Central Asia through the rubric of "religious revival" rather than perceiving it as embedded in a complex web of historical continuity and change.[2] Alikhon's mother expressed the temporal complexity that underlies these processes of change by indicating that Ismailis along the Pamir Highway, who were part and parcel of Soviet efforts at modernization, had at the same time become religiously "backward" compared to Ismailis abroad.[3]

Against this backdrop, religious practice along the Pamir Highway in the Soviet period should be revisited as a social phenomenon that was as complex and multidimensional as it is today. Pilgrimage, life-cycle rituals, and individual practice were existent throughout the twentieth century, and my interlocutors often emphasized that the transmission of knowledge about Islam (*Islam dini*) was an important part of their lives in Soviet times.[4] As in other parts of the Soviet Union, the public display of religiosity was suppressed along the highway, but practices in private homes were a different story altogether. For instance, Kamal still has detailed childhood memories of fasting (*orozo*) during Ramadan in his home village close to the Chinese border in the 1970s: while his father, himself a supporter of Soviet rule and a local government employee, strived to maintain the fast at home, teachers gave Kamal bread and water at school and carefully watched the intake of food.

The example of Alikhon's mother's and Kamal's experiences both underscore the contradictory interrelationship between public and private spheres. They also highlight the Soviet distinction between religious practice as connected to "backward customs" (Jacquesson 2008, 289), at most to be condoned in private, and the state's secular aspirations, forcefully asserted in the modernized spheres under its control. This argument ties in with a wealth of studies, prominently represented by Talal Asad's (2003) *Formations of the Secular* and Saba Mahmood's (2005) *Politics of Piety*, that critically assess the pervasiveness of the "secular imaginary" and question its analytical usefulness.[5] In this chapter, I seek to take such a critical perspective to the places along the highway and look at religious change in the region as an ongoing historical process. Rather than taking the prefabricated categories of Soviet and post-Soviet for granted and aligning change to them, I suggest approaching this process as the aggregation of effects of fine-grained encounters between particular actors. People along the Pamir Highway engage with these protagonists of religious transformation—ranging from government representatives, Islamic missionaries, and development institutions to alleged "terrorists"—in creative ways, often (but not always) going beyond the boundaries of the streamlined "official story" (Scott 1990).

Banning *Daavat*

When I first attended Friday prayers in the central mosque of Murghab at the very beginning of my fieldwork in 2008, the prayer hall was packed with men of different ages, hairstyles, and fashion. Some of them

FIGURE 4.1. The Friday mosque in Alichor. Photograph © Bernd Hrdy, 2008.

wore *kalpaks*—the distinctive Kyrgyz felt hats—and were clean-shaven, some had come in tracksuits and baseball caps, and others wore the south Asian *shalwar kameez* (long shirt and loose trousers) and had beards. All of these men were Kyrgyz, but what counted in the moment of prayer was not necessarily their ethnic identity but the fact that they all followed the Sunni Hanafi school (*Imam Azam maskhaby*).

When we all left the yurt-shaped mosque after the prayers, a group of young men in *shalwar kameez* followed me on my way home and asked me why I had come to Murghab. After I explained to them that I was researching local everyday life and would be staying in Murghab for some time, they reacted enthusiastically and invited me to join them on a preaching tour to the most distant villages of the district. The young men wore beards and smelled of alcohol-free cologne that "the prophet Muhammad himself had used," as one of them explained. They would, they emphasized, just wait for a group of men coming from Osh to Murghab later that month and then head to a number of villages close to the Chinese border in order to "invite people to Islam."

When I heard them call their tour *daavat* and themselves *daavatchy*s, I realized that the young men had activities in mind that have gained in importance all over Central Asia since the turn of the millennium. The organization to which the young men belonged was the Tablighi Jama'at, whose presence in Kyrgyzstan has been a story of success and expansion but which has come under increasing political pressure in Central Asia more generally.[6] My first encounters with members of the Tablighi Ja-ma'at, who usually call themselves *daavatchys* in a Kyrgyz context, date back to fieldwork that I conducted in 2005. Later, in 2006, I had the op-portunity to accompany a group of *daavatchys* on a tour through the district of Kochkor in central Kyrgyzstan. Again in Murghab in 2008, many people along the Pamir Highway sympathized with efforts to renew faith and enthusiastically talked about Tablighi literature as "books that explain Islam." Some also likened *daavatchys* to pre-Soviet "dervishes" (*derbishter*) and "holy men" (*yiyk adamdar*) who roamed the region for God's sake. Back then Gulira, for instance, referred to *daavatchys* as *du-banalar* and *derbishter*, both Kyrgyz terms for dervishes, and to *daavat* as purifying "the soul" (*jan*). A neighbor agreed with Gulira's interpre-tation and added that the new Kulma road to China would provide the *daavatchys* with the means to easily access remote villages in the border triangle where Tajikistan, Afghanistan, and China meet. This would, the neighbor emphasized in a discussion with Gulira, facilitate the work of the *daavatchys*, whom she thought of as belonging to a class of religious specialists that had already existed "in ancient times" (*kadim chakta*). It appeared to her that through *daavat*, people along the highway now had the chance to establish a bridge between pre-Soviet holy men—*eshan*s and dervishes—and contemporary Sunnis in Murghab.

While the Tablighi Jama'at has its historical roots in the Deobandi movement in India and has developed a strong institutional base in Pa-kistan (Masud 2000a), it is also a globally oriented organization that is active in many countries around the world.[7] By promoting a lifestyle that is supposed to imitate the life of the Prophet Muhammad, *daavatchys* evoke an image of tradition and historical authenticity (Metcalf 1993, 601). This image is furthermore supported by practices such as wearing the *shalwar kameez* and using tooth-cleaning twigs (*miswak*) instead of toothbrushes.

When I first encountered *davaatchys* in Murghab in 2008, they rep-resented a historically legitimate and authentic form of Islam, particular-ly in the eyes of many Kyrgyz.[8] As a result, people bought and read the Tablighi Jama'at's foundational literature by Muhammad Zakariya Kan-dhalawi (Zakariia 2005–2008), and referred to the works simply as "Mus-lim books" (*busurman kitepteri*). Soon, however, *daavat* as an endeavor to renew and purify people's faith and religious practice became increasingly politicized and polarized. Shortly after I met the group of young men who had so much looked forward to going on *daavat* in summer 2008, government agencies started a campaign that aimed to discredit the *daavatchys*' reputation throughout the region.

An official ban on the Tablighi Jama'at in Tajikistan had already been declared in March 2006 ("'Dzhamo'ati Tablig'" 2009).[9] At that time, Tajikistan's Supreme Court had assessed the Tablighi Jama'at as an "extremist" organization and a threat to the constitutional order. But along the Pamir Highway, government agencies did not initiate a clampdown on the Tablighi Jama'at before late 2008.[10] Then from 2009 onward, the atmosphere for *daavatchys* became increasingly tense, as members of the Tablighi Jama'at in other parts of the country were taken to court on charges of extremism and participation in a banned organization, which is still happening as of this writing.[11] The clampdown on the Tablighi Jama'at can be situated in an overall government approach to religion in Tajikistan that John Heathershaw and Sophie Roche (2011, 18) label "militant secularism." In this regard, political struggles in the Rasht Valley in the northeastern part of the country turned into a fight against alleged "Islamists": police have forcefully shaved off thousands of beards, fined women for wearing the hijab, and closed dozens of mosques, while the government sought to prohibit giving Arabic names to newborn children and banned the Islamic Renaissance Party of Tajikistan (Hizbi Nahzati Islomii Tojikiston) (Swerdlow 2016). Explanations of why certain practices and organizations are banned and individuals imprisoned are often obscure and unconvincing. Such government actions have contributed significantly to the "divide between a religiously observant society and a state class which arbitrarily and instrumentally uses and abuses Islam" (Heathershaw and Roche 2011, 19).

Against this backdrop, the promised *daavat* tour on which the young Kyrgyz men in Murghab had invited me in the summer of 2008 never took place. The organizers from Osh and Murghab decided to cancel the trip because of the emerging tensions. By January 2009, I noticed that almost no *daavatchys* could be spotted in the streets and mosques, and people increasingly began to speak of *daavat* in disparaging terms. By spring, one could see only the odd individual wearing a beard and *shalwar kameez* in Murghab's small bazaar. Some people would then whisper "bin Laden" or *mudzhakhed* ("mujahid"), thereby expressing their public disrespect for the men who had only recently seemed to reconnect the Sunnis of the region with their religious past.

Leaving the Scene

The speed of the *daavatchys'* disappearance from public places along the Pamir Highway is linked to the force of government intervention and the spread of images of the "terrorist" threat that came with it. Nevertheless, some of the innovations that *daavat* had brought to the region remained untouched, such as the strong emphasis on "correct" (*tuura*) and "pure" (*taza*) individual faith and practice, as well as the idea of educating neighbors and friends in Islamic teachings. I also noticed that many people continued to read the Tablighi Jama'at's foundational literature despite government officials' attempts to confiscate "*daavat* books" from homes along the Pamir Highway. The literature has often remained a part of local religious practice, and I encountered people who thought about naming their children after the founders of the Tablighi Jama'at. People's negative comments about and growing annoyance with *daavatchys* stand in contrast to such practices. These contrasting yet not necessarily contradictory processes can be framed with reference to James Scott's distinction between public and hidden transcripts. In his study *Domination and the Art of Resistance* (1990), Scott argues that in constellations of domination, public transcripts denote a hegemonic conduct that is publicly permissible. Hidden transcripts are part of a "backstage discourse" that is constituted by acts that cannot be performed or "spoken in the face of power" (xii). Given that places along the Pamir Highway have been marked by a sharp distinction between public and private dimensions of Islam over most of the past century, I suggest that people's abilities to adapt, transform, and disguise religious practice are of pivotal importance to an understanding of the local setting. Thus, bearing in mind the fact that the public activities of the Tablighi Jama'at gradually faded in the course of 2009, in the following I present an ethnography of the *daavatchys'* disappearance from the scene and how they entered the backstage.

The discrediting of *daavat* activities along the Pamir Highway is embedded in an overall changing political climate concerning religion in Tajikistan, which I witnessed between 2008 and 2015. In this regard, several factors played a role. First, the conflict in the Rasht Valley in the north of the country gave the government an opportunity to demonstrate its willingness to engage in violent struggle against alleged "Islamists."[12] Second, in 2009 the government implemented a new law on religion that generally enlarged the discourse on terror, Islam, and the need for state control. Third, 2009 was officially declared the Year of Imomi A'zam (Abu

Hanifa), the founder of the Hanafi school of Islamic law, in celebration of the seventeen-year anniversary of Tajikistan's independence ("Imami A'zam" 2009). People along the Pamir Highway widely considered this to be President Rahmon's acknowledgment of Sunni Hanafi Islam as Tajikistan's official version of Islam. Across the country, many non-Hanafi Muslims and members of other religious denominations interpreted this as a form of exclusion. The resultant de facto declaration of a "state Islam" also increased the official awareness of competing groups and organizations, which were to be labeled as "terrorist" and a threat to "national security" (*amniyati millī*).

In Murghab, this combination of factors led to a discourse of danger that identified "foreign" (*khorijī*) influences as a major threat. In a declared "war" (*bor'ba*) against "terrorism" (*terrorizm*) and "extremism" (*ekstremizm*), government agencies attempted to explain a range of domestic disturbances by invoking the image of foreigners who had supposedly triggered unrest. And in order to stigmatize the members of the Tablighi Jama'at as followers of a potentially dangerous transnational organization with its headquarters in Pakistan, government officials used the vocabulary of the global "war on terror" to describe *daavat*.

In this regard, an autumn 2009 report by the government in Murghab to the higher authorities of Gorno-Badakhshan exemplifies how the Tablighi Jama'at was framed as a terrorist organization at the local level. The report addresses "Tajikistan's agenda on the war on terrorism and other extremist forces between 2006 and 2010." In the report, a government official states the following:

> The head of the Committee for Religious Affairs of the Ministry of Culture visited Murghab. He met with people from the communities of Murghab, Alichur, and G. Berdibaev and explained to them the requirements of the new law on religion, the ban of the Tablighi Jama'at, and the reregistration of mosques and prayer houses. However, no Tablighi activities could be observed during 2009. According to the local department of the secret service (GKNB), the situation is now fully under control. Furthermore, all prayer houses within the territory of Murghab district were reregistered. Generally, the political situation in the region is stable and there have been no signs of terrorism and extremism recently. Law and order are strictly implemented in the region. (Murghab 2009, 2)

The encounter between *daavatchy*s and government officials cannot be considered merely a local phenomenon and an endeavor that aimed at limiting the intrusion of "foreigners" who potentially brought destabilization to the border region. The language of the "war on terror," as used in the extract just presented, also resonates with broader discourses on terror in Central Asia and indeed around the globe.[13] As a result, with members of the Tablighi Jama'at being defined as "terrorists" (*terrorist-ter*) from abroad, any claims to continuity between local holy men from the past and *daavatchy*s became discredited. The following extract from a conversation among four Kyrgyz elders at a large memorial feast in early 2010 illustrates how *daavat* as an initially locally supported practice for faith renewal became publicly reinterpreted through the prism of international terrorism.

> Elder 1: They say the English influence Hizb-ut-Tahrir.
>
> Elder 2: And there is the influence of *daavat* in Murghab. Many bad things are done under the cover of *daavat*.
>
> Elder 3: Terrorists support *daavat*. It's like a green traffic light and if you're a *daavatchy*, then you can pass.
>
> Elder 2: It's also about the call to religion (*din*). I have to say we all accepted it ourselves.
>
> Elder 4: The literal translation of *daavat* is "call to religion." They said, "Come to Islam." Now most of the people are performing prayers, doing ablutions. There is no need for a call to religion in Murghab.

The association between *daavatchy*s and organizations that openly promote political visions of Islam, such as the Hizb-ut-Tahrir,[14] derived from the *daavatchy*s' appearance rather than from the contents of their teachings. The *daavatchy*s whom I met along the Pamir Highway had a decisively apolitical attitude and expressed their wish to transform individual religious practice, not the whole country. To be sure, *daavat* works toward the reform and purification of individuals and thus aims for a utopian society in which every member participates in this practice. However, this is hypothetical, and the *daavatchy*s along the Pamir Highway with whom I spoke about their aims expressed their interest in current affairs rather than in an unknown future. As one *daavatchy* told me in 2008, when thinking of where to travel on *daavat,* he made a distinction between places with "Mecca order" (*Meke tartip*) and those with "religious order" (*din tartip*). In this framework, "Mecca order" stands for a place that is hostile to *daavatchy*s, invoking early Islamic history and Mecca's inhabitants who rejected Muhammad and Islam. *Din tartip*, or "religious order," however, stands for an environment that is favorable to *daavatchy*s and in which, just like in Medina during Muhammad's time, Islam can flourish (Ismailbekova and Nasritdinov 2012, 188). In this *daavatchy*'s view, Tajikistan was a place of "Mecca order," where the government aggressively imposed its interests upon citizens. But when he referred to "religious order," he did not mean an Islamic state or sharia law. His prime example of "religious order" was Kyrgyzstan, a secular state in which comparatively free religious practice was possible and where the government watched but did not ban *daavat*.

In the process of enforcing the ban on the Tablighi Jama'at along the Pamir Highway, government officials rarely referred to the teachings of the *daavat*. Rather, they invoked an image of the *daavatchy* as a long-bearded, *shalwar kameez*–wearing "terrorist" who stands in a long historical lineage with the stereotypical Islamic fighter, the *mudzhakhed* and the contemporary Taliban whom people know from the 1980s Soviet war and the ongoing conflict in Afghanistan. The image of the *mudzhakhed*, or the alternate term "Wahhabi," tied in with people's anxieties about the uncontrollable movement of foreigners in the region. Despite the fact that the *daavatchy*s were either local or from nearby Osh, their public appearance—mainly their clothes and their beards—indicated difference and a sense of uprooting. Johan Rasanayagam (2006a, 100) has analyzed such processes of othering in the framework of Uzbekistan and notes that the term "Wahhabi" reflects struggles to define the "real" Islam. The drawing of boundaries between locally embedded Muslim practices and universalist interpretations of Islam is expressed through the rejection of "foreign" influences, which include certain outward manifestations and everyday practices. With reference to Michel Foucault (1994), Rasanayagam argues that in this way power, as a relationship between partners, is "dispersed throughout the whole society" (101). From this perspective, it is not only Tajikistan's government that has shaped the discourse on *daavatchy*s through the introduction of policies from above; people along the highway have themselves reconsidered their interpretations of public *daavat*, while nevertheless still integrating and normalizing Tablighi teachings and practices in their private everyday routines.

For instance, Mairambek, whom I regularly visited in a village at the Chinese border in the course of my fieldwork, had found *daavat* activities "interesting" (*kyzyktuu*) in the beginning. He also read Tablighi literature and found compelling the idea that modern life along the highway could be complemented by improved religious practice. To my knowledge he still keeps the books at home and has not stopped praying five times a day, followed by the practice of *zikr*, or remembrance, which *daavatchy*s introduced in mosque communities along the highway. Yet he also expressed his relief when he realized that the number of *daavatchy*s had decreased after the ban. Due to its alleged remoteness, his village at the Chinese border used to be a rather popular destination for *daavatchy*s. Assuming that religious knowledge would be especially scant in faraway places, *daavatchy*s had come to such villages along the Pamir Highway with the idea that local people would simply welcome and appreciate them as bearers of valuable information. While this might have been true in the beginning when there really was a gap in specialist knowledge on Islam, Mairambek also remembers *daavatchy*s as a nuisance. In the summer of 2010 he told me, "It's good that they stopped this kind of *daavat* now. It was like an invasion of the uneducated [*negramotnyi*]. Before you conduct *daavat* you should be educated yourself. How can you teach somebody without knowing yourself? *Daavat* should start in your family, with neighbors, the street, and the village. Only then can you travel to other villages and towns or even abroad." Similarly, in other encounters people emphasized the *daavatchy*s' hubris and lack of education. For instance, Baktygül had been interested in *daavat* from the start and reads a great deal about Islam. However, when I walked with her through the streets of Murghab in 2010, she reacted with annoyance when we saw one of the few remaining *daavatchy*s in the region who dared to appear in public.[15]

> Baktygül: Do you see this guy?
> Till: Who is he? Is he a Kyrgyz?
> Baktygül: He looks like a *mudzhakhed*, like bin Laden. He is a Kyrgyz.
> Till: Why does he wear those clothes?
> Baktygül: He wants to be a mullah [*moldo*]. They get these clothes from the market in Osh. Now he looks like a *mudzhakhed* from Pakistan or Afghanistan.
> Till: So is he a *daavatchy*?
> Baktygül: Yes, he is, but they are just pretending to be mullahs.

Baktygül's disdain for *daavatchy*s was, on the one hand, based on their alleged association with "terrorists" that has been promulgated through government propaganda. On the other hand, she was even more annoyed by the fact that they were trying to present themselves as mullahs and therefore as religious specialists with an education from a madrassa or a university. Baktygül was particularly irritated by the idea of these unprofessional young men seeking to teach others about the correct performance of religious practice and trying to transmit theological interpretations of foundational texts of Islam such as the Quran and Hadith. While they were trying to impersonate the holy men who had lived in Murghab in the past, *daavatchy*s were in fact incapable of taking their place in the present.

Remembering the *Eshan*s

To think of *daavatchy*s as comparable to the "holy men" (*yiyk adamdar*) of the past was, as Gulira pointed out in summer 2009, a naïve fallacy. Reflecting on her previous statement that *daavatchy*s were similar to the dervishes who had roamed the region until the 1930s, Gulira now disagreed with her former self. How could she have thought that it was possible to be born in the present and still have skills that were inextricably linked to a period of time that had passed "long ago" (*kadimta*)? Similarly, Mairambek argued that as people had become modern along the highway, the "old time" (*kadim chak*) could not return. While we were having tea in their living room, Mairambek and his wife comically enacted this past, thereby underscoring the change that had happened since "modernity" (*sovremennost'*) was introduced to Murghab. Mairambek said ironically, "As I told you, most parts of life used to be better. Even women. They used to follow orders and didn't try to impose their own will on their husbands. Look, that's how Kyrgyz women used to be before we became modern [*sovremennyi bolgon*]." At that very moment, Mairambek's wife put on a headscarf, performed an exaggeratedly graceful bow, and imitated an obedient wife who exits the room walking backward with her hands folded in front of her, never turning her back to her husband. After she had returned and sat down again, Mairambek told me that back then roles were clear and undisputed. This was true for men, women, and children; for different generations; and for religious specialists. Thus, just as the roles of individuals in the public sphere were strictly defined, so too were they within the family (*üi-bülö*). What mullahs (*moldo*) and judges (*kazy*) were to the public, the husband was to his family—a just authority with executive powers.

Mairambek perceived the period of modernity as a time in which jokes about traditional gender roles are welcome, yet he did not approve of the decay of authority when it came to Islam. He wished for the emergence of an educated and forceful class of religious specialists such as had existed up to the late 1930s. For Mairambek, this class was made up of a range of specialists, including dervishes, mullahs and, most importantly, *eshan*s, who disappeared from Murghab just prior to World War II. According to Mairambek, it was not political pressure or deportation that led to their disappearance but the fact that people progressively adopted a modern lifestyle that included the consumption of alcohol, a different style of dress, and the abandonment of ancient cultural skills.

The Kyrgyz word *eshan* derives from the Persian *ishān*, which had long been used with an honorific significance in the sense of *shaykh* or *murshid* ("teacher" or "guide") in Central Asia. In contrast to *murīd* ("disciple" or "pupil"), the term implies a higher rank in the religious hierarchy and is sometimes attributed to specialists at the tomb of a saint (Barthold and Wheeler 2012). The notion of an *eshan* as a "holy man" (*yiyk adam*) who lives nearby or at a tomb or a *mazar* is an integral part of how Kyrgyz along the Pamir Highway remember such individuals.

In the course of my fieldwork, people who conducted healing rituals in Murghab, such as *emchi*s and *bakshy*s, also viewed *eshan*s as bearers of esoteric religious knowledge who provided a link to a past of the "pure Kyrgyz" (*taza Kyrgyz*). Baktygül, whom I have already introduced as an herbalist and healer, is such an *emchi*. When she talked about her profession and explained how she acquired the power of healing, Baktygül often mentioned childhood memories that were related to an *eshan* called Moldosultan who used to live in Bash Gümböz, a village close to Alichor. When I asked her if *eshan*s were still active in the region, the following conversation ensued:

> Baktygül: They don't exist anymore.
> Till: Why not?
> Baktygül: Now people aren't pure [*taza*]. For example, if I were a man I would take another's wife. If I were a woman, I would take someone's husband. People aren't pure. They slaughter someone's horse or kill people. My children watch American movies. I also watch them sometimes when I lie down. This is a sin [*künöö*]. For example, there is a movie called *Police Wars* [*Mentovskie voiny*]. They steal young children there. It's not pure.

The lack of purity (*tazalyk*) that Baktygül mentioned is a defining marker of modernity that infused the region when settlements were built and people were employed within the Soviet system and became "mixed" (*aralash*). Aigül, who is the granddaughter of an *eshan* and now an elderly lady, expressed the same opinion when I met her during a memorial feast at her house. Gulira, whom I accompanied to the feast, approached Aigül during lunch and took the opportunity to start a conversation about *esh-ans* in the region:

> Gulira: Eshan Ata used to read his prayers [*namaz*] and didn't do any-thing bad. But did he look at women's faces? For example, at young daughters-in-law [*kelin*] or girls? Or did he not look, saying it was a sin [*künöö*]?
>
> Aigül: He used to look.
>
> Gulira: Yes, but at that time daughters-in-law used to appear this way? Right? [*She covers her face with her hands and indicates long sleeves.*] They didn't show their hair, right? It was a sin, right? We also need to have such clothing during *namaz*.
>
> Till [*turning to Aigül*]: When was that time?
>
> Gulira [*interrupting*]: It wouldn't be allowed for us either! It would be a sin for us.
>
> Aigül: Earlier . . . a long time ago . . . Now we have become modern [*sovre-mennyi*] and it's bad. We've become really bad. In earlier times, we used to wear long dresses.

While Aigül presented modernity as a period of bad behavior and moral decay, she did not view modernity as entirely negative; she also expressed her satisfaction with changes that have been introduced in the course of the twentieth century. Thus, she went on talking and said, turning to Mairam, Gulira's teenage daughter, "A long time ago twelve-year-old boys married and had wives. In earlier times [*kadim chakta*], people gave their daughters for marriage at the age of nine. We are very modern [*sovremen-nyi*] now." And she smiled and leaned back.

Both Aigül and Baktygül agreed that modernity was an irrevocable fact. For them, the modern condition was not merely associated with de-cay but also with a contemporary reality in all its material dimensions. People had made their decision to change from "old time" to modernity by altering their diet, wearing different clothes, using new technology, and developing alternative forms of entertainment. Thus, modernity is not a condition that was superficially adopted and can easily be changed. It is ingrained in human bodies, and people along the Pamir Highway eat, wear, watch, and interact in "modern" ways. As elderly ladies, both Aigül and Baktygül had witnessed the last representatives of the "old time" in their childhood, and these memories reminded them of the loss that their disappearance meant to people along the highway. The *eshan*s knew more than others and sometimes had a clear (*achyk*) vision of future events.

Residing at tombs (*gümböz*) and *mazars*, they not only helped the living with the provision of spiritual blessings (*bereke*) but also honored the dead ancestors. In the present time, no such individuals can be found, and spiritual guidance comes from various, often unreliable, sources.

Blazing a Trail

After the stigmatization of the *daavatchy*s as "terrorists," the main Sunni influences in Murghab became imams in governmental service, self-appointed mullahs, and a vast number of books and booklets that travel on the highway from Osh. Traders often bring these materials from southern Kyrgyzstan and sell them at the bazaar in Murghab. Sometimes people buy them for themselves in Osh or Bishkek; on some occasions, I have seen piles of printed-out Islamic Internet resources in Russian or Kyrgyz that people had collected in Kyrgyzstan.

To a large extent, the origins of the books and booklets that are sold in Osh represent the diversity within the Sunni Muslim world itself.[16] At the beginning of my fieldwork, books translated from Turkish, Arabic, and Urdu into Russian and Kyrgyz could be found there. Recently, Kyrgyz authors have started to contribute more to the field. The topics of these books and advice booklets range from descriptions of correct prayer practice, obeisance to parents, and commentaries on the hadith to Tablighi literature, the life of the Prophet, and collections of *masala* (teachings explaining different aspects of religious practice). Among my Kyrgyz friends, such collections of *masala* were especially popular, as they utlized anecdotes and stories to exemplify the merits of faith.[17] At the same time, the opening of a free market for religious literature often appeared odd, confusing, and counterproductive. After the *daavatchy*s had been written off, many people along the Pamir Highway complained to me about the lack of authoritative sources when it came to access to information on Islam. Even though the Muftiyat in Bishkek attempted to gain some degree of control over the publications that were sold in the bazaars in Kyrgyzstan by using stamps to indicate quality, the range of contradictory opinions on Islamic practice remained an obstacle. Some of my Ismaili friends in Murghab ironically called the Sunni transmission of knowledge "a bit of a mess," but even Nursultan, who was seriously concerned with correct prayer practice, stated that he suffered from a lack of direction:

> Most of these booklets are bad and not thought through enough. First, they're full of contradictions. There is no order anymore and you don't

know to which *maskhab* [school of Islam] the authors belong. People have become really confused with *maskhabs* recently. They will tell you that it's Imam Azam, but in fact it's not. For instance, about ritual purity [*ta-arat*] . . . some claim that you can smoke and chew tobacco [*nos*] between prayers and that's Imam Azam's way. But it's not . . . Anybody can publish such a booklet and make money with it. Most of the people will treat booklets with *suras* respectfully, but some may use them as toilet paper. That's wrong.

In a situation where information on Islam seemed to spiral out of control, Nursultan wished for mullahs who could lead people and give clear directions about how to distinguish good content from bad. Many men in Murghab in particular were on the lookout for a mullah whom they considered knowledgeable and trustworthy. They would sometimes travel to distant villages to seek advice regarding prayer practice, lifestyle, and the upbringing of children. In order to orient themselves within a confusing field of knowledge, they sought guidance from somebody who had the ability to distinguish right from wrong. Nursultan and Gulira, too, tried out various paths to find a way through the thicket of global Islam that they encountered along the highway. They went to imams from different mosques, mullahs based in villages outside the town, and healers. They participated in reading groups, joined discussions and instructional sessions (*mashvara*) that were organized by neighbors, and looked for somebody who could provide direction in all this.[18] While Gulira settled for the healer Baktygül as her main source of advice on religious matters, in the summer of 2010, Nursultan finally found a man he thought would meet his requirements. When Nursultan came back from one of the consultancies with the promising mullah, I had the following conversation with him:

> Nursultan: Till, I have to tell you a funny story about that *moldo*. As you
> know, there are many girls who cover their faces to protect it from
> the sun, but who wear tight jeans at the same time. That's actually not
> right and the *moldo* told us many *masalas* about this issue. But then a
> funny event occurred.
> Till: What happened?
> Nursultan: The *moldo* told us to be careful what clothes our wives and
> daughters wear. The clothes shouldn't be too short and tight. Then he
> said, "You're just walking down the street and then you suddenly see

the shape of a woman's body." The *moldo* really drew the shape of a female body in the air [*with his hands Nursultan carves out the shape of a voluptuous body in the air himself*] and told us, "This isn't the way it is supposed to be!" We all laughed. He really is a modern [*sovremennyi*] *moldo*. He knows us well.

Nursultan's modern mullah, and other contemporary Sunni specialists along the Pamir Highway, were expected to provide people with a sense of correct and inappropriate practices. They assessed teaching materials, interpreted and clarified vaguely formulated rules, and signposted Sunni Hanafi doctrine as the right version of Islam. In this process, I saw a mullah in Alichor being confronted with the question of whether Kyrgyz children were allowed to play with a talking Jesus doll that had been distributed by Ukrainian Christian missionaries. The mullah found this permissible because Jesus, or rather Isa, is recognized in Islam as a prophet and the doll's battery, allowing it to utter parts of the Sermon on the Mount, had long been dead. I also witnessed a Kyrgyz imam in Murghab reacting to the hotly debated question of whether it was permissible for Kyrgyz to lend each other large amounts of money that they had received as loans from an Ismaili microfinance program. While the imam told the mosque community that they could lend money to each other without interest, he deemed it un-Islamic to get money from a microfinance program. The issue was not that the program was Ismaili funded (as long as nobody asked them to become Ismaili); rather, he was of the opinion that receiving the loans was problematic because they entailed interest payments.

As these examples suggest, religious specialists were expected to direct the people living along the Pamir Highway through the complexities of everyday life and help them face challenging questions to which no booklet or commentary could provide a precise answer. In these encounters, the issue of difference between Sunnis and Ismailis came up frequently. As the following example shows, this sectarian difference went beyond simplistic binary oppositions because it was embedded in a maze of identities in which religion, ethnicity, and regional belonging often intersected.[19]

Many of my talks with Baktygül were embedded in the context of house calls. Sometimes people in Murghab would call her while we were chatting about the Pamirs, Tajikistan, and Switzerland, and then we would go see her patients together. During these walks through town, the most meaningful conversations and encounters with and about other people in Murghab arose. In such a moment, Baktygül came up with the topic of other healers in the region and the significance of their work from her point of view. One day in the summer of 2010, she suddenly began to talk about healing practices of Ismaili *khalifa*s and the reasons why such practices were not compatible with her own herbal healing methods:

> Baktygül: Tajiks here have a different religion [*Tajiktin dini bashka*]. They're not Muslims [*busurman emes*]. They're Shia Tajiks. They're black [*kara*]. It's not possible to mix the two [ways of healing].
>
> Till: Black . . . ?
>
> Bakytgül: . . . Shia. If the two get mixed, then they will work against each other. For example, if you don't go to a Kyrgyz, it's possible to go to a Tajik. But after having visited a Kyrgyz then it wouldn't be possible. It would get mixed up. Then they would get sick. They would have more sicknesses and would eventually die.

Having said this, Baktygül asked me not to mention our discussion to *khalifa*s or other Ismaili specialists in particular. She sensed the potential for conflict in what she had said, and her relationships with Ismailis had always been friendly and respectful. At the same time, her healing practices were organized along sectarian boundaries; one could choose only one direction, and that choice had to be made at the beginning of a healing procedure.[20] Baktygül considered it crucial to choose one way when it came to health issues. If they got "mixed" (*aralash*), it would cause nothing less than death.

To consider sectarian difference a central theme for Baktygül, however, would not do justice to her way of thinking. Sectarian difference counted when it came to healing, marriage, and the performance of rituals. But it was nothing that, in her opinion, would prevent Kyrgyz and Pamiris from living side by side along the highway. On the contrary, when we arrived at her patient's house after our walk and the conversation that I have just recounted, Baktygül repeatedly emphasized that "Khorogi Tajiks" (*Khorogdun Tajikteri*), as she often called Pamiris, were "educated" (*gramotnyi*) and "humane" (*adamkerchiliktüü*). During her treatment of Tajigül, her middle-aged patient, they began to discuss politics and the difference between Pamiris and Tajiks from western Tajikistan.

> Baktygül: Here Khorogi Tajiks are good. . . . If you don't have a place to sleep, they will let you in their houses. If you stay out, Dushanbe Tajiks [*Dushanbelik*] will kill you. People from Dushanbe push others.

Tajigül: People from Dushanbe don't agree with us. It's said they will destroy the Kyrgyz.

Baktygül: If they start to destroy us we will rise up. We aren't afraid of Tajiks. It's true. We will confront each other. If they start a fight we will also fight. We should have had a hunger strike in the past. I didn't have the opportunity, otherwise I would have organized one. And we have children studying in Dushanbe; they will go against them.

Tajigül: We are afraid of this. Generally, Tajiks are bad.

Baktygül: Khorogi Tajiks are good. How many years have we lived together! Such a long time.

On the one hand, Baktygül draws a distinction between Pamiris and Kyrgyz on the basis of sectarian difference. On the other hand, she also views people along the highway, both Kyrgyz and Pamiris, as distinct from the Tajiks of western Tajikistan based on ethnicity and regional belonging. Thus, the fact that Kyrgyz and Tajiks are Sunnis does not necessarily foster intimacy, and the difference between Sunnis and Shia Ismailis does not necessarily interfere with local identity. Quite the contrary—Baktygül attributes education and a humane attitude to Pamiris, which she juxtaposes to the image of oppressive Tajiks from Dushanbe. In the recent history of places along the Pamir Highway, this emphasis on "the humane" (*adamkerchilik*), uniting local people across difference, played a pivotal role as the region experienced a shift from Soviet provisioning to humanitarian aid and international development.

ISMAILI PATHWAYS

*Daavatchy*s come from Pakistan, the imam's edicts from France. Laws come from Dushanbe and goods from China. War comes from Afghanistan, risky experiments with democracy and freedom from Kyrgyzstan. Remittances come from Russia. Purity comes from the mountain pastures and the best technology comes from Germany. Kyrgyz books come from Osh and Bishkek.

This short and eclectic extract comes from a longer passage in my field notes in which I describe how people along the Pamir Highway mapped their world in the course of my fieldwork. The attribution of certain things or people to specific places was based on particular encounters in everyday life: Kyrgyz books could be found in the bazaar, and Germans were attempting to build a new hydroelectric power plant in Murghab. Soviet Germans also used to build the best houses during the time of the

Union. Troubling news came from Kyrgyzstan, but even more so from Afghanistan. Sons and daughters migrated to Russia to work and sent money home, and laws in the unknown, bureaucratic Tajik language made officials sweat. The Ismaili imam, the Aga Khan IV, transmitted his edicts (*farmon*) from Europe, and huge Chinese trucks filled with goods thundered past Murghabi houses from spring to autumn. And who did not long to spend some days on a serene mountain pasture?

This description of how people along the Pamir Highway trace the movement of things, humans, and ideas into the region highlights particular trajectories that were salient when I wrote the note in 2010. It also shows that such trajectories are historically situated, often bound to change, and sometimes persist: *daavatchy*s are no longer to be seen in Murghab; since 2013, Chinese trucks speed along the Pamir Highway all year round; laws are still sent from Dushanbe; the power plant has not progressed; labor migration has declined due to the crisis in Russia; the Aga Khan IV's edicts keep arriving from Aiglemont near Paris; and Kyrgyzstan has become a lot calmer. Similarly, we can go back in recent history and look at how these trajectories have changed over the course of the twentieth century. We then, for instance, see Soviet soldiers from various republics taking up their positions at posts on the borders with China and Afghanistan in the 1930s; foodstuffs and fashion clothing from Moscow in Murghabi shop windows in the 1960s and then the lack thereof when civil war started in Tajikistan in 1992; and subsequent humanitarian aid, predominantly provided through institutions chaired by the Aga Khan IV.

The political inevitably meanders through these examples from my ethnography, resulting in multiple "faces of the state" (Navaro-Yashin 2002) that people along the Pamir Highway see reflected in actors, things, and ideas moving in and out of the region. During my fieldwork time, Ismailis in Murghab commented on the fact that presidential decrees and the Aga Khan's edicts, often addressing ritual, social issues, and morality in one message, are both called *farmon* in Tajik. For instance, Alikhon told me that he thought the president tried to emulate the Aga Khan in order to reach out to the Pamiris. The Kyrgyz in Murghab, on the one hand, perceived the Aga Khan and Ismaili institutions as having contributed in important ways to survival along the highway in the years of the civil war between 1992 and 1997. On the other hand, they also saw him as representative of Ismailis in the region and, as Gulira told me, having no real interest in the Kyrgyz. Against this backdrop, Ismailism, humanitarian aid, and development along the Pamir Highway are embedded within complex political and religious genealogies. These genealogies are informed by the shared experience of having received aid and survived together. At the same time, they are marked by a particular Ismaili civil war and post–civil war history that has provided the grounds for distinction within this shared experience.

Saving the Pamirs

In 1992, newly independent Tajikistan sank into the chaos of a civil war that lasted until 1997.[21] At the outset of the conflict, there were politicized regional identities that had already gained public relevance in the last years of the Soviet Union. In the case of Gorno-Badakhshan, this resulted in the founding of the La'li Badakhshan (The Ruby of Badakhshan) movement, which envisaged a future Badakhshan as an independent republic with its own economic ties. Even in the early stages of conflict, regional identities had already started to intersect with religious belonging, and questions of sectarian difference began to play an important role in public discourse. Kirill Nourzhanov and Christian Bleuer (2013, 290) highlight the complexity of these categories by way of the example of Tajikistan's first presidential elections in 1991: while candidate Davlat Khudonazarov, a Pamiri Ismaili, allied himself with Islamists from Gharm, his opponent Rahmon Nabiev launched a smear campaign, supported by mullahs in Kulob, labeling Khudonazarov a Badakhshani infidel (*kofir*). In the civil war that soon followed, religion, alongside regional belonging, became, as Jonah Steinberg (2011, 25) argues, "a key element." War factions took shape along the lines of religious, ethnic, and regional categories, and many people were killed because of their origin and faith.

With the majority of inhabitants of Gorno-Badakhshan being Ismaili, the suffering of the people in the region immediately became a high priority on the agenda of the Aga Khan Development Network (AKDN), whose chairman is the Aga Khan IV. The AKDN is a group of development agencies with mandates that include the environment, health, education, architecture, culture, microfinance, rural development, disaster reduction, the promotion of private-sector enterprise, and the revitalization of historic cities.[22] In 1993, the Aga Khan Foundation (AKF), an agency of the AKDN, established the Pamir Relief and Development Program. This program later became the Mountain Societies Development Support Program (MSDSP) when in 1997 activities expanded outside Gorno-Badakhshan to the Rasht Valley and the region of Khatlon.[23] The renam-

FIGURE 4.2. Flour from Kazakhstan being unloaded from rail wagons at the Osh depot of the Mountain Societies Development Support Program (MSDSP). © Robert Middleton, 1994.

ing of the program signified a shift from short-term humanitarian aid and relief in the context of civil war to a development program that aimed to implement long-term projects.

The initial relief program run by AKF during the war was generally seen as essential for survival. In the eyes of both Pamiris and Kyrgyz along the Pamir Highway, the provision of food supplies and heating fuel from 1993 onward largely secured people's lives in the region.[24] Using the same infrastructure of provisioning via the road as the Soviet administration had previously, the program imported basic necessities that could not be produced in the Pamirs. The establishment and presence of the Aga Khan Development Network along the Pamir Highway did not exclusively target Ismailis but included other people living in Gorno-Badakhshan as well. At the same time, Ismaili institutions arriving in Gorno-Badakhshan in the early 1990s did not find a tabula rasa but had to position themselves against the backdrop of an already existing history of Ismaili interaction and disconnection in the region. For instance, as Aliaa Remtilla (2012, 46) notes, many Pamiris still remember the historic visit of the Ismaili missionary Pirsabzali, who traveled in 1923 from Bombay—then the seat of the Aga Khan III—to Badakhshan, including territories in today's Afghanistan, China, Pakistan, and Tajikistan. Pirsabzali's message from the imam not to resist the Russians and to productively engage with Soviet rule still reverberates widely in the region.[25] Yet now that the Soviet empire had crumbled, as the imam had "foreshadowed" (Remtilla 2012, 46), Ismaili institutions were for the first time facing actual encounters across difference in Gorno-Badakhshan. People in the region had become used to services provided by the Soviet state and were following a local tradition of Ismailism that differed from practices performed in other regions.

Jonah Steinberg (2011, 169) argues that Aga Khan institutions in Gorno-Badakhshan have exhibited only some "superficial continuity" with Soviet forms of organization. He mentions that the institutions brought a crucial shift from Soviet structures of "collective organization" to participatory developmental approaches. This entailed a strengthened focus on individual effort, meritocracy, and a take on economics that, as Salmaan Keshavjee (2014) highlights with regard to medical projects, is oriented toward neoliberal governmentality.[26] Thus when the MSDSP and related programs began their work in Gorno-Badakhshan and other places in Tajikistan, they did not simply take over the role of patron that they inherited from the Soviet state, but sought to transform and educate individuals in skills that would prepare them for an entrepreneurial world. In doing so, the institutions of the AKDN addressed people of different ethnic and religious identities. At the same time, however, they also established exclusive links between Ismaili communities in different parts of Gorno-Badakhshan and the global Ismaili network, with its headquarters in Geneva, London, and Aiglemont just outside Paris.

Facing and Crafting the State

On 26 May 1995, the Aga Khan IV made Murghab his first stop on a visit to Gorno-Badakshan and addressed the local population in the form of an edict (*farmon*) in which he advised his followers to contribute to a peaceful Tajikistan; to cherish the transition to "modern statehood," including free-market economy, democracy, and equal rights; and to peacefully live alongside the country's other Muslims in one *ummah* ("community") of Islam (Al Hussaini 2009, 927). The content of this edict has resonated in a myriad of *farmon*s and speeches that the Aga Khan IV and other Ismaili representatives have delivered to the people of Gorno-Badakshan over the past twenty years. In many of these speeches, the *farmon*s' salient language of political and social vision is supplemented by an explicit call for Ismailis to be loyal citizens of Tajikistan.[27] In this public discourse, Ismaili institutions, most importantly personified by the Aga Khan

IV, enact the state through the services they perform and by emulating nation-state symbolism, including governing bodies, an Ismaili constitution, and a flag.[28] Yet they also reject the explicit "face of the state" (Navaro-Yashin 2002) that is associated with *davlat* or *mamleket*, the terms most often used by people along the Pamir Highway to refer to the state of Tajikistan and its territoriality. While the question of political power—expressed in diplomacy, provisioning, and the struggle for religious legitimacy—is omnipresent in Ismaili discourse, Aga Khan institutions depict interference with state affairs as an undesired form of action. In everyday practice, the official Ismaili refusal to wear the "face of the state" is complicated by the fact that both the president's and the Aga Khan's formal appearances are similarly festooned with the trappings that people along the Pamir Highway associate with "statist" (*davlati*) displays: both are patriarchal male figures; the edicts they send are labeled *farmon* and are reminiscent of the Soviet bureaucratic top-down vocabulary of decrees (*prikaz, ukaz*); their visits are celebrated in a festive manner with large crowds and "traditional" music and dancing; both inaugurate infrastructure projects such as bridges, power plants, and hospitals; and both send gifts to places along the road.

In his study of an apartment complex in Sarajevo, Stef Jansen (2015, 12) proposes a distinction between statehood and statecraft as a means to navigate different analytical dimensions of the state. "Statehood" refers to "what the state is, claims to be, and should be"; "statecraft" denotes "what the state does, claims to do, and should do." While the first is concerned with a state's legitimacy as a polity and its "administrative-territorial anatomy," the latter is linked to its rooting in material conditions and temporal structures that enable "normal lives." Jansen's distinction sheds light on why Ismaili and government institutions frequently appear to overlap in form and practice but should be regarded as different on many levels. Their practices of statecraft sometimes indeed coincide and foster a sense of institutional competition. Yet the ways in which they conceptualize their own roles and claims along the road and their aspirations for the future are distinct and point to rather divergent ideas of statehood.

Gifts from the Master

The distribution of food, fuel, and technology along the Pamir Highway had a long history throughout the twentieth century, and current practices of statecraft can be measured against the ideal of "Moscow provisioning," an ideal that has never since been achieved in the same way as during the late Soviet period.[29] In early summer 2010, I visited Sultonsho in his house in Murghab and encountered the outcome of recent gifting by Ismaili and government institutions. I had not seen Sultonsho in a while, and upon my arrival he proudly pointed to two new technical devices that were resting under the roof of his veranda.

> Sultonsho: Look, we've got two solar panels now. When you were here earlier we didn't have either of them.
> Till: Where did you get them from? China?
> Sultonsho: No, no . . . one is a present from the Imam. There was a raffle because they didn't have enough for all. The other is a present from [President] Emomali [Rahmon].
> Till: What do you need them for?
> Sultonsho: Television, lamps, radio . . . the thing from the Imam works with all of them and is long-lasting. The other panel from [President] Emomali [Rahmon], naturally, doesn't really work anymore. It's broken. It's a cheap one.

The interpretation of the opposing nature of Sultonsho's solar panels touches upon different dimensions in which Ismaili institutions operate along the Pamir Highway. First, relations between Ismaili institutions and the Aga Khan's "spiritual children" in the region are based on a close material relationship between local Ismailis and their imam. In her study of communities in the western Pamirs, Aliaa Remtilla (2012, 82) reveals that this relationship has its origins in the "economy of grace" that Pamiri Ismailis attributed to the Soviet state and the continuation of which they have found in Ismaili rather than in government institutions. In this regard, the imam has stepped in as *soheb*, the master and a father figure. Thus the fact that Sultonsho identified the Imam's solar panel as superior in quality to the president's gift is linked to the juxtaposition of a capable master and the government's incapacity to make things work in Gorno-Badakhshan.[30] It also, however, relates to the esoteric aspects of the Aga Khan's relationship with his followers, who experience the work of Ismaili institutions as deeply interconnected with the Aga Khan's duties as their imam. In this regard, Aliaa Remtilla argues that many studies on the influence of the Aga Khan in contemporary Gorno-Badakhshan focus mainly on *zahiri* ("exoteric") aspects of his presence and neglect *batini* ("esoteric") aspects. In her opinion, this does not take into account the fact that, conceptually speaking, *zahir* and *batin* are deeply connected in a way that reflects the relationship between the current Aga Khan and past and future imams: "This totality of all Imams is referred to as the Imamate and it is in the Imamate that the *nur* (lit. light) of God is reflected. This eternal, *bāteni* Imamate is made visible in the human, *zāheri* manifestations of each individual Imam in such a way that the *nur* of all Imams—the institution of the Imamate—is present in its entirety in each one. In this way, the *bāten* is in opposition to, constitutive of, and inherent within the *zāher*" (Remtilla 2011, 191).

The multidimensionality that is inherent in Ismaili institutions and the humanitarian aid and development work they have delivered along the Pamir Highway allows them to speak with one voice and yet convey rather different meanings to different people. This is also exemplified by the way the aforementioned concepts from Ismaili theology have been translated into the institutional setup and distribution of responsibilities. Ismaili institutions are officially and explicitly separated into a secular wing, which works in the development sector (e.g., AKDN), and a wing that administers the religious activities (e.g., the Ismaili Tariqah and Religious Education Committee/Board, ITREC/ITREB).[31] This provides Ismaili institutions with the opportunity to position themselves in the field of international development, where religious language has long been marginalized.[32] At the same time, in Gorno-Badakhshan the mutually constitutive realms of Ismaili presence have resulted in the emergence of powerful institutions and are now regarded by people in Gorno-Badakhshan as inseparably intertwined.

An Official Odyssey

On a cold, sunny winter day in January 2009, I sought to find out more about Ismaili institutions and their presence along the Pamir Highway. I had been studying the region for a while and had made friends with many Pamiris, but I had not yet had the chance to talk to representatives of these organizations that played such an influential role in Gorno-Badakhshan's recent history. I started my inquiry with the usually kind and helpful Ismaili neighbor families. Yet our conversations about official Ismaili presence in Murghab turned out to be a failure. As I put down in my field notes that afternoon, they "all said that they didn't know anything" and that I should "ask the *khalifa* or some Pamiri elders." Slightly disconcerted by people's reluctance to talk, I plodded through the cold and snowy streets to the house of the *khalifa*.

A *khalifa* is an Ismaili religious specialist and community leader in a Pamiri context who performs rituals and healing procedures. He also plays a central role as the liaison between Ismailis and the Aga Khan, in which role he conveys *farmon*s from the Aga Khan to the community.[33] When I entered the elderly *khalifa*'s house in Murghab, he was polite but immediately made his point clear: he would not talk to me about Ismaili presence in the region. As I found out later, he had a number of reasons for not wanting to talk to me. First, Pamiri friends told me a while after my visit that he had no intention of talking openly about Ismaili affairs because of his former involvement in the Soviet system. As a high-ranking car mechanic along the highway, he had been professionally involved in state structures for many years and was well advised to keep silent because of Soviet antireligious policies. In addition, changes in Ismaili rituals and prayer practice had caused disturbances among Ismailis in the Pamirs in 2009. These changes had been initiated by Ismaili institutions in an attempt to alter and standardize particular aspects of local religious practice, including prayers and marriage ceremonies, and were hotly debated in the region. The *khalifa*, embedded in the structure of Ismaili institutions, preferred to refer me to what he considered the next level in the hierarchy. He advised me to go to the head of the Mountain Societies Development Support Program (MSDSP) who, in his opinion, had more authority to reply to my questions.

I went directly from the *khalifa*'s house to the office of the MSDSP near the bazaar, where I met the two local heads of the program (who shared a heated room). One of them was the Pamiri man whom the *khalifa* had recommended, the other a Kyrgyz elder who seemed a bit surprised to hear me asking him questions about official Ismaili presence in the region. Leaving me no time to start a dialogue, they quickly presented me with an overview of MSDSP's development projects in Murghab in the form of a well-prepared and streamlined briefing. At the very end of their talk, they pointed out that for further information I should go to their superiors or directly to the Ismaili Tariqah and Religious Education Committee (ITREC) in Khorog, which they considered more suitable for any questions that did not relate to "development" (*razvitie*) but, rather, to "religion" (*religiia*).

At the end of my odyssey through official Ismaili Murghab, I arrived back at Nursultan and Gulira's house. That evening Nursultan was lying in the living room and asked me how my day had been. I then told him my story: that our neighbors sent me to the *khalifa*, the *khalifa* sent me to the MSDSP, and the MSDSP finally suggested I should contact the ITREC in Khorog. After having carefully listened, Nursultan laughed and said

FIGURE 4.3. The gate of a house in Murghab made of vegetable oil barrels from humanitarian aid. Photograph © Till Mostowlansky, 2011.

ironically, "And in Khorog they'll say, 'Go ask the Imam,' because they aren't willing to talk! You see, that's the way things are around here. It's our mentality [*mentalitet*]."

My official odyssey and Nursultan's remark highlight several points with regard to the statecraft of Ismaili institutions and the closely interwoven secular and religious dimensions of their work. First, Nursultan's statement indicates that the lack of willingness to speak in Murghab is not simply restricted to Ismaili institutions but is part of a broader attitude toward institutional hierarchy in Gorno-Badakhshan. It is a widespread opinion in Murghab that the district was utterly law-abiding and oriented toward centers of political power throughout the Soviet period, and in the course of my fieldwork government officials frequently referred me to higher levels of authority when I had questions or requests concerning my research. I was never quite sure if this was done to avoid the burden of responsibility or just in the hope that I would shrug my shoulders and give up. With regard to Ismaili institutions, Murghab's distance from and dependence on Khorog and the local Ismailis' "diasporic" situation among a majority of Kyrgyz might have added to this already hierarchically stratified constellation. In this sense, the Aga Khan's stepping into the footsteps of the Soviet paternalistic state as *soheb*—the master—has brought with it a whole set of hierarchically organized institutional practices. Yet the realm of Ismaili statecraft has been, as is the case with many international organizations, restricted to particular fields in the provisioning of humanitarian aid and development. Unlike the government, Ismaili institutions neither issued passports nor did they man border posts or train a police force. However, Ismaili institutions have established, among other things, educational facilities, hospitals, bridges, markets, and parks. The locally inextricably entangled spheres of Ismaili secularity and religion have provided them with a powerful narrative to get things done along the Pamir Highway. Among many of my Pamiri friends, this has also fostered an inclusivist discourse based on rumors of clandestine Kyrgyz conversion to Ismailism, allegedly inspired by the imam's humanitarian aid. For instance, Holiknazar and his wife Malohat, my neighbors in Murghab, explained to me that the Kyrgyz had somehow become Ismailis during the years of civil war provisioning. Since in their opinion Ismaili faith had become stronger as a result of the imam's aid, the same must have been true for the Kyrgyz. Others referred to eyewitnesses who had seen Kyrgyz attending events during the Aga Khan's visit (*didor*) to Tajikistan in November 2008 and silently admiring him.[34]

When confronted with such narratives of conversion, my Kyrgyz friends usually laughed and dismissed them as a Pamiri "dream" (*mechta*). They seemed too far removed from everyday reality even to be discussed. Yet these narratives also included nostalgia for lost forms of conviviality and the striving for future ones. When Holiknazar and Malohat told me about the Kyrgyz conversions, Holiknazar hooked his forefingers into each other to conjure up the image of the state of interdependency in which people along the Pamir Highway lived thanks to the imam. By employing the two intimately linked forefingers, Holiknazar was replicating a common way to depict how different peoples had lived together as "brothers and sisters" in the Soviet Union. However, in the present, the more common gesture used to signify communal relationships in the region is to hold the two forefingers parallel to each other, not interlinked. In this sense, one can also read these narratives of conversion as an expression of the wish to overcome present difference and to revive past forms of community. In contrast, public displays of Muslim identities along the Pamir Highway, and their entanglements with political processes, provisioning, and transnational actors, have not only resulted in a sense of solidarity but have also invoked new forms of distinction.

CHAPTER 5

THE GOLDEN GATE OF TAJIKISTAN

TRANSLATING THE LAW

Along the Pamir Highway and in other places in Gorno-Badakhshan, painted signs in Tajik and sometimes in Russian read, *Badakhshon darvozai tilloii Tojikiston*—"Badakhshan is the golden gate of Tajikistan." As a political slogan, the golden gate metaphor has been around since the beginning of my fieldwork in the region and was, as presidential speeches demonstrate, sanctioned by the government. For instance, in a speech in Khorog in July 2008, Emomali Rahmon used the expression while envisaging a revival of Badakhshan's Silk Road history and past connectivity with China, the Middle East, and the Indian subcontinent (Prezident 2008). In another speech in September 2012, he reminded his audience that the region's developing status as the golden gate of the country had only recently been achieved with the government-enforced construction of "modern motorways" (*rohhoi muosir*) and bridges in the 2000s (Prezident 2012).

Invoking Silk Road romanticism, very present in both orientalist literature and China's recent One Belt, One Road strategy, the golden gate metaphor tells several stories about Gorno-Badakhshan's status within Tajikistan.[1] Official discourse praises the region as essential and valuable to the country. This value holds the promise of a flourishing future amid global connections. At the same time, the state comes across as a modernizing force that, by ostentatiously advertising newly built infrastructure and connectivity, reinscribes backwardness into the Soviet past. Finally, the golden gate metaphor spatially situates Gorno-Badakshan where

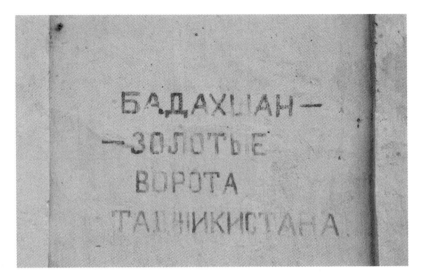

FIGURE 5.1. A sign in Russian that reads, "Badakhshan is the golden gate of Tajikistan." Photograph © Till Mostowlansky, 2008.

gates are usually located: in the margins, on the fringes, and at places of economic passing-through.

People along the Pamir Highway relate to the different dimensions of this metaphor in various ways. Some told me with excitement that Gorno-Badakhshan would become an important "center" (*markaz*) for trade with China in the future, with roads, railways, and a renovated Murghabi airport. Others thought that the region did not need Tajikistan and could sustain itself on the ruby pits in the border zone with China, the Kūhi La'l (the "ruby mountain" in the western Pamirs), and minerals that allegedly remain undiscovered in the ground.[2] Yet all of them agreed that what the president promoted as ongoing modernization and future prosperity rarely benefited them in their present everyday lives. Instead, when talking to me they often painted a picture of a political elite, personified by the presidential family, that came to Gorno-Badakhshan to build, extract resources, and trade for their own sake.

The government's ambivalent presence along the Pamir Highway ties in directly with my discussion of statehood and statecraft at the end of chapter 4. In this regard, Stef Jansen's (2015) analytical distinction between discourses on the nature and representation of the state ("statehood") and past, present, and future state practices ("statecraft") is particularly helpful in making sense of how various actors in Gorno-Badakhshan simultaneously align with, reject, envisage, and "do" the state.[3] Thus, I suggest thinking of people along the highway as having long and consistently been involved in the making of the state in Tajikistan, albeit in historically changing and transformative ways. With regard to the practicalities of analyzing these processes, I follow Akhil Gupta's (1995, 375) argument that "studying the state ethnographically involves both the analysis of the *everyday practices* of local bureaucracies and the *discursive construction* of the state in public culture" (emphasis in the original). During my fieldwork, themes that have been of particular salience to an understanding of the state along the Pamir Highway include the troubling question of language and administration; encounters in the process of implementing laws; the meaning of existing, deficient, transforming, and desired economic opportunities; and debates on the ideal form of rule.

Russian as an Achievement

Landscapes of language along the Pamir Highway are multilayered and change from settlement to settlement and even sometimes from street to street and house to house within settlements. For people living in the district center of Murghab, Kyrgyz has been the most important language for everyday communication in public and in Kyrgyz homes. Pamir languages are mostly spoken in Pamiri homes and are again divided into several different languages. In this setting, Russian has historically had an important status as a lingua franca throughout the region. The Soviet army, and later the Russian army, provided a range of employment opportunities that required knowledge of Russian, and the district—like the rest of Gorno-Badakhshan—was generally administered in Russian. Even though Tajik was defined as the official language of the Tajik SSR, and Russian and Uzbek as its other languages of administration in 1989, this did not have any significant influence on the way people along the Pamir Highway communicated or submitted official documents. Tajikistan's new constitution, which was adopted by popular referendum in 1994, did not introduce any major changes to this practice and largely took over the content of the 1989 law on language (Landau and Kellner-Heinkele 2001, 123): Tajik was considered the state language and Russian the language of interethnic communication. Members of every ethnic group were given the right to use their native language freely. However, in October 2009, the lower house and the upper chamber of Tajikistan's parliament passed a new law on language that made it mandatory to use Tajik in official communications. At the same time, Russian ceased to be the language of interethnic communication (Kellner-Heinkele and Landau 2012, 178). Even in elite offices in Dushanbe, where Tajik had been gaining in importance since the early 1990s, the introduction of the new law turned well-educated specialists into illiterate dabblers desperately trying to catch up with the new, hastily constructed language of administration. Along the Pamir Highway, the new law on language considerably changed people's perceptions of the state and the ways in which they situated themselves within it. In Dushanbe, language specialists and translators could be found and employed to redesign and translate official reports, but no such cadres found their way up to Murghab. To my friends who worked within government institutions and those who had to engage within the bureaucracy, "the state" (*davlat, mamleket*) turned into an assemblage of illegible acts that had to be translated, interpreted, and pondered.

In the winter of 2010, shortly after the Tajikistani parliament had passed the law on language, I had tea with Kamal, the Murghabi official who worked for the local government. He had already started to learn Tajik in order to be able to submit his reports in the new language. As he stated, however, he felt he was too old to learn Tajik properly despite the fact that his intentions were serious, and he felt threatened by the announcement that reports in bad Tajik or any language other than Tajik would cause ruinous fines. Even if he did not manage to successfully learn Tajik, he hoped he would still make his way without being fined. Yet his major concern was for the future of his children. "Our children have to learn the state language," he repeatedly emphasized, noting the general difficulty of learning Tajik along the Pamir Highway.

Since the local Pamiris, who are officially defined as Tajiks, speak a range of southeastern Iranian languages but not Tajik, it was difficult to find Tajik first-language speakers in the region who could act as teachers and translators. In the district center of Murghab, only one Tajik school provided an entire study program in Tajik in 2011, and even that had the reputation of being badly suited to everyday requirements. Parents often sent their children to study in Khorog or Dushanbe in order to attain a better knowledge of the state language, but instead of moving back to Murghab as well-educated experts, they sought job opportunities abroad or in the place of their studies.

Yet it was not only insufficient access to Tajik study programs that caused consternation along the Pamir Highway. The use of Russian as the language of administration and the perfect mastery of it contributed to a sense of pride that was closely linked to modern self-representations. In this regard, I would like to call to mind Nursultan's army story that I briefly mentioned at the beginning of chapter 1: While talking about his time in the Soviet army, Nursultan referred to differing degrees of human development, which he attributed to place and ethnicity. Russians and people from the Baltic countries seemed more modern to him than Central Asians, while people from the Pamirs were higher up in the hierarchy of progress than Turkmen and other Central Asians. The knowledge of Russian played an important role in defining these stages of development. In Nursultan's opinion, people from the Pamirs—be they Kyrgyz or Pamiri—were not naturally more modern than others but had become more modern as an effect of modernization in the course of the twentieth century. As in many other places in Central Asia, modernization was based not only on the reorganization of living space, diet, clothing style, changing gender roles, and involvement in technical professions, but also on higher Soviet education for which the acquisition of Russian was a basic precondition.[4] In addition, the perception of "Tajiks from Dushanbe" (*dushanbelikter, Dushanbe Tajikteri, dushanbinskie*) as being of rural origin, uneducated, and less civilized has increasingly contributed to the distinction between Gorno-Badakhshan and western Tajikistan. Conceptualized as a realm of the modern with a potentially well-educated, Russian-speaking population, Gorno-Badakhshan was confronted with laws and cultural influences that, while undermining its modernity, simultaneously drew attention to it. To many people along the Pamir Highway, learning Tajik as the sole state language not only seemed like an impossible endeavor due to the lack of adequate learning opportunities but also constituted a threat to the status they had achieved in the Soviet past. Reactions ranged from criticism of the new language policy as constituting a loss of access to people in Russian-speaking countries (mostly uttered privately in people's homes) to supportive public statements emphasizing the need for national "unity" (*vahdat*) on the road to progress.

Understanding What Needs to Be Done

The year 2009 brought some political changes that people along the Pamir Highway frequently discussed. Not only was the law on language passed but also the aforementioned new law on religion which, in the Year of Imomi A'zam, presented Sunni Hanafi Islam as the country's official teaching.[5] One effect of the new law on religion was that religious communities and mosques had to be reregistered in order to remain legal. As Tim Epkenhans (2010, 99) notes, the process of registration required "the completion of comprehensive documentation, giving not just a demonstration that building and sanitation regulations have been fulfilled, but also a detailed description of religious beliefs."[6] For religious specialists as well as for officials working for government institutions along the highway, this procedure meant long work hours, trips to and receiving official delegations from Dushanbe, and confusion over extensive reporting in the unfamiliar new state language.

On one of Kamal's rare free Saturday afternoons, when we were sitting on mats on the floor of his house and having tea, two men unexpectedly entered and asked for his support. The two men turned out to be mullahs who were concerned with the implementation of the new law on religion. Since they did not understand the text of the law in Tajik and had become confused by contradictory comments by other officials, they had finally come to Kamal, whom they considered the most reliable source of information in such matters. At a certain point during the conversation the question of how to best reregister mosques arose. A charter with the specific requirements, which was to include a list of central documents, had to be established. Yet it was unclear in which language the charter was to be issued:

> Kamal: Is the charter in Kyrgyz and Russian?
> Mullah 1: No, it's fully in Kyrgyz. Who is going to understand it if we make it in Tajik? Nobody will understand. Moreover, it would be better for us if the charter were in Kyrgyz because people will understand what we are doing and what needs to be done. It's not right to force people to learn Tajik today.

As it turned out, a delegation of officials had been sent from Murghab to Dushanbe to get instructions on how to proceed regarding the implementation of the law on religion. But despite their efforts none of them could recall having ever fully read the original Tajik text version of the law. Thus, Kamal was relieved to hear that the two mullahs had at least understood the importance of reregistering their mosque, albeit not in the required language. For him, most problems with implementing the law were related to a lack of understanding Tajik, as his response to the mullahs illustrates: "All this happened just because of not knowing the language. It would be very good if we could understand the language.

At least we could finish the central points after so many people have been to Dushanbe recently."

As they were struggling to fully understand the law, which no one had seen the original version of, Kamal and the two mullahs conferred on how best to proceed. Then Kamal had an idea and fished a copy of *Asia Plus*, Tajikistan's major Russian-language newspaper, out of his folder. The latest edition included a report on the new law on religion, quotes from the original text in Russian translation, and reflections on the Year of Imomi A'zam and on the ban of the Tablighi Jama'at ("'Dzhamo'ati Tablig'" 2009; "Imami A'zam" 2009). He handed the newspaper to the mullahs and told them to work with it. When I met the mullahs in the bazaar a couple of weeks later, they told me that the article in Russian in *Asia Plus* had given them more insight into the content of the new law on religion than meetings with officials in Dushanbe. They had also managed to submit their documents in Tajik even though they had to pay to have the documents translated.

Similarly, I met many people along the Pamir Highway, both those working within government institutions and others engaging with them in bureaucratic encounters, who somehow managed to get their things done in Tajik. However, they needed proxies, either friends or professionals, to do so. For instance, Kamal told me that the language situation embarrassed him. He experienced it as a loss of control over basic bureaucratic procedures and he mourned the time when he was part of an outstanding district administration. Kamal often referred to Murghab as "the district that first implemented laws coming from Dushanbe and Moscow" during the Soviet period. For others, Tajik was just the rather useless and backward language of an administrative sphere from which they found themselves disconnected. Gulira, for instance, once told me with horror about one of her nephews who had spent a summer in Dushanbe and returned to Murghab after three months. While his Tajik had substantially improved, he had given up his modest knowledge of Russian in exchange. "How can this kid now ever become somebody beyond Dushanbe?" she asked me. For her, Russian was still linked to mobility, literature, and modernity at large.

Within this framework, the Kyrgyz in particular felt "harshly" (*kattuu*) treated by the government, a statement that was often accompanied by the gesture of choking a person. Within an official environment that heavily favored the Tajik language and ethnicity, access to the center became increasingly dependent on people who could match linguistic and ethnic requirements. For most Kyrgyz along the Pamir Highway it seemed impossible to become such a person, and many of my interlocutors were keen on maintaining good relationships with the Pamiri minority. Even though they were not native Tajik speakers, Pamiris were at least officially defined as Tajik in their passports. It was therefore hoped that they would have better connections to the capital. A frequently voiced sentiment by Kyrgyz along the Pamir Highway was that they needed the Pamiris in order "to pave the way to Dushanbe and speak for Murghab." However, the fact that Pamiris, despite these expectations, often also felt alienated from Dushanbe and had similar difficulties speaking Tajik at official events highlights the complexity of state encounters in Tajikistan.

Veena Das and Deborah Poole (2004, 8) argue that the illegibility of the state's "practices, documents, and words" constitutes spaces that can be defined as the margins of the state. Within these margins, the state is continually experienced, made, and undone. From such a perspective, people along the Pamir Highway are not only located in the geographical margins of Tajikistan, as is often suggested by reference to the long distance to the capital, the high-altitude environment, and the surrounding borderlands. They are also subjected to often violent forms of exclusion around which many people with minority ethnic, linguistic, regional, and religious identities must organize their everyday lives throughout the country. For instance, most of my Uzbek friends in Dushanbe have by now "bought" through bribes the ethnic label Tajik to be included in their IDs and passports. They hope to thereby create a better future for themselves and their children as legible citizens of Tajikistan. I have also met pious young Tajik men in Dushanbe who decided to shave off their beards before entering university courses in economics in order to improve their chances of succeeding in a government career. The literal illegibility of the law on religion in Murghab, as exemplified by Kamal and the two mullahs, is therefore only one effect within a larger project of statecraft that aims to turn "unruly subjects" (Das and Poole 2004, 7) in the margins into legible and lawful ones.

"WE HAVEN'T LEARNED TO TRADE"

Holiknazar was not in a good mood when we walked through the bazaar in Murghab in the summer of 2010. He had wanted to go to Osh and start importing Chinese clothes from southern Kyrgyzstan to Murghab, where he planned to sell them to villagers from the region. But due to the violent conflict in Osh, his plan was about to fail. The markets in Osh were closed and the city was in turmoil. The loan he had received from the microfinance bank founded by the Aga Khan was now useless, and he had to pay the first installment with interest by the end of the month. And so we walked and I listened to his sorrowful tale of the failure of his first entrepreneurial attempt. At a market stall he bought a watermelon that had been brought from distant western Tajikistan instead of from Osh, and then a box of cigarettes. Just as Holiknazar was looking for a match, a Chinese driver walked by. Holiknazar turned to him and said in Russian:

> Holiknazar: Eh, gook [*uzkiglaz*, lit. "slant-eye"], you got a light?
> *The Chinese driver remains silent, ignores Holiknazar, and turns away.*
> Till: What did you just call him?
> Holiknazar: Gook. That's what we call them here. Chinese are just fucked up [*khuevyi*] people.

Holiknazar's offensive remark about the Chinese was certainly a result of his frustration and financial worries. At the same time, it also reflects common opinions along the Pamir Highway, which links Chinese presence in the region to anxieties of cultural, economic, and political takeover.[7] For instance, I met shepherds on the summer pastures who claimed that mosquitos and horseflies had grown to much more aggressive and poisonous dimensions since the Chinese kept coming to Murghab. One of the shepherds reasoned that the Chinese government bred them and then sent them to make people vacate the eastern Pamirs. Chinese goods, too, were a topic of constant debate along the highway. Many of my interlocutors were convinced that China only exported the lowest-quality foodstuffs and plastic items to Tajikistan, following a hierarchy of trade that put poor Central Asian countries at the lower end of the quality scale. Discussing this issue at a wedding, some guests savored and compared Uzbek and Chinese rice and eventually concluded that the Chinese brand was of inferior quality and speculated that Chinese products were intended to damage people's health. These everyday worries about Chinese presence in the region were predominantly informed by encounters with goods—and perhaps insects—but seldom with people. Very few of my acquaintances had personally met and interacted with Chinese drivers and road construction workers. At the same time, these anxieties were also embedded within broader political developments that had emerged since the opening of the road to the Kulma pass in 2004 and which triggered the circulation of facts and rumors through newspapers and mundane conversations. Among these was, for instance, the

FIGURE 5.2. A delivery of Chinese city buses on its way to Dushanbe. Photograph © Bernd Hrdy, 2009.

2004 Sino-Tajik agreement on the final demarcation of the disputed Badakhshani border, in the course of which Tajikistan ceded 980 square kilometers of land to China (Kraudzun 2011, 176).[8] People along the Pamir
Highway perceived this agreement as a loss of land, as they did upon
hearing the news that Tajikistan would lease additional land to China for
farming in the country's west in 2011.[9] To them the Chinese seemed over-
ly powerful, and it was felt that they were entering Tajikistan in endless,
uncontrollable numbers.

People along road also frequently juxtaposed Chinese presence to that
of Russians in the Soviet Union. While Russians had brought with them
"good quality" (*kachestvennye*) products and institutions, the Chinese
seemed worlds apart and with no intention of leaving behind anything
of permanence. This notion of lost permanence partly emerged from remembering how well supplied places along the highway used to be. Back
then, subsidized shops sold goods at prices that were no more expensive
than those in the surrounding flatlands. It was only after the collapse of
the Soviet supply chain that bazaar trade and bargaining were introduced
to communities along the Pamir Highway. Prior to that, shops used to be
well equipped and were replenished on a regular basis (Kraudzun 2012,
96). Even among younger people, memories of such wealth are still pres-

ent in everyday life. On walks through the district center of Murghab and her home village, Gulira often pointed to deserted or converted shops and abandoned gas stations and told me what kind of clothes, cookies, soft drinks, and sausages had been sold there.

Mamadjuma, an elderly Pamiri who used to be responsible for the organization of cargo transport on the Pamir Highway in the 1970s and 1980s, described the contrasting and transforming ways of supply to Gorno-Badakhshan as follows:

> At that time [1980s] there was a lot of movement and transport . . . because cargo was brought by car from Osh to Murghab and Gorno-Badakhshan . . . from Osh, from the Kyrgyz republic. All according to a plan—there was a fixed plan of cargo delivery to each district. For example, to the districts of Murghab, Shugnan, Vanj, and many more. It means there was delivery of foodstuffs, clothing, coal, fuel. All these things were transported on the road non-stop. Drivers drove their cars without using the brakes . . . all the time. There were heavily loaded trucks coming from Osh; people unloaded cargo and then the trucks returned to Osh immediately. It was a never-ending movement. Finally, the movement stopped because the Union collapsed. Each republic was interested in its own economy, its own problems, its own foodstuffs, its own clothing—generally things that people need for everyday life. And then traders came and began to sell things in the bazaar for exorbitant prices.

The traders (or *kommersanty* as Mamadjuma called them in Russian) who came to trade in Murghab and Khorog often were not from the region. In the beginning, traders from the Ferghana Valley were predominant, and after the civil war in 1997, when the road between Dushanbe and Khorog began to improve, traders from western Tajikistan, and occasionally from Afghanistan, sought business opportunities up in the Pamirs. Thus, woeful references to the development of commerce along the Pamir Highway such as Mamadjuma's should not be read simply as expressions of nostalgia for a well-supplied past, but also as sentiments of present loss of control on the local level. When the habitual way of delivering goods to places along the highway ceased in the 1990s (Kraudzun 2012, 93–96), the profiteers of change were not from Murghab. With the disappearance of Soviet central planning and the emergence of new, confusing rules of economic exchange, the environment became "wild" (*dikii*), as Mamadjuma put it.

Into the Wild

Securing survival by delivering goods to the communities along the Pamir Highway had been an important aspect of statecraft in Soviet times. Tajikistan's civil war and the delivery of humanitarian aid by Ismaili institutions emulated and prolonged this supply chain, symbolized by a seemingly never-ending movement of trucks and goods. A former truck driver who commuted between Osh and Khorog delivering humanitarian aid during the war told me in 2013 that he and many others in Murghab had hoped that this system would persist. In contrast to these local expectations, however, Ismaili institutions have always thought of humanitarian relief as a temporary solution on the way to a market economy (AKDN 2016a).[10] The fact that this path has been neither straight, smooth, nor prosperous for people along the Pamir Highway is linked to what Mamadjuma invoked by the term "wild": as the Soviet supply chain and its successors reduced the flow of consumer goods and regular salaries into the region, economic practices that had previously been deemed "illegal" became part of an expected everyday normalcy. For instance, only a few years earlier in the Soviet Union individual trade had been banned and branded as *spekulatsiia* ("speculation"; see Kraudzun 2011, 178). Alongside these now normalized individual economic transactions, other practices that are perceived locally as morally corrupt, such as drug trafficking and "bribery" (*vziatka*), became entangled with actors of statecraft. Within this emerging "wild" environment, the distinction between statecraft and crime seemed increasingly blurry.[11]

Caroline Humphrey (1999, 199) argues that in the Soviet Union, criminals established moral codes that they contrasted to those of the Soviet state. In this context, they offered a "roof" (*krysha*) of protection to enterprises, for which they received payments. For post-Soviet Russia, Humphrey mentions that such "racketeering has burst the boundaries of the criminal groups, with a variety of 'roofs' found among the police, politicians and private security firms, as well as among the traditional criminal bosses." Humphrey's image of bursting the boundaries of "state versus crime" and embracing an intermingling of "state and crime" reflects how people along the highway frame the developments of the 1990s. An example of this is the interconnection between humanitarian aid and drug trafficking during the civil war. Both humanitarian aid and drug trafficking were gendered fields of practice, and it was mainly my male interlocutors who expressed their opinions of how these seemingly contradictory fields were inextricably linked. Drivers, administrators, and soldiers often got closely involved in these businesses when they had to drive trucks, organize logistics, and run checkpoints from 1993 onward.

Holiknazar, like many other men from the region, served as a contract soldier in the Russian army and was later employed by transport agencies as a driver. As he explained to me on a trip to Kyrgyzstan, trucks were loaded in Osh with flour, oil, fuel, and other goods that were designated as aid for Gorno-Badakhshan. The trucks left from their base in Osh, drove through the Alai range, and finally entered Tajikistan just after Sary-Tash. Then the trucks proceeded on Tajikistan's Pamir Highway to Murghab and on to Khorog in Shughnan and to all other districts of the region. After having unloaded the trucks at their point of destination, drivers were supposed to return to Osh with empty vehicles for reloading. However, the trucks often transported opium from Afghanistan, providing huge profits to those involved. Despite occasional arrests, the fact that the trucks could get loaded and pass through military checkpoints and the international border with Kyrgyzstan indicates the fluid boundary between statecraft and illicit practices in Tajikistan.[12] When talking about their witnessing of or, less frequently, participation in drug trafficking, people along the Pamir Highway referred to the past and attributed it to the civil war. Yet illicit trade in gemstones and in the meat of the endangered and officially protected Marco Polo sheep were practices that were closely linked to local people's everyday lives and the experience of contradictory dimensions of statecraft. It was not only government officials who seemed to be switching between different modes of law and enforcement and communicating contradictory moralities; as Gulira once noted, "the people" (*kalk*) along the Pamir Highway were doing it, too.

The development of bazaar trade between Osh and Murghab was another dimension of an economic environment that people along the highway deemed "wild" and chaotic, even though they eventually participated in it themselves. People's ambivalent attitudes toward trade that I encountered in the course of my fieldwork correspond to descriptions of the social, cultural, and political effects of the rising post-Soviet bazaar in other places in Central Asia.[13] In this regard, Morgan Liu (2011, 118) frames the Central Asian bazaar as a "microcosm" of contemporary life in the region that makes visible the juxtaposition of "free-market chaos, dispossession, predatory opportunism, and immoral disregard for the common good" on the one hand, and "possibilities for wealth, consumption, globalizing tastes, and aspirations" on the other. As Liu further notes, post-Soviet economic change, with the creation of "a new wealthy class of traders and political elite," could perhaps be seen as a bigger threat to the "local community fabric" than the "intentionally transformative non-market modernization" of the Soviet Union. For people along the Pamir Highway, the threat of newly emerging practices was largely based on the fact that traders making their fortunes in the region came from "other places" (*bashka jerden*). In the beginning locals neither had the skills nor the resources to trade, but the embarrassment of engaging in "old" and seemingly backward economic practices also played a role. As Güljan, the swearing female trader from chapter 2, explained to me,

> They [people along the Pamir Highway] were embarrassed to trade. The Uzbeks' ancestors were already doing this in ancient times. People here have started it recently. Young people are learning it now. We know that our bazaar was small after the Union's collapse. And only later did our people start to learn. Now there are so many traders that they cannot fit into the small bazaar. Now there are more people than last year. Have you noticed? Now anyone can sell goods. Now there are more people than in previous years. If we want to buy something we go to the bazaar, and we sell there too. Now, every single one of us has started to use the bazaar.

As Güljan's statement highlights, bazaar trade has been both a source of embarrassment and a necessity. Trading, selling goods on the bazaar, and bargaining were not considered appropriate during the Soviet period; they seemed like ancient ways of making do that only those who had inherited them from their ancestors could perform. According to Güljan, neither in pre-Soviet times nor during the Soviet period was trade a practice in which local people engaged. In this regard, neither Kyrgyz nor Pamiris considered themselves especially gifted businessmen or businesswomen. This was an ability that was often attributed to Uzbeks, city-dwelling Kyrgyz from Osh who had learned it from Uzbeks, and sometimes to Tajiks from western Tajikistan as a heritage from the past. Even though the traders in the bazaar of Murghab were of fairly mixed ethnic backgrounds and geographic origins at the time of my fieldwork, it was a common opinion that trade was a practice that was forced upon them from the outside. Kamal, for instance, explained the Kyrgyz's difficulties in overcoming their embarrassment to trade by the fact that related vocabulary originated from Persian and Arabic and could therefore essentially not be Kyrgyz:

In Murghab, we haven't learned issues related to trade. Have you noticed? Basically, trade must be this way: there are at least two people involved in trade. For example, the first one is the buyer [*kardar*]. Then there's the seller. He's the trader [*soodager*]. The word *sooda* comes from *savdo* in Persian. It's *sauda* in Arabic and it's *sooda* here. *Sauda* is *sooda* in Kyrgyz. . . . And now the relationship between these two: the buyer talks to the seller about goods. The communication begins and they have to agree on something—the price for instance. The word *nark* for price also isn't a Kyrgyz word. The word is also from Persian and Tajik. There's no Kyrgyz word for this here. It's *nark* or *savdo*. It means these words came from Arabic or Persian. And this means that Kyrgyz people didn't run businesses or trade. The terms themselves prove it.

While, as Kamal emphasized, trade-related vocabulary did not exist in Kyrgyz "originally," the Pamiris as mountain dwellers (*gortsy*) were also not used to trade. Trade was, in Kamal's opinion, a profession that was typical of settled people from the flatlands of Central Asia. When I asked him why Kyrgyz did not have any trade-related vocabulary, he replied that it was because of their nomadic way of life (*köchmön turmushu*). In his opinion, the Kyrgyz in the region did not learn to trade because when they were nomads, traders from the Ferghana Valley or Kashgar in China used to visit their pastures and exchange goods and flour for livestock. Then, in the Soviet period people got involved in a completely new economic system that was based on the presence of the state (*mamleket*). As Kamal explained, "We don't trade in our family . . . we buy things with the salary we get from the government. We're just not used to it."

During the course of my fieldwork, the bazaar in Murghab grew. New houses were constructed and multiple rows of additional shipping containers were put in place to serve as small retail shops. In the bazaar, Kyrgyz sold clothes and foodstuffs alongside Pamiris, Uzbeks, and Tajiks. I also got to know one Afghan trader who sold secondhand clothes and cell phones, occasionally swapping them for rubies from the region. In contrast to this varied picture of the bazaar, people who lived in the district center or in villages along the road insisted that they, as Kyrgyz or mountain dwellers more generally, were just not so good at trading. The prevalence of this view might be linked in part to their limited access to broader trade networks and lack of contacts in Dushanbe. Most local businessmen strictly focused their activities on the stretch of road

FIGURE 5.3. The bazaar in Murghab. Photograph © Bernd Hrdy, 2009.

between Osh and Murghab, with which they were well accustomed and along which they knew people and could navigate linguistically. I met and accompanied traders and drivers on their way from Osh to Murghab. These journeys were frequently slowed down by overloaded passenger jeeps unsuitable for cargo, long checks at the border, and the bad state of the road between the border and Murghab. For instance, Akylbek, whom I joined several times at the *Alai baza* just outside Osh, where drivers rest and ready their cars for the journey, usually filled his Mitsubishi Pajero to the brim with sacks of rice and flour, clothes, toilet paper, spare parts, fruit, and wedding cakes. As Akylbek did not have the required certificates to import these goods into Tajikistan, he had to pay around $20 in bribes at each border post in addition to costs for fuel, accommodation, car repair, and spoiled goods, leaving him with no or modest profits in the end. He told me that he was sick of being stuck to the stretch of road between Osh and Murghab and that he dreamed of owning a transport company, importing goods from China to Tajikistan. However, as for most traders from Murghab whom I got to know, Akylbek's dream has not materialized—in all likelihood not because he would not be good at doing it, but due to the highly regulated economic-political setting in Tajikistan that prevents him from even trying.

Unprofitable Endeavors

To Kamal, the economic success and expansion of China seemed powerful (*küchtüü*), and for people along the Pamir Highway prospects could have been excellent. He once told me that the Kashgar-Murghab-Khorog-Dushanbe connection could have replaced the Pamir Highway to Osh as Gorno-Badakhshan's main artery. But in 2013, nine years after the opening in 2004, the economic situation had not changed much and, except for lines of trucks driving through Murghab, China trade remained a rather abstract prospect for most people.

The cross-border movement of local people with Tajikistan passports was unrestricted in the first year after the opening of the road. Passports could be sent to Dushanbe and, after having obtained a Chinese visa, people from Murghab were free to travel to nearby China. But these regulations changed, and from 2006 onward a trip from Murghab to Kashgar became so expensive that not even trade generated enough profit to pay for it. For example, Güljan, the trading lady who commuted between Osh and Murghab, had planned to start doing business with Kashgar at that time in order to shift from the uneasy Pamir Highway to the Chinese road. To her, China had appeared like the promise of a bright future. Yet the fact that she now had to travel to Dushanbe to apply for a visa in person, which took days and cost hundreds of dollars, turned her business idea into an unprofitable endeavor. Güljan put it this way:

> Whoever has money can go. But a lot of money is needed for the transportation to Dushanbe, money is needed to stay there. It's expensive. Earlier, if I was planning to go to China I would send all of my documents with you. Let's say you're going to Dushanbe. I would tell you to finish up these things and would give you my passport and money. You would go and finish things. I would put all these documents into my pocket and leave. It's not that way now. Now it's done individually. For example, you have 5,000 dollars: just go [to China]! Let's say I only have 2,000 dollars. I would have just enough money for transportation. That way my money wouldn't be enough. So now, if you have money, you can go.

In addition to these centralized bureaucratic formalities, one was also not allowed to bring vehicles with Tajikistan number plates into China, which made the purchase of an expensive air ticket inevitable. Thus altogether, in order to realize a business trip to the neighboring country, even people living literally at the border had to travel all the way to Dushanbe to organize bureaucratic formalities and then to catch an airplane to Urumqi in Xinjiang just to enter Gorno-Badakhshan overland via Kashgar. For Güljan, the cost of this procedure would have far exceeded the profit she could have made from such a journey. In contrast, traders from Khorog who run transport businesses to Dushanbe and those from western Tajikistan with bases in Dushanbe or Khujand were much more deeply involved in China trade than people living along the Pamir Highway.

Güljan and many others in the region suspected that the family of President Rahmon, who owns the airline Somon Air and several transport companies, supported trade-related restrictions for its own benefit.[14] In her opinion, Rahmon's family had shaped regulations according to its business interests, so that "the law was now like this" (*myizam azyr oshondoi*). A confidential 2009 cable from the U.S. embassy in Dushanbe published on WikiLeaks supports my interlocutors' perception of trade between China and Tajikistan as an affair that is regulated by the presidential family: "Chinese sources put trade turnover in 2008 at $1.2 billion, dramatically higher than the official Tajik figure. According to business contacts, Tajik customs officials may not report a good deal of trade with China, especially that conducted by people closely tied to the presidential administration. President Rahmon's daughter herself is reputedly heavily involved in the China trade, bringing containers over the border at Kulma without being examined by customs agents or assessed import tariffs" (U.S. Embassy cable 2009).[15] Similarly, a World Bank (2007, 24) report on trade in Central Asia from 2007 argues that bilateral transport agreements between Tajikistan and China, including restrictions on vehicles and costly bureaucratic processes, "discriminate" against local traders. In places along the Pamir Highway, this discrimination was amplified by the image of a presidential elite who run Tajikistan as a family business. Just like the smaller-scale traders from the outside, they had reactivated ancient trader heritage, which appeared somewhat "wild" to people along the road. In the one-way trade from China to Tajikistan (although occasionally in the other direction), an abundance of goods had once again begun to enter the country, evoking historical experiences of provisioning. In this sense, the never-ending movement of trucks had returned, yet under rather different economic and political auspices and not meant to sustain people's lives along the road but to enrich the lives of others in Dushanbe and beyond.[16]

The oppressive quality of exclusion, both economic and cultural, has had very different effects in Murghab. Contemporary statecraft in the region has fostered, as Anna Tsing has put it (1994, 279), forms of marginality that make evident constraints on local life as well as "the creative potential of rearticulating, enlivening, and rearranging" of social categories that peripheralize people along the highway. While claiming not to be talented in trade, they have visibly proved otherwise; despite their modern self-representations, they have been able to engage in "old" and foreign economic practices. At the same time, they have also been restricted to performing these practices on the decaying stretch of Soviet road between Osh and Murghab, while the presidential family, personifying the state, feeds on the modernizing lifeline from China.

We might think of these two roads as standing for two rather different stories of economic and political modernization. On the one hand, people at the crossroads of these two stretches experienced during Soviet times what James Ferguson (2006, 197) calls, with reference to the Zambian Copperbelt, a socially "thick" project of modernization that bundled up diverse social and political needs. In contrast, the Kulma road to and from China stands for a socially "thin" economic project which, looking at Ferguson's example of oil extraction in Angola, caters to a small elite and, despite huge profits, brings little benefit on a local level. In her study of Meratus in Indonesia, Anna Tsing (1993, 8) reminds us not to forget that marginality is always a contradictory rubric. While people along the highway might have been excluded and "marginalized," actors of statecraft are still "rarely absent from local discussions of local culture and community," and authority often remains defined through ties to them. It is in the course of such discussions and public performances that people along the Pamir Highway negotiate statehood, debating, in the words of Stef Jansen (2015, 12), "what the state is, claims to be, and should be."

A REAL KHAN

Nowruz is a celebration on the twenty-first of March that marks the spring solstice and serves as an alternative New Year's Eve in Central Asia, as well as in many other countries in the Middle East and Asia. In Tajikistan, Nowruz is a national holiday and is often used to celebrate Persian cultural heritage.[17] Yet it also serves as an opportunity to publicly display different ethnic and local identities through dances, costumes, food, and music. For many people along the Pamir Highway, Nowruz is a day of leisure and family with the thrill of anticipation for the upcoming spring. At the same time, Nowruz festivities are marked by speeches and public performances that convey messages of statehood.

On the twenty-first of March 2010, a large crowd of Murghabi town dwellers and many more guests from villages all over the district joined the official celebration of Nowruz. Families and crowds of young people assembled in the stadium at the southern end of the district center, and those who could not be accommodated watched the festivities from the road above the stadium. Together with Nursultan, Gulira, and their relatives, as well as with Holiknazar and Sultonsho, I stood there and tried to follow the show, which consisted of choreographed children's dances and political speeches. Government officials delivered their speeches in Tajik and, occasionally, Kyrgyz members of the local administration spoke in Kyrgyz so that the audience could better understand the content of the messages.

Two of the Nowruz speeches gave rise to lively discussions among my friends after the celebration. The first one was that of the district's head imam (*rayonduk imam*). In his speech in Kyrgyz, the imam attempted to remind people in Murghab of their important role in contributing to a good and peaceful life in Tajikistan. On the one hand, his speech reflected the aspiration for unity, harmony, and peace among the country's regions and ethnicities. On the other hand, it suggested that unity within the state can emerge only from unity within the family. Thus, the family was presented as the state's smallest unit, a nucleus that represents the state in miniature.

> Dear fellow inhabitants [*jerdeshter*] of Murghab, dear guests, I congratulate you on Nowruz. Let us be thankful to God for bringing us such a day. Let us celebrate this holiday. Of course, everything happens according to God's will. As I am allowed to speak on the occasion of this celebration, I would like to call for unity [*birimdüülük*], harmony [*yntymaktuuluk*], and mercy [*kairymduuluk*]. Let us respect each other, keep our relationships friendly, and maintain these relationships in the future. Of course, I would also like to call for peace [*tynchtyk*] in our land even though two peoples [*eki kalk*, i.e., Kyrgyz and Pamiris] live here together. Of course this is a good thing and we call for peace in the future. The state [*mamleket*] is based on peace within the family [*üi-bülö*]. Whenever there is peace in the family, the state is peaceful. Whenever there is unity in the family, the state becomes united. The state starts with the family.

Then, in a further speech in Kyrgyz that immediately followed the district imam's words, a female member of the local government turned to Murghab's youth and invoked the image of Tajikistan's president as a patriarchal father figure and modernizer who provided them with science and technology as a means of development:

> Dear participants of today's celebration, on behalf of the district government we congratulate you all on the holiday of Nowruz. Nowruz comes from our ancestors and it has been celebrated every year. Every year on Nowruz we step into a new day and into a new season. Nowruz is reformation. As our dearest President Emomali Rahmon stated, 2010 is the Year of Sciences and Computer Technologies. Dear young people who are now stepping into the future: please contribute to the development of our country. At this moment our mothers are cooking *sümölok* [a dish prepared for Nowruz] and our friends are celebrating this holiday. Let Nowruz be blissful, dear people of Murghab. Let us hope this year will be a productive year. Let us have peace and blessings for our land. Let us develop Tajikistan, our country, every day, and let there be good wishes for that. Let the Year of the Tiger bring only good things.

Discussing the speeches shortly afterwards, Gulira, Nursultan, Sultonsho, and Holiknazar agreed with the imam's plea for the interdependence of state (*mamleket*) and family (*üi-bülö*). At the same time, they also questioned the president's role as a capable leader. Referring to the announcement of 2010 as the Year of Sciences and Computer Technologies in Tajikistan, Nursultan and Sultonsho countered that there was not even sufficient electricity in Murghab to use technology, let alone to practice science. To this, Holiknazar nodded his approval and said the president could not "make people work," and Gulira concluded that the president had really squandered his chance to become "strong" and "remembered in history" like Genghis Khan and Alexander the Great.[18]

The underlying idea that Tajikistan was supposed to function in a manner analogous to that of a family was an image that I encountered quite often along the highway.[19] In this analogy, the type of leadership deemed necessary to establish harmonious and peaceful relations played an important role. In order to secure peace and prosperity within a family, there was the need for a strong father and patriarch who could nurture and guide his wife, or wives, and children. This hierarchy went from the family to elders to the local government and the governor of the province, and at the top of the hierarchy stood the president as the head of the nation (*millat*), representing the highest figure defending his people's best inter-

FIGURE 5.4. A placard signed by President Emomali Rahmon that says in Tajik, "Respect for the state language is the duty of every citizen of the Republic of Tajikistan." Photograph © Till Mostowlansky, 2015.

ests.[20] Terms used to denote such a leader included father (*ata*), president (*prezident*), boss (*nachal'nik*), head (*rais*), and khan, and could be ascribed to a father, a husband, an elder, a religious leader, or a political figure. As a gendered concept, such leadership was usually imagined as paternal and male. In the Kyrgyz context, however, an elderly woman (*kempir*) could also perform similar duties.[21] Focusing on Tajik contexts in the western part of the country, Colette Harris (2004, 40) showed that this concept of leadership is closely linked to a form of gender performance to which "generation and sex are both integral." The patrilineal and patrilocal organization of the family favors men in leadership positions. At the same time, the role of mature women is ambiguous because "their generational position gives them partial membership in the dominant group, while their sex places them in a subordinate position to the males" (39).

As a result of the conceptual interdependency between micro- and macrolevels of rule, public discourse on statehood in Tajikistan maps gendered notions of honor and space from household onto nation and vice versa.[22] While the nation (*millat*) and its father (*padar*) are envisaged as male, the homeland or motherland (*vatan*) is conceptualized as female. In this constellation the male leader, and the nation more generally, ought to protect the motherland's honor (*nomus*), just as the male head of a family needs "to protect the sexual integrity of the female members of the household" (Epkenhans 2016, 256).[23] In her study of *namus* in Iraqi Kurdistan, Diane King (2008) shows that this particular notion of honor is meant to preserve reproductive sovereignty on different scales. While the father, grandfather, brother, and—among Kyrgyz along the highway—the *kempir* need to protect the actual sexual integrity of female family members, political actors are equally supposed to put this concept into practice. This includes taking measures to protect national borders, to provide grounds for overarching unity, and to establish prosperity.

Public discourse on statecraft in Tajikistan depicts President Emomali Rahmon as fulfilling his duties as the father of the nation (*padari millat*) to the highest standard. Places along the Pamir Highway as well as in all the country's other regions are plastered with billboards on which the president is shown relentlessly working for the benefit of the nation and proffering aphorisms through which he reminds citizens to work hard and be unified. Huge placards portray him in particular contexts of action: Rahmon as a construction worker, Rahmon as a farmer in a field, Rahmon surrounded by schoolchildren, Rahmon in a line with historical heroes of the country, Rahmon as a statesman on a par with the president of Russia.[24] In this regard, they also often show him posing in front of the construction sites of large infrastructure projects, such as the Roghun dam, that will presumably preserve Tajikistan's sovereignty by bringing progress, prosperity, and national honor (*nomusi millī*).[25]

People along the Pamir Highway evaluated Rahmon's quest for legitimacy, based on attempts at political-reproductive sovereignty and established with the help of infrastructure to come, against the backdrop of past Soviet presence and, in the case of the Pamiris, the Aga Khan's actions. They also frequently discussed what an ideal ruler would be like and whether there were any prospects of encountering such a leader soon. When Gulira, Nursultan, Holiknazar, and Sultonsho talked about the Nowruz speeches in March 2010, they were quite disillusioned with what officials had presented as future progress and innovation. They listened and agreed with the head imam's vision of the state as a family and the family as a state, and they were convinced that harmony (*yntymak*) between the two peoples (*eki kalk*) of Murghab—the Kyrgyz and the Pamiris—was indispensable. Yet they also did not see any strong and just leaders outside their families that could make things work in Murghab. In his work on Uzbeks in Osh, Morgan Liu (2012, 175) frames such

Figure 5.5. A placard with President Rahmon that says in Tajik, "[The] Roghun [dam] is vital for Tajikistan." Photograph © Till Mostowlansky, 2010.

reasoning on ideal rule involving a benevolent, patriarchal leader as a
"khan-centered imaginary."[26] In the course of my fieldwork, people along
the Pamir Highway at times juxtaposed a particular imaginary khan
to the president's deeds, as the example of the 2010 Nowruz celebration
demonstrates. Yet in other instances and as time went by, they seemed to
identify Rahmon with exactly that leader. In this regard, people's ideas
about statehood, and indeed their evaluations of statecraft, were embedded within temporality and could change because the world around them
changed, too.

Democracy and Danger

When debating their own place in Tajikistan, people along the highway frequently referred to events that had happened outside Gorno-
Badakhshan—in the country, the broader region, and indeed around the
world. For instance, in 2009 riots in Xinjiang caused anxieties in Murghab; from 2011 onward the civil wars and the rise of the Islamic State (*Islam
mamleketi*) in Syria and Iraq influenced perceptions of terrorism; and the
2011 earthquake, tsunami, and nuclear catastrophe in Fukushima raised
the question of whether something had been wrong on the "moral side"
(*moral'nyi chak*) in Japan. At the same time, news from and political

developments in Kyrgyzstan had a much more immediate influence on people's opinions and often stood on a par with events in other parts of Gorno-Badakhshan or Tajikistan. With plenty of relatives all over Kyrgyzstan and with Osh still being an important economic point of reference, people in Murghab, both Kyrgyz and Pamiris, were often eager to discuss politics in the neighboring country.

In such discussions between 2008 and 2010, politics in Kyrgyzstan had always featured as benign and peaceful, though slightly messy, in contrast to the violent civil war period and current rule in Tajikistan. Rahmon usually appeared to be harder (*kattuu*) on his subjects than Kyrgyzstan's president Kurmanbek Bakiev, and life in Osh seemed to be more predictable than in Gorno-Badakhshan. Shortly after the Nowruz celebration in March 2010, however, this attitude toward politics in Kyrgyzstan began to change. In April, demonstrations and riots in Bishkek led to the ousting of President Bakiev, and just two months later ethnicized conflict in Osh shattered the country's image as intrinsically peaceful. In that summer, videos of horrifying atrocities circulated from mobile phone to mobile phone along the Pamir Highway, showing images of both Kyrgyz and Uzbeks mistreating each other. Images of rape, torture, execution, and people being burned alive were distributed via Bluetooth and DVD and played on TVs and computer screens all over the region. In this way, even people who had not been present during the fighting in the city began to consume the effects of, as Gulira put it, a "state that was no more" (*azyr mamleket jok*). While Gulira clearly took the side of the Kyrgyz in the conflict and believed that the Uzbeks of southern Kyrgyzstan had started the disturbances, she generally defined everyone who had committed these atrocities—whether Kyrgyz or Uzbek—as "not being humans" (*alar adamdar emes*). As a consequence, Gulira thought that Kyrgyzstan was in need of a leader who could control the country in its entirety and punish those who had committed the atrocities. And it was at that time when several of my interlocutors, including her husband Nursultan, expressed their wish for a "real khan" (*nastoiashii khan*). As I discussed in chapter 3 by way of the example of the TV series *Genghis Khan*, the "real khan" was imagined to be a strong, strict, and just president who would establish order and wisely rule the country with an iron fist. In light of the events in Kyrgyzstan, Tajikistan's president began to appear more capable and more likely to attain this ideal than the government in Kyrgyzstan, which found itself in the middle of a political experiment with an unpredictable outcome.

It was in the course of these political events in Kyrgyzstan that President Rahmon visited places along the highway on the occasion of the national Day of Unity (*Rūzi Vahdat*) on 27 June 2010. As I discussed in chapter 2, Rahmon seemed well aware of the civil war memories that the violence in Osh had brought back to people in Tajikistan and gave speeches all over Gorno-Badakhshan calling for peace and unity among the different ethnic groups and the country's regions. In the context of the presidential journey to places along the highway, Rahmon also briefly visited Mairambek's village near the Chinese border. While Mairambek had been rather critical of the president prior to the summer of 2010, he now told me that Rahmon had begun to behave differently toward people along the Pamir Highway. To Mairambek, he seemed more caring, more concerned, and more generous, as shown in the following conversation we had shortly after Rahmon's visit.

> Mairambek: He [Rahmon] really attracts people. . . . He speaks well, and even if he speaks in Tajik it's possible to understand the meaning. He didn't speak in Russian or Uzbek. [During the visit] he spoke only Tajik.
>
> Till: Nobody spoke Russian during the meeting?
>
> Mairambek: One of us was allowed to speak Russian. He [Rahmon] gave permission to one person. He was a World War II veteran. He spoke in Russian. I told him to speak in Kyrgyz so that it would be understandable, but he spoke in Russian. If he had talked in Kyrgyz, the president would have understood because he knows Uzbek very well. . . . Then he left. Our *rais* [district governor] is a cow. When the president came he went to meet him once only. He didn't accompany the president, even though he himself is the president of the district.
>
> Till: The *rais* is a cow?
>
> Mairambek: He [Rahmon] cannot handle these people. The *rais* doesn't know his job. Otherwise Rahmon is a good person. He's on the people's side. The president said that he's for Murghab and that he would help. Now Kyrgyzstan has had these events. He said we wouldn't have to worry. He said Tajikistan also experienced similar things in the past. This would stop. He told us to be calm. He brought 70 kilos of flour [per household] and put it into stores. Now, for example, the best flour costs 110 somoni; otherwise [if Rahmon hadn't brought it] people would bring it from Osh and sell it for 130 somoni. It's white, first-class flour.

Mairambek's transforming perception of the president reflects the change of demands in a climate of anxiety. While he had often complained about the political and economic situation in Murghab prior to the violence in Osh in June 2010, he now advocated a strong president who guaranteed peace. The erstwhile notion of Rahmon as a failed modernizer who could not make things work in Murghab faded into the background. At the same time, in the course of that violent spring in Kyrgyzstan, Rahmon was increasingly constructed as a khan-like ruler. In his study of Uzbek men in Osh, Morgan Liu shows how their perceptions of Uzbekistan's president Islam Karimov changed as a result of political events from "a benevolent despot whose harsh way worked for his people's long term good" at the turn of the millennium (Liu 2002, 2) to a rather critical assessment as a result of the improving economic situation in Kyrgyzstan and the so-called Andijan massacre in Uzbekistan's Ferghana Valley in 2005 (Liu 2012, 44). Quite the contrary, along the Pamir Highway people's assessment of the president's performance, and the government more generally, improved in the wake of the violence in Osh.

Later in the same year, Nursultan told me that there were two possible paths to a good government (*hukumat*): either a "real khan" who would be harsh but who would also be expected to bring prosperity by making his subjects follow his orders, or the introduction of "real democracy" (*nastoiashaia demokratiia*), which meant more than just formal participation and having the same president for decades, as was the case in Tajikistan. As he understood it, Kyrgyzstan had attempted to introduce "real democracy" but failed and paid a bloody price for it with outbursts of violence. In addition, from December 2010 onward, Russian TV channels carried extensive coverage of the Arab Spring, and throughout 2011 people along the highway watched the fierce conflict in Libya. Nursultan saw these events as a result of the struggle for participation and questioned if this was really the right way to go. Shortly afterward, in addition to the disturbing news from the region and beyond, local prospects also took a worrying turn. After the events in Osh in the summer of 2010, narratives of possible conflict seeped into various places in Tajikistan and added to the lengthy discourses of danger of interethnic conflict and fragmentation in Central Asia.[27] Such narratives also found their way into ethnically and religiously divided places along the Pamir Highway. For instance, in the summer of 2011, Sultonsho told me that he had heard rumors of upcoming armed conflict between Kyrgyz and Pamiris in Murghab. Allegations that members of the other group were stockpiling weapons had led to a tense atmosphere and prompted government officials to intervene when the situation turned critical. As Sultonsho explained, and Kamal later confirmed, the president himself sent officials from Dushanbe to Murghab, who then threatened to step in violently if the situation did not cool down. He expected the president to act and show strength in a moment of disintegration.

Sultonsho's words reveal more about his particular vision of an ideal leader and wish for stability than about the actual resolution of a close and threatening conflict that never quite materialized but that has held people along the Pamir Highway in its thrall. With the Osh violence still on his mind, Sultonsho's view in mid-2011 was that a benevolent despot was preferable to chaotic democracy and that a "modern state" was possible without participation. Rather than actually being a "yearning for old forms of authority," Morgan Liu (2012, 182) argues that such a conceptualization of statehood, particularly the idea of the khan's "transformative powers" over his citizens, responds to the conditions of modernity "in its own way." Sultonsho's various references to the Soviet state, which he believes would have intervened immediately and efficiently in such a situation, serve to reiterate this point.

War from a Distance

On 21 July 2012, General Abdullo Nazarov, the head of the regional office of the State Committee of National Security, was stabbed to death on the road just outside Khorog. In reaction, government forces moved into Khorog to take into custody the alleged murderers of Nazarov. Initial negotiations with the civil war veteran and militia commander Tolib Ayombekov, who was suspected of having been involved with the alleged perpetrators, failed. As later investigations revealed, Ayombekov feared that the operation would be used as a cover to move on him and other local commanders. They had been integrated into Tajikistan's army after the civil war but felt increasingly alienated as a result of Rahmon's efforts to centralize his power. Then on 24 July, government forces launched assaults on the bases of these commanders in different districts of Khorog, employing grenade fire and snipers. According to international observers, the operation ended unsuccessfully for the government in Dushanbe, with at least 22 documented civilian casualties and dozens of fallen soldiers (Kerymov et al. 2013).

At the beginning of the military operation in Khorog, government forces closed the borders of Gorno-Badakhshan and cut lines of communication into the region. Thus only several days later, toward the end of July 2012, did I receive replies to the worried messages that I had sent from Kyrgyzstan to people along the Pamir Highway during the days of fighting. The tone of these replies varied greatly depending on whether they came from Khorog or Murghab. A friend from Khorog wrote that his motherland (*vatan*), meaning Badakhshan and not Tajikistan, was under attack and that Pamiris needed to defend themselves against the Sunni invaders. At the same time, people from Murghab let me know that the district was under curfew but that everything was peaceful (*tynch*). Nursultan wrote to me saying that there was war (*voina*) in Khorog; that it, as usual, had come from the flatlands (*pas jerlerden*); and that he did not know what would happen to Tajikistan. When I returned to Gorno-Badakhshan for fieldwork the following year (2013), these contrasting interpretations were still present. On the one hand, I met young men in Khorog who, full of resentment after the fighting the previous year, considered the government operation an abomination and sought revenge. They fervently listened to the Shughni singer-songwriter Sash and sang his religiously inspired anthem "I love you, oh Motherland" (*Uzum zhivj to ey vatan*), which invokes an epic image of Badakhshan as a rough and beautiful land in need of the protection of martyrs and the Ismaili faith. On the other hand, up in Murghab I was told by Kyrgyz friends that peace had prevailed and that they had paid their respects to the Pamiri families who had lost relatives in the fighting. Baktygül and Dinara, a woman in her forties who worked in a medical facility in the district, discussed these matters with me over lunch in November 2013. Dinara said that Kyrgyz and Pamiris in Murghab had once again become close (*jakyn*). In contrast, politics (*saiasat*) were bad now (*jaman bolgon*), with ever-increasing restrictions on public prayers in mosques and on what one was allowed to say openly in the streets of Murghab. And when I met Mairam-bek in his village at the Chinese border, he told me that Rahmon tried to be "a Stalin" but that he could not do it because, as the events in Khorog had shown, he was simply not strong enough.

The ways in which people along the Pamir Highway navigated through economic, legal, and political change throughout my fieldwork were informed by instability. At the same time, the resulting uncertainty was not a condition in which they simply situated themselves passively. Often, they tended to doubt the nature of the government's intentions and actions, and the modernity of Tajikistan's statehood more generally. Mathijs Pelkmans (2013, 16–17) identifies four qualities of doubt: doubt is activated uncertainty; it is ephemeral; it embodies contradictory energy; and it implies "a relational and temporal dimension in which doubt, certainty, disillusionment and resolution feed into and give way to each other." To conceive of doubt as giving a sense of direction and order to uncertainty is a helpful take on how people along the highway make sense of their lives in Tajikistan. By doubting the government's deeds, but also those of others within and outside the country, they practiced a form of political action. "Lived doubt," as Pelkmans (2013, 2) argues, relates not only to the questions of "What is?" and "What is true?" but also "What to do?" People along the Pamir Highway have had a pragmatic approach to this question that reaches far back into the twentieth century. After all, they have stayed up on the moon where conflict is less likely to reach while establishing strong ties to valleys and flatlands near and far. Yet, most importantly, through turbulent times they have carefully maintained social relations in places along the Pamir Highway that are bound together by the shared experience of distinction from surrounding regions.

EPILOGUE

Over the years of my research in Tajikistan and Central Asia more generally, I have interacted with people from places along the Pamir Highway in cities outside their home villages, the country, and the region. I met students from Alichor in Osh and Dushanbe, men and women from Murghab working in Bishkek, and people from villages at the Chinese border in Europe. In the course of our encounters, many of them mentioned that their classmates, coworkers, neighbors, and friends in these places beyond the highway thought of them as coming from a distant and disconnected region. Those from outside the region expected them to be surprised by the amenities and pace of city life, by the opportunities and the bustling markets, by escalators and haute cuisine. Yet as a matter of fact, they were not. Au contraire, these people from along the Pamir Highway surprised others simply by not being particularly surprised. After all, they knew a good part of "modern life," drawing on their own and their families' historical memories of Soviet mobility and the experience of having lived "urban" lives in Gorno-Badakhshan. For instance, I still vividly remember the comment of a friend visiting Europe who was asked her opinion of life in Switzerland. To the puzzlement of her hosts, she dryly replied that the country as a whole reminded her of a very calm and well-organized Central Asian sanatorium.

These encounters beyond the Pamir Highway highlight an argument that runs through the chapters of this book. Modernity and marginality are not a priori on opposite sides of a dichotomy. Their relationship is instead subject to particular historical processes. Yet they are closely intertwined, not only across a range of places tied together by asphalt but also across time. The Soviet construction of the highway in the 1930s stands at the beginning of this relationship, but people along the road also situate themselves within much longer histories in the region. Against this backdrop, they have used variously entangling "projects" of modernity to express both locality and universality, emphasizing the specificity of the places they inhabit as well as their own ability to connect to worlds beyond. The story of Neil Armstrong and the *azan*, the call to prayer, that opens this book is part of such an expression, and it reflects the ways people along the Pamir Highway perceive of modernity as nonlinear, overlaying, and in need of perfection. According to the narrative, which features in many Muslim contexts around the globe, Armstrong recognizes the *azan* during a visit to Cairo and converts to Islam because he had heard the same melody when he first stepped on the moon. Using the most sophisticated means of modern technology, the first man on the moon arrived on the lunar landscape only to find out that God was already there.

The image of the moon resonates in places along the highway for a number of reasons. The rocky, arid landscape resembles lunar formations, the lack of oxygen signals high altitude, the sky and clouds appear closer than elsewhere, and vast parts of the thinly populated region remain seemingly untouched by human hands. People along the highway think of their earthly moon in terms of a positive marginality and, in combination with claims to being modern, link it to a sense of distinction. On the one hand, being different, more modern, more civilized, and more peaceful than the surrounding flatlands is an important aspect of life along the Pamir Highway. In this regard, people's points of comparison often lie beyond the Pamirs and Tajikistan, in other places to which they attribute modernity. On the other hand, people along the road are aware of the fact that their marginality is not just an effect of their own decision to be different. Rather, they navigate through the constraints and oppression that are inherent to their marginality by renegotiating and reinterpreting the very rubrics that have put them up on the moon in the first place.

The processes of renegotiation and reinterpretation span various dimensions of sociality along the Pamir Highway. They include encounters in spoken and written language as expressed in everyday conversations and debates, political speeches, pamphlets, and local histories. These processes also encompass engagements with movies, TV shows, development projects, political slogans, and new laws. And they involve the way people position themselves vis-à-vis material forms such as large infrastructure projects, cars, asphalt, roads, communication technology, consumer goods, hot springs, and martyrs' graves. We could perhaps understand peoples' navigation through these dimensions of sociality along the road as, to echo Bruno Latour (2005, 70), different "modes of action." While each of these "modes of action" has very different affordances, their totality provides us with a sense of how deeply ingrained the rubrics of modernity and marginality are in everyday life along the Pamir Highway.

During my frequent visits to Dushanbe over the past decade, I met many development consultants assessing the quality and effects of Tajikistan's internationally funded projects in such diverse fields as health, economy, energy, and environment. With some of them I discussed my work, and quite a few met my standpoints with interest and respect. However, I also met those who could not understand why looking at Tajikistan's eastern "periphery" was of any relevance. To them, the state was represented by officials in the capital who worked toward bilateral agreements with their peers in Beijing, Bishkek, Kabul, and Moscow. Places in between were simply part of a transit zone that would only warrant their interest if there were unrest. The dynamics in the district of Murghab thus appeared quite negligible to any understanding of Tajikistan at large, although the study of Khorog was viewed as comparatively more legitimate due to its history of civil war and recent conflict. One consultant who had once worked in Gorno-Badakhshan even told me that people along the Pamir Highway should be resettled to the flatlands or lower mountain valleys, as they only lived high up in the Pamirs as a result of past Soviet geopolitics and could not survive there on their own without state subsidies.

This book is not simply an attempt to contradict and redefine such views, which range from reflections on "the center" and "the nation" as prisms of analysis to the open advocacy of mountain dwellers' deportability, itself reminiscent of Soviet policies of resettlement. Instead I suggest that this book, by looking at particular forms of modernity and marginality along the Pamir Highway, makes up one piece of the jigsaw puzzle that we call Tajikistan. If we follow Veena Das and Deborah Poole (2004) in their reasoning that a state is made up of its margins—ranging from citizenship and gender to geography—then people and places along the road are not anomalous but part of the country's normalcy. Such an approach allows for a differentiated view of geographical remoteness as influencing but not determining everyday life along the Pamir Highway. At the same time, this take emphasizes the importance of marginality along the road, which cannot simply be mapped onto geographical space but is rather embedded in political and economic processes.

Sarah Green (2005, 1) calls marginality "a tricky word" precisely due to its frequent conflation with geographical remoteness and disconnection. While "being where you are and being from somewhere" certainly "always matters," as Green emphasizes, the purpose of this book is to say more than that. In order to understand marginality along the Pamir Highway and the insistence on modernity as a form of local self-representation, we might rather focus on forms of inequality that are not inherent to Murghab or Gorno-Badakhshan but which constitute different margins across Tajikistan. In this regard, Green (2005, 1) speaks of marginality as the negatively affected "ability to have a name that could be used to challenge whatever center happens to be significant at the moment."

For people along the Pamir Highway, this ability to have a name, or not, is tied to different roads with multiple histories and divergent roles in the present. When talking about, for instance, the Soviet road between Osh and Khorog, sometimes referring to a period well into the 1990s, they often emphasized the social, the *affect* that was inextricably bound up with this highway. They had lived along, with, and through this road. The opening of the Kulma road in 2004 altered these dynamics quite dramatically and established an alternative narrative for what sociality along the highway might look like. People in Murghab were not very much involved in the construction of the link to China, nor was there any attempt to promote "local cadres," as the Soviets did, that could look after, administer, and make use of the new road. The fact that the Kulma road directly feeds into the Pamir Highway points to the multiple meanings that one stretch of asphalt can have: while the road link to the Chinese border is of very limited local value, on the Pamir Highway rather different visions of connectivity, economy, and political rule materialize and become entangled.

During my research and my many encounters with people along the Pamir Highway, the idea that the present and future of the region would be determined by China was consistently expressed. With a vast majority of consumer goods being of Chinese origin and with an endless procession of trucks passing through the district of Murghab on their way from the Kulma pass to Dushanbe, this is hardly surprising. On the one hand, people's anxieties of what this influence might mean were informed by the pronounced absence of Han Chinese from everyday interactions, as well as by a notion of linguistic and cultural difference. For instance, when I moved from Europe to Hong Kong in the course of my research, Sultonsho and other friends along the highway were concerned about my health because they identified China, and Chinese places in general, with cramped living conditions and a lack of "pure" (*chistyi*, *taza*) food products. At the same time, others like Kamal saw Gorno-Badakhshan's growing interconnection with China as an impending opportunity and as a future one needed to be prepared for. In any case—anxiety or future opportunity—the implication of both has been that the present is not necessarily desirable and is often uneasy.

The marginality that emerges from Murghab's situatedness in an economically and politically contested transit zone has as much to do with the flow of Chinese goods into the region as with domestic politics in Tajikistan. In a constellation in which the ruling elite perceives the new Kulma link and parts of the Pamir Highway as a mere strip of asphalt supporting their trade endeavors, people who live along the road take a backseat as unskilled laborers who reload trucks. This image of the road as a means to "extract" resources might help us reassess the triumphalist narrative of global connectivity along contemporary "Silk Roads" that has dominated the discourse in recent years. In this regard, the U.S.-launched New Silk Road initiative to integrate and connect Afghanistan and Central Asia with Europe and East Asia has attracted little attention along the Pamir Highway. However, recent road construction in Gorno-Badakhshan, as well as in other regions of Central Asia, is part of the materialization of China's Silk Road Economic Belt component of the One Belt, One Road (*yidai yilu*) strategy, which aims at integrating sea and land routes across Asia, Europe, Africa, and the Middle East. While the Kulma road was opened more than a decade ago in order to link China's and Tajikistan's road networks, it has now become part of a grand vision that maps China's connections and supply chains throughout Eurasia and beyond. Academic supporters of this vision of economic globalization at large, such as Parag Khanna (2016), have seen this as a positive, if not always benign, process of connecting urbanizing places. Such a perspective entails the conclusion that inequity will not necessarily decrease in this process but that, as Khanna (2016, 381) argues, "too little trade is a much bigger problem than unfair trade" and "too little wealth creation is a much bigger problem than high inequality." Both historical and contemporary social transformations along the Pamir Highway call into question the linear

FIGURE E.1. A Chinese truck in Murghab. Photograph © Bernd Hrdy, 2009.

vision of modernity, development, and connectivity that underlies this perspective. People along the highway did not gratefully wait for China to build a road, nor do they see themselves as being lifted out of backwardness in the present. As I have outlined in the chapters of this book, they rather expect modernity to already be there. To them modernity is an endangered condition that is in need of revival, reconfiguration, and improvement. In this regard, any contemporary actor of statecraft in the region needs to live up to the work that the Soviet Union accomplished in terms of provisioning, infrastructure, and social cohesion. As this book endeavors to demonstrate, that has not been the case in recent years, and the present is marked by the absence of a force that is capable of putting Gorno-Badakhshan back in the center again. Instead, the Pamir Highway constitutes one of the many sites upon which the state is both made and undone. By taking a stance that views Tajikistan as constituted by its margins, this book hopes to make the case for the importance of looking at the places and lives in between and along the road.

NOTES

PROLOGUE

1. For studies on internal migration and resettlement in Tajikistan and Gorno-Badakhshan see, e.g., Abulhaev (2009), Bliss (2006), Ferrando (2011), Kassymbekova (2011), Kreutzmann (1996, 2015), Loy (2005a, 2005b), and Schoeberlein (2000).

2. On local "projects" of modernity, see Randeria, Fuchs, and Linkenbach (2004); on the dynamics of marginality see, in particular, Green (2005, 1–39) and Tsing (1993, 51–71).

INTRODUCTION: TRAVELING INTO THIN AIR

1. Although the official Tajik name for the region is Viloyati Mukhtori Kūhistoni Badakhshon, the most commonly used terms are still GBAO or Gorno-Badakhshan, both of which derive from the Russian Gorno-Badakhshanskaia avtonomnaia oblast'. This is not only true in everyday communication but also in more official settings such as Tajik embassies and offices, where the terms GBAO, Gorno-Badakhshan, or simply *Pomir* are widely used.

2. Soviet discourses on the Pamirs have also contributed to such images. For instance, as early as 1935 the *Lenfilm'* production *Lunyi kamen'* (*The Moonstone*), in which scientists travel to the Pamirs in search of a valuable mineral, depicts a remote and dangerous region.

3. See Said (1979). On orientalism in the Pamirs, see also Mostowlansky (2014).

4. Among the existing studies on Murghab, see in particular Bubnova (2005), Maanaev and Ploskikh (1983), Pirumshoev and Iusufbekov (2005), Saparbaev and Temirkulov (2003), and Taipov (2002).

5. Siegelbaum (2008a) provides an insightful history of the Lada and other Soviet automobiles.

6. For more details on my work in Kyrgyzstan, see Mostowlansky (2007).

7. This perspective ties in with Ingold's (2009) notion of repeated wayfaring as iteration and Saxer's (2016) suggestion to speak of the study of pathways as co-itinerant rather than multisited.

8. See in particular Weber (1976, 206).

9. There is also great diversity within the Pamir languages, which include Bartangi, Ishkoshimi, Khufi, Roshorvi, Rushoni, Sariqoli, Shughni, Wakhi, and Yazghulomi (Dodykhudoeva 2002; Bahry 2016). Not all Pamir languages are mutually intelligible. Along the Pamir Highway I generally encountered Bartangi and Shughni, which are mutually intelligible, as well as Wakhi, which is not.

10. On the question of "Pamiri" as an ethnic identity, see Davlatshoev (2006).

11. For studies on the linguistic setting in Gorno-Badakhshan (and Murghab more specifically), see Bahry (2016), Karabaev and Ahn (2016), and Mostowlansky (2017).

12. On exploring and spying in the Pamirs, see Hopkirk (1992, 465–82; 1995), Johnson (2006), Kreutzmann (2015, 69–121), and Middleton and Huw (2012). In addition, the 1985 American comedy film *Spies Like Us* explicitly plays with the image of the Pamirs as fertile ground for espionage in a cold war context.

13. For academic studies of the conflict in the Rasht Valley, see Heathershaw and Roche (2011) and Roche and Heathershaw (2011).

14. On the 2009 riots in Urumqi and other places in Xinjiang, see Li (2009), Millward (2009), and Ryono and Galway (2015).

15. See Liu (2012), Megoran (2013), McBrien (2013, 257–66), and Reeves (2010a, 2010b, 2014a).

16. For a survey of ethnography in unstable places, see Greenhouse, Mertz, and Warren (2002).

17. On the conflict in Khorog, see Devji (2012a, 2012b) and Kerymov, Bakhrieva, and Akdodova (2013).

18. For an analysis of why historically parts of the Pamirs have developed into an "area of no concern," see Kreutzmann (2015, 33). For an in-depth discussion of Van Schendel's (2002) and Scott's (2009) original works on such dynamics in the highlands of Southeast Asia, see Jonsson (2010), Michaud (2010), and Sidaway (2013).

19. On the distinction between the Tajik and Afghan parts of Badakh-shan as marked by developmental and temporal differences, see Manetta (2011).

20. See in particular Conrad and Randeria (2002, 10 and 17–22) and Randeria (1999).

CHAPTER 1. MODERNITY AND THE ROAD

1. Regarding the use of cradles, people in Murghab sometimes also speak of clean, new, beautifully painted cradles from Osh as modern in contrast to used, dirty, local ones. Such a view contributes to the under-standing of modernity as a relational category that is embedded in con-crete interactional contexts.

2. For an overview of the history of Ismaili communities worldwide, see Daftary (2011) and Steinberg (2011).

3. Data on the demography of Gorno-Badakhshan are notoriously in-consistent, and information on different periods of time is sketchy (Bliss 2006, 46). Kreutzmann (2015, 373) notes that census counts throughout the twentieth century indicate that around 90 percent of the population of Gorno-Badakhshan is Tajik (see also Kreutzmann 1996, 169). I suggest that a vast majority of these Tajiks identify as Ismailis.

4. For an overview and critique of existing studies, see Houben and Schrempf (2008). A selection of important studies on modernity includes Appadurai (2008), Arnason (2000), Bauman (2000), Collier (2011), En-glund and Leach (2000), Faubion (1988), Ferguson (2001), Heinlein et al. (2012), Kandiyoti (2007), Knauft (2002), Mitchell (2000), Schelkle (2000), and Spitulnik (2002). In addition, Abashin (2015) provides a fine-grained social history of a village in the Ferghana Valley from the nineteenth cen-tury to the present day that addresses the transformative force of "mod-ernization" under colonial, Soviet, and present-day conditions.

5. See Chari and Verdery (2009), Ibañez-Tirado (2015a), Kwon (2010), Marsden (2012), and Mostowlansky (2014).

6. On this particular point see also Massey (2005, 63).

7. Expressing a similar epistemological interest, Randeria, Fuchs, and Linkenbach (2004, 17) characterize an anthropology of modernity as put-ting "an emphasis on the performance of definition and the formation of social actors on the level of local and regional life-worlds. In doing so, diverse approaches of concrete actors with a concrete and empirically ex-perienced modernity are brought to the forefront, as are ideas about one's own (local, regional) 'projects' of modernity. Furthermore, strategies by

means of which such 'projects' are negotiated and asserted in the context of multi-layered constellations of power are taken into consideration" (translation from the German by the author).

8. On material dimensions of modernity, see in particular Guldi (2012), Mitchell (2002), and Weber (1976).

9. For studies on unstable, transforming, and transformative infrastructures, see Barry (2001, 2013), Bennett (2010), and Harvey and Knox (2012, 2015).

10. See Savvaitova and Petr (1999).

11. On the politics of space under Stalin, see Dobrenko and Naiman (2003).

12. On this specific argument see also Reeves (2011a).

13. See in particular Bliss (2006), Bubnova (2005), and Kreutzmann (2015).

14. For the most prominent locally produced scholarly works in recent years, see Chokoev (2007, 2015), Jumabaev and Parmanov (2002), Saparbaev and Temirkulov (2003), Tadzhidinov and Parmanov (2007), and Taipov (2002).

15. China's One Belt, One Road strategy (Belt and Road 2016) seeks to integrate various previously existing land and sea connections across Asia, Europe, the Middle East, and Africa within one large economic and political framework. In this regard, Silk Road rhetoric has not only become increasingly popular to address China's Central Asian neighbors but also to refer to "maritime silk routes" throughout Southeast Asia and the Indian Ocean.

16. This observation ties in with a large body of anthropological literature on time and temporality; see Gell (1992), Ibañez-Tirado (2013, 2015a), Munn (1992), and Owen Hughes (1995).

17. For historical accounts of these events, see Ismoilov and Suptsepin (1974, 13) and Nazrulloev (1979, 92). For a general take on the history of Soviet road construction, see Siegelbaum (2008a, 125–72).

18. See in particular Kraudzun (2016, 163–64) and Straub (2013, 70–81).

19. For Soviet depictions of development along the Pamir Highway, see Avtomagistral' Osh-Khorog (1974), Ismoilov (1962), Nazrulloev (1979), and Popov (1935).

20. On the construction of roads across the border in Xinjiang, see Joniak (2016).

21. For studies on the construction and social significance of the Karakoram Highway, see Khan (2006), Kreutzmann (1993, 2004, 2009), and Rippa (2015).

22. In Russian and former Soviet contexts, the term "road of life" is a powerful reference to a channel of supplies that helped the besieged city of Leningrad survive in World War II. World War II veterans and those watching Russian coverage of the "Great Patriotic War" on television in Gorno-Badakhshan were particularly aware of this reference to the road that was constructed across frozen Lake Ladoga in the 1940s. On the symbolism of the "road of life," see Siegelbaum (2008a, 158).

23. See Nikolai Ssorin-Chaikov's (2003) work on subarctic Siberia for an insightful study on a part of the Soviet periphery that was presented as a timeless and recurring "snapshot boundary between tradition and modernity" (139), always in the process of modernization but never actually reaching modernity.

24. On Soviet visions of secularity, see in particular Luehrmann (2011) and Scott (1998, 195).

25. See the studies by Augé (2008), Harvey (2004), and Lefebvre ([1974] 1991). The past two decades have furthermore brought forth an increasing number of anthropological studies on roads. An overview of the existing body of literature gives an impressive account of cross-cultural perspectives on roads and of the people who live near them. See Colombijn (2002), Baptista (2016), Broz and Habeck (2015), Dalakoglou (2010, 2012), Dalakoglou and Harvey (2012), Green (2013), Harms (2011), Harvey (2005, 2010, 2012), Harvey and Knox (2012, 2015), Hayano (1990), Khan (2006), Kirksey and van Bilsen (2002), Klaeger (2013a, 2013b), Masquelier (1992, 2002), McGee (2002), O'Hanlon and Frankland (2003), Pedersen and Bunkenborg (2012), Pina-Cabral (1987), Reeves (2014b, 2016), Rippa (2015), Roseman (1996), Snead, Erickson, and Darling (2009), and Thomas (2002).

26. A similar notion is also reflected in Harvey (2004).

27. For a fundamental critique of the human–matter binary, see Latour (2007).

28. On this point, see also Barry (2001, 12).

CHAPTER 2. MAKING MURGHAB

1. See Féaux (2011a, 2011b, 2016) on dams in Kyrgyzstan, Reid (2017) on railroads in Tajikistan, and Kotkin (1997) on the construction of Magnitogorsk in Russia.

2. On "roadlessness" in early Soviet Russia, see Siegelbaum (2008b).

3. Studies on cross-border communities in Afghanistan, China and, to a lesser extent, Pakistan include Callahan (2007, 2012, 2013), Dor and Naumann (1978), Kraudzun (2011), Kreutzmann (2003, 2012, 2015), Levi-Sanchez (2017), and Shahrani (2002).

4. For an account of the German-Russian Pamir-Alai Expedition whose members visited the region at the end of the 1920s before the construction of the highway, see Rickmer Rickmers (1930). Luknizki (1972) provides a description of change between the 1930s and the 1950s. On the construction and militarization of borders in the region, see in particular Kraudzun (2011, 2016), Kreutzmann (2015), Rowe (2010), and Straub (2013). In addition, Kassymbekova (2016) provides a detailed picture of early Soviet rule in Tajikistan.

5. Despite its importance in everyday life and its transformative force, there is very little detailed information, not to mention published material, available on "Moscow provisioning" beyond Reeves (2014c, 110–18). As Sergei Abashin has pointed out to me in personal communication, the scarcity of information on the phenomenon can be partly explained by its informal character as an overarching category. In his view, *Moskovskoe obespechenie/snabzhenie* ("Moscow provisioning/supply") is a colloquially used term that summarizes different practices of privileged "supply" orchestrated by the Ministry of Commerce in Moscow, particularly from the 1960s onward. According to Abashin, the label "Moscow" perhaps derives from the postal addresses of individual enterprises engaged in the process of provisioning that read "Moscow-39," "Moscow-40," and so forth. Literature on the closed atomic cities (*zakrytye goroda*) of the Soviet Union furthermore suggests conceptual origins in the 1940s and 1950s, when the system of "state supply" (*Gossnab*) was introduced to strategically important places that existed secretly and off the map (see Brown 2013, Mel'nikova 2006, and Tolstikov 2012).

6. On the affective quality of infrastructure, see Bennett (2001), De Boeck (2011), Harvey and Knox (2012), Reeves (2014b), Sneath (2009), and Street (2012).

7. *Dormaster* is a common abbreviation for the complete Russian term *dorozhnyi master* ("road foreman").

8. Bartangi is one of the numerous Pamir languages that are spoken along the Pamir Highway. The term denotes belonging to the mountain valley of Bartang but has—due to migration—developed away from re-

ferring to a particular territory to carrying the meaning of being a speaker of the language of the Bartang Valley even when not living there. At times, the association of Bartangis with a territory, language, and distinct cultural practices has led to the use of the term "Bartangi" as an ethnic category in its own right in Gorno-Badakhshan. On the formation of different ethnic identities among Pamiris, see Kalandarov (2004).

9. In their study on migration in twentieth-century Russia, Siegelbaum and Moch (2014) establish a typology of migrants that includes resettlers, seasonal migrants, migrants to the city, career migrants, military migrants, refugees and evacuees, deportees, and itinerants. The case of Sultonsho's family, and those of many others along the highway, does not fit into any of these categories. However, in historical perspective we can understand them as resettlers who came from Bartang to the Ghunt Valley in search of land and later as migrants from a rural environment to a place of relative urbanity (Murghab), and as career migrants who moved there for work.

10. On modernity and nostalgia, see Boym (2001), Pickering and Keightley (2006), Piot (2010), and Bonnett (2016). For discussions on the particularities of post-Soviet/postsocialist nostalgia, see Nadkarni and Shevchenko (2004) and Todorova and Gille (2010).

11. On *basmachi*s in Tajikistan, see Bergne (2007, 28) and Nourzhanov (2015).

12. For an extended version of Gulira's and Nursultan's story, see Mostowlansky (2013).

13. The examples of Sultonsho and Gulira also challenge Russian-centric takes on the late Soviet period such as Yurchak's (2006) frequently cited study of late socialism and the last Soviet generation, which suggests the existence of a generic late Soviet modernity. They also challenge McBrien's (2008, 144) assumption that there are "specificities of Soviet/post-Soviet modernity."

14. On space and place, see Cresswell (1996, 2004), Escobar (2001), and Ingold (2009). In an earlier, published version of this analysis (Mostowlansky 2012), I used Henri Lefebvre's term "spatial practice" to describe this process. For the sake of terminological clarity, I have recently begun to employ the term "place making" instead, thereby following Cresswell (2004, 10), who notes that Lefebvre's (1974, 1991, 33) classic definition of "spatial practice" as embracing "production and reproduction" as well as "particular locations and spatial sets characteristic of each social forma-

tion" corresponds to the notion of place making. For a fundamental critique of space, see Ingold (2009).

15. On Tajikistan's civil war and its uneasy resolution, see Djalili, Grare, and Akiner (1998), Heathershaw (2009), and Nourzhanov and Bleuer (2013, 335).

16. For an edited and translated version of the story, see Hatto (1990, 87 and 122).

17. On the role of the Manas epic in everyday life and political contexts in Kyrgyzstan, see Gullette (2008, 2010) and Van der Heide (2015).

18. The production of books on local history and culture in Murghab is largely determined by age and gender. This is predominantly because authority is established through "being elder" (Beyer 2010, 81) and because of the image of the male Kyrgyz elder (*aksakal*) as someone who ideally represents knowledge and wisdom. However, it has to be emphasized that in Murghabi everyday life, both men and women discuss local history and culture and transmit respective knowledge. Thus, it is not the practice of constructing historical time and space as such that is gendered but its formalization in journals and books.

19. The Kyrgyz word *kairyk* means "song" or "tune." It furthermore signifies a specific tune for the *komuz*, a stringed instrument considered part of Kyrgyz culture in Murghab.

20. Sariqoli is a Pamir language and therefore part of the southeastern Iranian languages. In China, Sariqoli is referred to as "Tajik" despite being distinct from Tajik in Tajikistan.

21. The term *Alai baza* is an umbrella term for a cluster of houses on the M41 a few kilometers outside Osh. Several families manage the individual houses in which drivers and passengers headed southward ready their cars and trucks, rest, and exchange news and goods. The house from which transport to Murghab and Khorog leaves is called *Kashka-suu baza*.

22. On pilgrimage sites in the southwestern and western Pamirs see Gross (2013) and Iloliev (2008, 44–46).

23. A look across the border to Kyrgyzstan shows that the search for "authentic" Kyrgyz spiritual culture is closely linked to *mazar*s (Aitpaeva 2007). While pilgrimage sites in Murghab are currently not the object of cultural revival activities, NGOs such as The Christensen Fund have financed local study initiatives and publications on *mazar*s in Kyrgyzstan (Mostowlansky 2011a, 295–99).

24. *Zyiarat* is also embedded in broader Islamic practices of pilgrimage across sectarian and regional boundaries; see Meri et al. (2012).

25. On this point, see Starks (2008), Geisler (2014), and Conterio (2015).

CHAPTER 3. *NASHA–VASHA*: OURS AND YOURS

1. On harmony ideology more generally, see Nader (1990). On harmony and *yntymak* in particular, see Beyer (2013), Beyer and Girke (2015), Mostowlansky (2013), and Reeves (2014c, 156–57).

2. In this regard, Verdery seeks to go beyond what she calls the anthropological "cataloguing" of time (e.g., Evans-Pritchard 1940; Leach 1971 [1961], 124–36) and to highlight the cultural making of time through politics.

3. On political centralization and time, see in particular Verdery (1996, 39–57).

4. While in the conversation presented here, Ajmi's statement was clearly a reference to Nursultan's use of the words *nasha* and *vasha* (to be grammatically correct, these should be spelled *nashoe* and *vashoe* to agree with the neutral gender of *vremia* ["time"], but the pronunciation is identical), similar expressions are also used in different linguistic contexts. The corresponding phrase *bizdiki–sizdiki*, for instance, can be heard at times in colloquial Kyrgyz.

5. In this regard, see in particular Beatty's (2002) study of diversity in Java and Marsden (2005, 197–204) on Chitral in northern Pakistan.

6. The two characters were able to stir emotions to such a degree that the all-Russian movement Tajik Labor Migrants (*Tadzhikskie trudovye migranty*) even demanded that the TV show be officially banned in Russia (Tsentraziia 2010). This discourse not only reflects the social impact of migration flows and the underdog status of Tajikistani citizens in Russia (often connected to the everyday experience of violence), but also a representation of Tajikistan that leaves little space for its internal complexity. In this regard, the Russian embassy's reaction to the official Tajikistani accusation of *Nasha Russia* as "moral genocide of the Tajik nation" (*moral'nyi genotsid tadzhikskoi natsii*) emphasizes to what extent the public discourse about the TV show draws on the image of the two nations as essentialized entities: "The persistent effort of certain media of the Republic of Tajikistan to present an image of Russia as an enemy of the Tajik people fundamentally opposes the traditional spirit of friendship and cooperation that unites our countries and peoples" (Tsentraziia 2010).

7. Ravshan and Dzhamshut's origin is never mentioned throughout the series. However, anyone who carefully watches the movie *Nasha Russia: Balls of Fate* will see that their passports say "Republic of Nubarashen."

8. For a discussion of this point, see International Crisis Group (2010, 12).

9. For coverage of the death threats to Mikhail Galustian, see "Tojikon Galustianro" (2009).

10. On (il)legality and migration from Central Asia to Russia, see Reeves (2013); for a study of the history of racialization in Soviet Leningrad and Moscow, see Sahadeo (2012).

11. Following Herzfeld (2005, 3), cultural intimacy is "the recognition of those aspects of cultural identity that are considered a source of external embarrassment but that nevertheless provide insiders with their assurance of common sociality, the familiarity with the bases of power that may at one moment assure the disenfranchised a degree of creative irreverence and at the next moment reinforce the effectiveness of intimidation." In the case of *Nasha Russia*, Herzfeld's concept sheds light on why people along the Pamir Highway frequently expressed superiority and embarrassment simultaneously. Even though they considered themselves different (i.e., more modern) from western Tajiks, they still identified as Tajikistani citizens in many situations.

12. See also the discussion of the role of Brazilian soap operas in southern Kyrgyzstan in McBrien (2012).

13. Yountchi (2011) importantly argues that the Rahmon government has attempted to balance sectarian fragmentation in Tajikistan by depicting Tajiks as part of the Persianate sphere with a long history of religious diversity (e.g., Zoroastrianism, Mazdaism, and Islam); see also Stephan 2010a, 140–48). However, a number of Pamiris along the Pamir Highway told me that such efforts have been partly undone by the official declaration of 2009 as the Year of Imomi A'zam (Abu Hanifa), the founder of Hanafi Sunni Islam (see chapter 4).

14. On the global Jamat, see Daftary (2007, 2011), Steinberg (2011), and Van Grondelle (2009).

15. For instance, Aliaa Remtilla (2011) emphasizes the salient role of images of the Aga Khan in the lives of Ismailis at the Tajikistan-Afghanistan border in Gorno-Badakhshan.

16. For a recent study looking at Sunni-Ismaili interaction in Darvoz in Gorno-Badakhshan, see Lashkariev (2016).

17. See Smith (2007) on the history of personal hygiene and purity.

18. Ostergaard (2012, 142–45) points out the significance of the often academically neglected and understudied visit to the toilet in Islamic practice.

19. Men, especially drivers, along the Pamir Highway frequently use the word *bliad'* to express anger or dissatisfaction with a situation. The euphemistic version *blin* (literally "pancake") is in use among females and has a similar function. While *bliad'* means "bitch," "slut," or "whore," in most cases the word is not applied to address a specific woman but to express frustration or exasperation with a situation, much like the English "shit" or "fuck."

20. See Beyer (2009, 2016) on customary law in Kyrgyzstan.

21. The public discourse on the meaning of "the Kyrgyz way" is particularly present in Kyrgyzstan, and opinions on the meaning of the term vary greatly. Aitpaeva and Molchanova (2007) provide a discussion of the topic using the Kyrgyz term *kyrgyzchylyk*. For statements about *kyrgyzchylyk* in regard to pilgrimage sites, see Aitpaeva (2007).

22. As Roche and Hohmann (2011) argue in regard to weddings in Tajikistan, processes of standardization have been ongoing since the early Soviet period. The past and present state-driven fight against "backward practices" suggests that from a historical perspective, there is little ground for a distinction between "Soviet" and "customary." In contrast, my interlocutors referred to these spheres as related but separate entities.

23. On the role of elders as guardians of cultural knowledge, see Beyer (2009, 2) and Ellen (1993, 231).

24. For studies of interethnic intimacy and the "friendship of peoples" in the Soviet Union, see Edgar (2007) and Tillett (1968).

CHAPTER 4. MUSLIMS ON THE ROOF OF THE WORLD

1. In her study on Islam and change at the Tajikistan-Afghanistan border in the western part of Gorno-Badakhshan, Aliaa Remtilla (2012, 148) presents a detailed story of an Ismaili man's first encounter with images of the current imam in the 1970s which, as in the case of Alikhon's mother, he saw in a magazine. On the role of the imam's image in everyday life, see Remtilla (2011).

2. For studies using the rubric of revival in regard to post-Soviet Islam, see Haghayeghi (1994), Karagiannis (2010), Naumkin (2005), and Olimova and Tolipov (2011). For a critique of approaches that look at Soviet/post-Soviet Islam, and religion more generally, in the sense of a

dichotomy, see Abashin (2014), Pelkmans (2009), and Pelkmans and Mc-Brien (2008).

3. This point also emphasizes the importance of avoiding the perception of Central Asian societies as persistently "traditional" and based on antimodern tendencies that are expressed through religion (as purported by Poliakov 1992). For a critique of such interpretations, see Rasanayagam (2006b).

4. On everyday religious practice in Central Asia, see Jacquesson (2008), Louw (2007), Montgomery (2007, 2016), and Rasanayagam (2011).

5. See also Asad (1993) and Van der Veer (2001, 2013).

6. According to Balci (2015, 25), the Tablighi Jama'at dates the first Tablighi activities in Central Asia back to the 1960s and 1970s, when students from the Indian subcontinent came to the Soviet Union on scholarships. Balci sees this as a strategy to seek historical legitimacy rather than as genuine evidence of a long history of the Tablighi Jama'at in Central Asia, which is actually very recent. Given this recent history, the extent of expansion is all the more striking. When I talked to Tablighi informants in Osh (Kyrgyzstan) in 2012, they proudly emphasized that they believed the Kyrgyz Jama'at to be the most significant in Central Asia. They furthermore told me that they had traveled to Tablighi gatherings in Bangladesh, where the Kyrgyz received honors for expanding *daavat* so rapidly in the country. For historical background on the Tablighi Jama'at, see Masud (2000a) and Metcalf (2002). Recent studies on the Tablighi Jama'at in Kyrgyzstan include Balci (2012, 2015), Ismailbekova and Nasritdinov (2012), Mostowlansky (2007, 93–115), Toktogulova (2007), and Nasritdinov (2012).

7. For detailed studies on the Tablighi Jama'at in various contexts, see Braam (2006), Gugler (2010), Janson (2005), Noor (2007), and Winkelmann (2005).

8. I have never encountered or heard of any Ismailis who were approached by *daavatchy*s and therefore assume that their focus lay on the Sunnis in Murghab. This also ties in with Tablighi efforts to avoid sectarianism by remaining silent about difference and by focusing on "merits" rather than "problems." However, the question of who should be targeted by the activities of the Tablighi Jama'at is contested. Generally, the organization addresses all Muslims, but theoretically no non-Muslims. As a result, this leaves room to exclude Muslims whom the Tablighi Jama'at does not recognize as such, e.g., Ahmadis (Masud 2000b, 96).

9. For a list of banned "extremist" groups in Tajikistan, see Taarnby (2012, 18–19).

10. It is unclear why the ban had no immediate effect, but in statements from May 2009, two officials of Tajikistan's Supreme Court explained that they were not aware of the ban (United States Commission on International Religious Freedom 2011, 311). The fact that two officials in Dushanbe were ill-informed suggests that the local government in Murghab had even less access to information.

11. See Central Asia Newswire (2012), Hamrabaeva (2009), Rafiyeva (2015), and Tokhiri (2009).

12. Insightful studies on the conflict in the Rasht Valley include Heathershaw and Roche (2011), Lemon (2014), and Roche and Heathershaw (2011).

13. Recent developments in Tajikistan also reflect processes in the broader region. Despite rather different societal and political contexts from Tashkent to Bishkek and from Astana to Dushanbe, the "war on terror" has become a tool to exert government control, sideline opposition, and brand deviance from the national norm as "terrorism" or "extremism." See in particular Khalid (2007, 168–203).

14. For a comprehensive study of the Hizb-ut Tahrir in Central Asia, see Karagiannis (2010).

15. While in the spring of 2010 I sometimes still spotted solitary men in *shalwar kameez* (especially in the bazaar in Murghab), by 2011 I no longer saw them. This does not, of course, prove that they had vanished completely. As I was repeatedly told in 2010, nobody in Murghab would consider these few remaining men "real" *daavatchy*s because they had stopped proselytizing. But they still wore their clothes and beards and therefore attracted attention in public.

16. On the transformative power of mass literacy and media in Islam, see Eickelman (1992) and Eickelman and Anderson (2003). For the role of media and Islam in Tajikistan, see Nozimova and Epkenhans (2013).

17. See Abdylda uulu (2005), Eratov (2005), Mametbakiev and Abdylda uulu (2004), Nabijan uulu (2008), and Nauka i fakty (2004).

18. On religious education in other parts of contemporary Tajikistan, see Roche (2013) and Stephan (2010b).

19. In this regard, Marsden (2005, 19) argues that the rise of "sectarian identities" in the sense of a "process whereby the boundaries between once fluid 'doctrinal clusters' are hardened" is closely linked to the systematization and objectification of religion.

20. I was not able to find out whether Baktygül actually treats Pamiri patients, too. While she told me that she had had some Ismaili patients in

the past, I did not witness such treatments myself. The flexibility of "the Kyrgyz way" would obviously allow such practices; however, remarks by other Kyrgyz interlocutors about the *khalifa*s being charlatans and by Pamiri interlocutors about Kyrgyz healing practices being "without effect" suggest that opening the field for the "sectarian other" is more a tool for the strengthening of a local bond than part of everyday practice.

21. Important studies on Tajikistan's civil war history include Epkenhans (2016) and Nourzhanov and Bleuer (2013, 323–35).

22. For a concise overview of AKDN's history, see Ruthven (2011).

23. On these processes of institutional change, see AKDN (2016a), De Cordier (2008), and Middleton (2016).

24. On provisioning during the years of war, see also Kraudzun (2012, 97).

25. Further details on Pirsabzali's journey are included in Steinberg (2011, 53) and Tajddin Sadik Ali (2016).

26. On this particular point and the early years of AKDN intervention in Gorno-Badakhshan, see also Keshavjee (1998).

27. Ismaili historiography has constructed this call for loyalty to the nation-state as a social fact. For instance, Daftary (2007, 504) notes that wherever Ismailis live in Asia, the Middle East, and Africa "as indigenous religious minorities and loyal citizens, they enjoy exemplary standards of living, and those who have immigrated to Western countries have readily adapted to their new environments."

28. Discourses on transnational statehood have long been present within Ismaili institutions. In his memoirs, the Aga Khan III notes that "it had been felt among the Ismaili community that it would be desirable to possess a national home . . . on the lines of Tangier or the Vatican" (1954, 286). The government of India, still under British rule in the 1930s, rejected such a request and Ismaili institutions steered toward the establishment of a "corporate community" (Steinberg 2011, 47).

29. I discuss "Moscow provisioning" in more detail in chapter 2.

30. Particularly in more recent years, my interlocutors along the Pamir Highway tended to contrast the government's incapacity to manage an organized and well-provisioned Gorno-Badakhshan to "spectacular" forms of state materialization (Laszczkowski 2014 and 2016) in western Tajikistan as signified by the recent construction boom in Dushanbe (Parshin 2012).

31. Official AKDN representation explicitly mentions this split and emphasizes that their "agencies conduct their programs without regard

to faith, origin or gender" (AKDN 2016b). On the AKDN website's "Frequently Asked Questions" section, the answer to "Are the AKDN and its agencies religious organizations?" is presented the following way: "A: *No. The work of the AKDN is underpinned by the ethical principles of Islam— particularly consultation, solidarity with those less fortunate, self-reliance and human dignity—but AKDN does not restrict its work to a particular community, country or region.* Its focus is on poor areas of the developing world, but it also conducts programs in North America and Europe. Pluralism is a central pillar of AKDN's ethical framework: AKDN aims to improve living conditions and opportunities for people regardless of their particular religion, race, ethnicity, or gender. AKDN employees are also of different faiths, origins and backgrounds" (AKDN 2016c; emphasis in original).

32. For a critique of the role of religious NGOs as "the other" of secularist international development, see Fountain (2013) and Fountain, Bush, and Feener (2015).

33. Boivin (2003, 277) and Steinberg (2011, 104) also emphasize that the *farmon* constitutes an important element in connecting Ismailis all over the world. As a spoken or written directive from the Aga Khan, a *farmon* not only provides guidance for his followers, but also engages with processes of modernization in various aspects. The Aga Khan's call to women not to wear the veil (Daftary 2007, 488; Steinberg 2011, 104) can be part of a *farmon*, as can more recent reforms in Gorno-Badakhshan, such as changes in prayer practice and the conduct of wedding ceremonies.

34. For an account of the Aga Khan's visit in 2008, see Remtilla (2012, 151–55).

CHAPTER 5. THE GOLDEN GATE OF TAJIKISTAN

1. There is an abundance of Silk Road literature mentioning the Jade Gate in China (see Hill 2009; Hopkirk 1980, 160) and, at a different geographical point, the Golden Horn in Constantinople (see Frankopan 2015, 154), which also inspired the name of San Francisco's Golden Gate as a gateway for trade (Brechin 2006, 5). Among people along the Pamir Highway, the golden gate metaphor also evoked associations with the Golden Gates in Kiev (Ukraine) and Vladimir (Russia).

2. Nourzhanov and Bleuer (2013, 202) mention that from the late 1980s onward, the political organization La'li Badakhshon (The Ruby of Badakhshan) promoted a similar vision of autonomy based on natural resources in the region.

3. Jansen's framework also provides an excellent starting point to think beyond James Scott's (2009) notion of "state evasion" and "non-state space." By looking at the shifting relations of statehood and statecraft in particular places, Jansen's differentiation allows for a refined take on the areas in between "state" and "non-state."

4. See Baldauf (2006, 2007).

5. On the Law on Freedom of Conscience and Religious Associations, see Epkenhans (2009, 2010, 2011), and Thibault (2014, 105–36).

6. This process of documentation was not simply a bureaucratic formality but included an official judgment on permissible and undesirable religious contents and practices. Epkenhans (2010, 99) states that the law allowed "state authorities to pass judgement on the character of a religion, i.e., to evaluate a given dogma as 'good' or 'bad' and to rule on the ethical and moral views of a faith."

7. On Chinese presence in Central Asia more generally, see Laruelle et al. (2010), Pantucci et al. (2016), and Peyrouse (2011). For an insightful study on the dynamics of "Sinophobia," employing the example of Mongolia, see Billé (2015).

8. The cession of land to China was the result of resolving a long-standing territorial dispute between China and the Soviet Union that had its origins in colonial and Soviet boundary making in the region (Garver 1981).

9. On Chinese land investments and farming in Tajikistan, see Hofman (2015, 2016), Hofman and Ho (2012), and Pannier (2011).

10. For critical assessments of the idea of a teleological transition from communism to capitalism in Central Asia, see Grzymala-Busse and Jones Luong (2002), Jones Luong (2004), and Wooden and Stefes (2009).

11. On entanglements of state and illicit practices see Heyman (1999) and Van Schendel and Abraham (2005).

12. See also De Danieli (2011), Kraudzun (2011), and Townsend (2006).

13. There is a growing body of work on bazaar trade in Central Asia. Important studies include Alff (2013), Karrar (2013, 2016), Marsden (2016), Nasritdinov and O'Connor (2010), Spector (2009), and Stephan and Mirzoev (2016). On the salient role of female traders in the Central Asian bazaar, see Werner (2004).

14. The issue of the presidential family's involvement in various businesses in Tajikistan has been addressed in a range of newspaper articles

as well as in a communiqué from the U.S. Embassy in Dushanbe that was published by WikiLeaks. See Kamilov (2014) and U.S. Embassy cable (2008). For academic studies of broader economic entanglements in Tajikistan and beyond, see Heathershaw (2011) and Heathershaw and Cooley (2015).

15. Additional data for previous years are provided by Asanova (2007) and Kaminski and Mitra (2012, 160), who state that trade turnover through the Kulma pass increased from zero in 2003 to $400 million in 2006.

16. Attempts at enriching the ruling family in Tajikistan do not seem to be restricted to China trade on the Pamir Highway. As Cooley and Heathershaw (2017, 180) show, the largely Chinese-funded Dushanbe–Chanak highway in the western part of the country has served to funnel a yearly revenue stream of up to 30 million USD from tollbooths into government circles via a company registered in the British Virgin Islands.

17. Local spellings include *Navruz* in Tajik and *Nooruz* in Kyrgyz. On Nowruz in Tajikistan and beyond, see Attar (1998), Levy et al. (2012), and Stephan (2010a, 89–94).

18. In her study on Talas in northwestern Kyrgyzstan, Beyer (2009, 155) argues that her interlocutors had experienced the state as being "there" during the Soviet Union. But then it "must have left some time after the country became independent." They associated order with the Soviet state because "there had been strong individuals in the kolkhoz who 'made people work.'" People along the highway, too, perceived the lack of such "strong individuals" in Tajikistan as a central problem that hindered the establishment of order (*tartip*) in the country at large.

19. Similarly, in his study on post-conflict Tajikistan, Heathershaw (2009, 69) describes the Tajikistani state as "personified" by paternal images of the president. Furthermore, Heathershaw states that "in the case of Tajikistan, the person of authority is habitually referred to as the rais (head)" who "exists at all levels of 'the state' from the unofficial authority of the mahalla to the presidency." On gender politics and everyday practices in Tajikistan, see also Cleuziou and Direnberger (2016).

20. In her study on Ishkashim in western Gorno-Badakhshan, Remtilla (2012, 65) mentions that the notion of the master (*soheb*) as a male figure who "defends one's best interest" plays an influential role in people's everyday lives, ranging from the family context with fathers and husbands to discourses on the paternalistic state and to the presence of the Ismaili imam.

21. Beyer (2009, 105) notes with regard to the region of Talas in Kyrgyzstan that widows in particular can become heads of household (*bash*) after the death of their husbands.

22. For a detailed description of how *nomus* is spatialized in households in Sokh in the Ferghana Valley, see Reeves (2011b, 564).

23. On the eroticism of *vatan* as beloved and mother in Iran, see Nadjmabadi (1997).

24. On "personality cult" across Central Asia, see Adams (2010), Cummings (2002), Dagiev (2014), and Polese and Horak (2015).

25. For in-depth studies on Roghun, see Féaux and Suyarkulova (2015), Ibañez-Tirado (2015b), Menga (2015), and Suyarkulova (2014).

26. Liu developed his argument on the khan over the course of more than a decade. See, in addition to Liu (2012), and Liu (2002, 2006, 2014).

27. For studies on discourses of danger and conflict in Central Asia, see Heathershaw and Megoran (2011), Reeves (2005, 2014c, 205–40), and Thompson and Heathershaw (2005).

REFERENCES

Abashin, Sergei. 2014. "A Prayer for Rain: Practising Being Soviet and Muslim." *Journal of Islamic Studies* 25, no. 2: 178–200.

Abashin, Sergei. 2015. *Sovietskii kishlak: Mezhdu kolonializmom i modernizatsii*. Moskva: Novoe literaturnoe obozrenie.

Abdullaev, Kamoludin Nazhmudinovich. 2009. *Ot Sin'tsziania do Khorasana: Iz istorii sredneaziatskoi emigratsii XX veka*. Dushanbe: Irfon.

Abdullaev, Kamoludin, and Shahram Akbarzadeh. 2002. *Historical Dictionary of Tajikistan*. Lanham: Scarecrow Press.

Abdylda uulu, D. 2005. *Namazdy eng ongoi ürönüü*. Bishkek: Turar.

Abulhaev, R. A. 2009. *Ta'rikhi muhojirat dar Tojikiston (1924–2000)*. Dushanbe: Donish.

Abu-Lughod, Lila. 2004. *Dramas of Nationhood: The Politics of Television in Egypt*. Chicago: University of Chicago Press.

Adams, Laura L. 2010. *The Spectacular State: Culture and National Identity in Uzbekistan*. Durham: Duke University Press.

Aga Khan III. 1954. *The Memoirs of Aga Khan: Foreword by W. Somerset Maugham*. London: Cassell.

Aitpaeva, Gulnara, ed. 2007. *Mazar Worship in Kyrgyzstan: Rituals and Practitioners in Talas*. Bishkek: Maxprint.

Aitpaeva, Gulnara, and Elena Molchanova. 2007. "Kyrgyzchylyk: Searching Between Spirituality and Science." In *Mazar Worship in Kyrgyzstan: Rituals and Practitioners in Talas*, 395–411. Edited by Gulnara Aitpaeva. Bishkek: Maxprint.

AKDN. 2016a. "Rural Development in Tajikistan." Accessed 5 April 2016. http://www.akdn.org/rural_development/tajikistan.asp.

AKDN. 2016b. "Home Page." Accessed 6 April 2016. http://www.akdn .org.

AKDN. 2016c. "Frequent Questions." Accessed April 6, 2016. http:/www .akdn.org/faq.asp.

Alff, Henryk. 2013. "Basarökonomie im Wandel: Postsowjetische Perspektiven des Handels in Zentralasien." *Geographische Rundschau* 65, no. 11: 20–25.

Al Hussaini, Noor Mawlana Shah Karim. 2009. *Kalam-e Imam-e Zaman: Farmans 1957–2009, Golden Edition.* Canada: No publisher.

Appadurai, Arjun. 2008. *Modernity at Large: Cultural Dimensions of Globalization.* Minneapolis: University of Minnesota Press.

"Armian s tadzhikami ssoriat vragi Rossii: Sambel Garibian." 2010. *IA Regnum.* Accessed 18 May 2016. http://www.regnum.ru/news/1307459 .html.

Arnason, Johann P. 2000. "Communism and Modernity." *Daedalus* 129, no. 1: 61–90.

Asad, Talal. 1993. *Genealogies of Religion: Discipline and Reasons of Power in Christianity and Islam.* Baltimore: The Johns Hopkins University Press.

Asad, Talal. 2003. *Formations of the Secular: Christianity, Islam, Modernity.* Stanford: Stanford University Press.

Asanova, Saodat. 2007. "Tajiks Seek Permanent Gateway to China." *Institute for War and Peace Reporting RCA,* no. 495. Accessed 18 May 2016. http://iwpr.net/report-news/tajiks-seek-permanent-gateway-china.

Attar, Ali 1998. "Nawruz in Tajikistan: Ritual or Politics?" In *Post-Soviet Central Asia,* 231–47. Edited by Touraj Atabaki and John O'Kane. London and New York: I. B. Tauris.

Augé, Marc. 2008. *Non-places: An Introduction to Supermodernity.* London: Verso.

Avtomagistral' Osh-Khorog. 1974. *Avtomagistral' Osh-Khorog: Dela i liudi.* Osh: SSSR Ministerstvo transportnogo stroitel'stva glavdorstroi.

Bahry, Stephen A. 2016. "Societal Multilingualism and Personal Plurilingualism in Pamir Tajikistan's Complex Language Ecology." In *Language Change in Central Asia,* 125–48. Edited by Elise S. Ahn and Juldyz Smagulova. Berlin: DeGruyter.

Balci, Bayram. 2012. "The Rise of the Jama'at al Tabligh in Kyrgyzstan: The Revival of Islamic Ties Between the Indian Subcontinent and Central Asia?" *Central Asian Survey* 31, no. 1: 61–76.

Balci, Bayram. 2015. "Reviving Central Asia's Religious Ties with the Indian Subcontinent? The Jamaat al Tabligh." *Religion, State and Society* 43, no. 1: 20–34.

Baldauf, Ingeborg. 2006. "Mittelasien und Russland/Sowjetunion: Kulturelle Begegnungen von 1860 bis 1990." In *Zentralasien: 13. bis 20. Jahrhundert. Geschichte und Gesellschaft*, 183–204. Edited by Bert Fragner and Andreas Kappeler. Wien: Promedia.

Baldauf, Ingeborg. 2007. "Tradition, Revolution, Adaption: Die kulturelle Sowjetisierung Zentralasiens." *Osteuropa* 57, no. 8: 99–119.

Baptista, João Alfonso. 2016. "The Road of Progress: Individualisation and Interaction Agency in Southeast Angola." *Ethnos*. DOI: 10.1080/00141844.2016.1150312.

Barber, Karin. 2007. *The Anthropology of Texts, Persons and Publics: Oral and Written Culture in Africa and Beyond.* Cambridge: Cambridge University Press.

Barry, Andrew. 2001. *Political Machines: Governing a Technological Society.* London: Athlone Press.

Barry, Andrew. 2013. *Material Politics: Disputes Along the Pipeline.* Malden: Wiley Blackwell.

Barth, Fredrik. 1969. "Introduction." In *Ethnic Groups and Boundaries: The Social Organization of Cultural Difference*, 9–38. Edited by Fredrik Barth. Boston: Little, Brown and Company.

Barthold, Wilhelm, and Geoffrey E. Wheeler. 2012. "Is'h'ān." *Encyclopaedia of Islam*, 2nd ed. Accessed 18 May 2016. http://referencework s.brillonline.com/entries/encyclopaedia-of-islam-2/ishan-SIM_3621.

Bauman, Zygmunt. 2000. *Liquid Modernity.* Cambridge: Polity Press.

Beatty, Andrew. 2002. "Changing Places: Relatives and Relativism in Java." *Journal of the Royal Anthropological Institute* 8, no. 3: 469–91.

Belt and Road. 2016. "The Belt and Road Initiative." Accessed 18 May 2016. http://english.gov.cn/beltAndRoad/.

Bennett, Jane. 2001. *The Enchantment of Modern Life: Attachments, Crossings, and Ethics.* Princeton: Princeton University Press.

Bennett, Jane. 2010. *Vibrant Matter: A Political Ecology of Things.* Durham: Duke University Press.

Bergne, Paul. 2007. *The Birth of Tajikistan: National Identity and the Origins of the Republic.* London and New York: I. B. Tauris.

Beyer, Judith. 2009. *According to Salt: An Ethnography of Customary Law in Talas, Kyrgyzstan.* PhD diss., Martin-Luther-Universität.

Beyer, Judith. 2010. "Authority as Accomplishment: Intergenerational Dynamics in Talas, Northern Kyrgyzstan." In *Eurasian Perspectives: In Search for Alternatives*, 78–92. Edited by Anita Sengupta and Suchandana Chatterjee. Kolkata: Shipra.

Beyer, Judith. 2013. "Ordering Ideals: Accomplishing Well-Being in a Cooperative of Elders." *Central Asian Survey* 32, no. 4: 432–47.

Beyer, Judith. 2016. *The Force of Custom: Law and the Ordering of Everday Life in Kyrgyzstan*. Pittsburgh: University of Pittsburgh Press.

Beyer, Judith, and Felix Girke. 2015. "Practising Harmony Ideology: Ethnographic Reflections on Community and Coercion." *Common Knowledge* 21, no. 2: 196–235.

Billé, Franck. 2015. *Sinophobia: Anxiety, Violence, and the Making of Mongolian Identity*. Honolulu: University of Hawai'i Press.

Bliss, Frank. 2006. *Social and Economic Change in the Pamirs (Gorno-Badakhshan, Tajikistan)*. London and New York: Routledge.

Bloch, Maurice. 1977. "The Past and the Present in the Present." *Man* 12, no. 2: 278–92.

Boivin, Michel. 2003. *La Rénovation du Shi'isme Ismaélien en Inde et au Pakistan*. London: Routledge.

Bonnett, Alastair. 2016. *The Geography of Nostalgia: Global and Local Perspectives on Modernity and Loss*. London and New York: Routledge.

Boym, Svetlana. 2001. *The Future of Nostalgia*. New York: Basic Books.

Braam, Ernesto. 2006. "Travelling with the Tablighi Jamaat in South Thailand." *Isim Review* 17 (Spring 2006): 42–43.

Brechin, Gray. 2006. *Imperial San Francisco: Urban Power, Earthly Ruin*. Berkeley: University of California Press.

Breu, Thomas, and Hans Hurni. 2003. *The Tajik Pamirs: The Challenges of Sustainable Development in an Isolated Mountain Region*. Bern: Centre for Development and Environment, University of Bern.

Brown, Kate. 2013. *Plutopia: Nuclear Families, Atomic Cities, and the Great Soviet and American Plutonium Disasters*. Oxford: Oxford University Press.

Broz, Ludek, and Joachim Otto Habeck. 2015. "Siberian Automobility: From the Joy of Destination to the Joy of Driving There." *Mobilities* 10, no. 4: 552–70.

Bubnova, M. A. 2005. *Istoriia Gorno-Badakhshanskoi avtonomnoi oblasti: S drevneishikh vremen do noveishego perioda*. Dushanbe: Paivand.

Callahan, Ted. 2007. "The Kyrgyz of the Afghan Pamir Ride On." *Nomadic Peoples* 11, no. 1: 39–49.

Callahan, Ted. 2012. "Pastoral Production Strategies and Market Orientation of the Afghan Kirghiz." In *Pastoral Practices in High Asia: Agency of "Development" Effected by Modernization, Resettlement and Transformation*, 71–87. Edited by Hermann Kreutzmann. Dordrecht: Springer.

Callahan, Edward M., Jr. 2013. *To Rule the Roof of the World: Power and Patronage in Afghan Kyrgyz Society*. PhD diss., Boston University.

Candea, Matei. 2007. "Arbitrary Locations: In Defence of the Bounded Field-Site." *Journal of the Royal Anthropological Institute* 13, no. 1: 167–84.

"Central Asia and Turkey." 2014. The Christensen Fund. Accessed 5 March 2014. http://www.christensenfund.org/programs/central-asia -and-turkey.

Central Asia Newswire. 2012. "Sughd Court Sentences Seven Alleged Tajik Extremists." Accessed 5 March 2014. http://www.universalnews wires.com/centralasia/viewstory.aspx?id=11447.

Chari, Sharad, and Katherine Verdery. 2009. "Thinking Between the Posts: Postcolonialism, Postsocialism, and Ethnography After the Cold War." *Comparative Studies in Society and History* 51, no. 1: 6–34.

Chokoev, Abdikarim Mamatmusa uulu. 2007. *Jergemdin murastary je ötkön ömürgo kairylyp*. Khorog: Logos.

Chokoev, Abdikarim Mamatmusa uulu. 2015. *Dünkö sanjirasy*. Murghab: Oshbasmakana.

Cleuziou, Juliette, and Lucia Direnberger. 2016. "Gender and Nation in Post-Soviet Central Asia: From National Narratives to Women's Practices." *Nationalities Papers* 44, no. 2: 195–206.

Collier, Stephen J. 2011. *Post-Soviet Social: Neoliberalism, Social Modernity, Biopolitics*. Princeton: Princeton University Press.

Colombijn, Freek. 2002. "Introduction: On the Road." *Bijdragen tot de Taal-, Land- en Volkenkunde (On the Road: The Social Impact of New Roads in Southeast Asia)* 158, no. 4: 595–617.

Conrad, Sebastian, and Shalini Randeria. 2002. "Einleitung: Geteilte Geschichten: Europa in einer postkolonialen Welt." In *Jenseits des Eurozentrismus: Postkoloniale Perspektiven in den Geschichts- und Kulturwissenschaften*, 9–49. Edited by Sebastian Conrad and Shalini Randeria. Frankfurt am Main: Campus-Verlag.

Conterio, Johanna. 2015. "Inventing the Subtropics: An Environmental History of Sochi, 1929–36." *Ab Imperio* 16, no. 1: 91–120.

Cooley, Alexander A., and John Heathershaw. 2017. *Dictators Without Borders: Power and Money in Central Asia*. New Haven: Yale University Press.

Corbin, Henry. 1983. *Cyclical Time and Ismaili Gnosis*. London: Kegan Paul.

Cresswell, Tim. 1996. *In Place/Out of Place: Geography, Ideology, and Transgression*. Minneapolis and London: University of Minnesota Press.

Cresswell, Tim. 2004. *Place: A Short Introduction*. Malden: Blackwell.

Cummings, Sally N., ed. 2002. *Power and Change in Central Asia*. London and New York: Routledge.

Daftary, Farhad. 2007. *The Isma'ilis: Their History and Doctrines*. Cambridge: Cambridge University Press.

Daftary, Farhad, ed. 2011. *A Modern History of the Ismailis: Continuity and Change in a Muslim Community*. London and New York: I. B. Tauris.

Dagiev, Dagikhudo. 2014. *Regime Transition in Central Asia: Stateness, Nationalism and Political Change in Tajikistan and Uzbekistan*. London and New York: Routledge.

Dalakoglou, Dimitris. 2010. "The Road: An Ethnography of the Albanian–Greek Cross-Border Motorway." *American Ethnologist* 37, no. 1: 132–49.

Dalakoglou, Dimitris. 2012. "'The Road from Capitalism to Capitalism': Infrastructures of (Post)Socialism in Albania." *Mobilities* 7, no. 4: 571–86.

Dalakoglou, Dimitris, and Penny Harvey. 2012. "Roads and Anthropology: Ethnographic Perspectives on Space, Time and (Im)Mobility." *Mobilities* 7, no. 4: 459–65.

Das, Veena, and Deborah Poole. 2004. "State and Its Margins: Comparative Ethnographies." In *Anthropology in the Margins of the State*, 3–34. Edited by Veena Das and Deborah Poole. Santa Fe: School of American Research Press.

Davlatshoev, Shuhrobsho. 2006. *The Formation and Consolidation of Pamiri Ethnic Identity in Tajikistan*. Master's thesis, Middle East Technical University.

De Boeck, Filip. 2011. "Inhabiting Ocular Ground: Kinshasa's Future in the Light of Congo's Spectral Urban Politics." *Cultural Anthropology* 26, no. 2: 263–86.

De Cordier, Bruno. 2008. "Islamic Faith-Based Development Organizations in Former Soviet Muslim Environments: The Mountain Societies Development Support Programme in the Rasht Valley, Tajikistan." *Central Asian Survey* 27, no. 2: 169–84.

De Danieli, Filippo. 2011. "Counter-Narcotics Policies in Tajikistan and Their Impact on State Building." *Central Asian Survey* 30, no. 1: 129–45.

Devji, Faisal. 2012a. "Tajikistan: Power and the Aga Khan." *Current Intelligence* 4, no. 3. Accessed 27 January 2014. http://www.currentintelli gence.net/storage/issues/2012/CI-Summer2012.pdf.

Devji, Faisal. 2012b. "The Dictatorship of Civil Society in Tajikistan." *Current Intelligence* 4, no. 4. Accessed 27 January 2014. http://www .currentintelligence.net/storage/issues/2012/CI-Fall2012.pdf.

Djalili, Mohammed-Reza, Frédéric Grare, and Shirin Akiner, eds. 1998. *Tajikistan: The Trials of Independence*. Richmond: Curzon.

Dobrenko, Evgeny, and Eric Naiman, eds. 2003. *The Landscape of Stalinism: The Art and Ideology of Soviet Space*. Seattle and London: University of Washington Press.

Dodykhudoeva, Leila. 2002. "The Socio-Linguistic Situation and Language Policy of the Autonomous Region of Mountainous Badakhshan: The Case of the Tajik Language." Linguapax.org. Accessed 9 May 2016. http://www.linguapax.org/wp-content/uploads/2015/09/ CMPL2002_T2_Dodykhudoeva.pdf.

Dor, Rémy, and Clas M. Naumann. 1978. *Die Kirghisen des afghanischen Pamir*. Graz: Akademische Druck- u. Verlagsanstalt.

"'Dzhamo'ati Tablig' novaia ugroza Tadzhikistanu?" 2009. *Asia Plus*, May 27, 8.

Dzhumaev, D. 1984. *Doroga druzhby*. Khorog: Tipografiia Khorog.

Edgar, Adrienne L. 2007. "Marriage, Modernity, and the 'Friendship of Nations': Interethnic Intimacy in Post-War Central Asia in Comparative Perspective." *Central Asian Survey* 26, no. 4: 581–99.

Eickelman, Dale F. 1992. "Mass Higher Education and the Religious Imagination in Contemporary Arab Societies." *American Ethnologist* 19, no. 4: 643–55.

Eickelman, Dale F., and Jon W. Anderson, eds. 2003. *New Media in the Muslim World: The Emerging Public*. Bloomington: Indiana University Press.

Eisenstadt, Shmuel N. 2000. "Multiple Modernities." *Daedalus* 129, no. 1: 1–29.

Ellen, Roy. 1993. *The Cultural Relations of Classification: An Analysis of Nuaulu Animal Categories from Central Seram*. Cambridge: Cambridge University Press.

Englund, Harry, and James Leach. 2000. "Ethnography and the Meta-Narratives of Modernity." *Current Anthropology* 41, no. 2: 225–39.

Epkenhans, Tim. 2009. "Regulating Religion in Post-Soviet Central Asia: Some Remarks on Religious Association Law and 'Official' Islamic Institutions in Tajikistan." *Security and Human Rights* 20, no. 1: 94–99.

Epkenhans, Tim. 2010. "'Islam' in the Security Discourse of the Post-Soviet Republics of Central Asia." *OSCE Yearbook 2010.* Accessed 18 May 2016. https://ifsh.de/file-CORE/documents/yearbook/english/10/Epkenhans-en.pdf.

Epkenhans, Tim. 2011. "Defining Normative Islam: Some Remarks on Contemporary Islamic Thought in Tajikistan—Hoji Akbar Turajonzoda's Sharia and Society." *Central Asian Survey* 30, no. 1: 81–96.

Epkenhans, Tim. 2016. *The Origins of the Civil War in Tajikistan: Nationalism, Islamism, and Violent Conflict in Post-Soviet Space.* Lanham: Rowman & Littlefield.

Eratov, R. 2005. *Daavat jolu.* Bishkek: n.p.

Escobar, Arturo. 2001. "Culture Sits in Places: Reflections on Globalism and Subaltern Strategies on Localization." *Political Geography* 20: 139–74.

Evans-Pritchard, Edward E. 1940. *The Nuer.* Oxford: Clarendon Press.

Faubion, James. 1988. "Possible Modernities." *Cultural Anthropology* 3, no. 4: 365–78.

Féaux de la Croix, Jeanne. 2011a. *Moral Geographies in Kyrgyzstan: How Pastures, Dams and Holy Sites Matter in Striving for a Good Life.* PhD diss., University of St. Andrews.

Féaux de la Croix, Jeanne. 2011b. "Moving Metaphors We Live By: Water and Flow in the Social Sciences and Around Hydroelectric Dams in Kyrgyzstan." *Central Asian Survey* 30, nos. 3–4: 487–502.

Féaux de la Croix, Jeanne. 2016. *Iconic Places in Central Asia: The Moral Geography of Dams, Pastures, and Holy Sites.* Bielefeld: transcript Verlag.

Féaux de la Croix, Jeanne, and Mohira Suyarkulova. 2015. "The Roghun Complex: Public Roles and Historic Experiences of Dam-Building in Tajikistan and Kyrgyzstan." *Cahiers d'Asie Centrale* 25: 103–32.

Ferguson, James. 2001. *Expectations of Modernity: Myths and Meanings of Urban Life on the Zambian Copperbelt.* Berkeley: University of California Press.

Ferguson, James. 2006. *Global Shadows: Africa in the Neoliberal World Order.* Durham: Duke University Press.

Ferrando, Olivier. 2011. "Soviet Population Transfers and Interethnic Relations in Tajikistan: Assessing the Concept of Ethnicity." *Central Asian Survey* 30, no. 1: 39–52.

Foucault, Michel. 1984. "Space, Knowledge, and Power." In *The Foucault Reader*, 239–56. Edited by Paul Rabinow. New York: Pantheon.

Foucault, Michel. 1994. "The Subject and Power." In *The Essential Foucault: Selections from Essential Works of Foucault, 1954–1984*, 126–44. Edited by Paul Rabinow and Nikolas Rose. New York: New Press.

Fountain, Philip. 2013. "The Myth of Religious NGOs: Development Studies and the Return of Religion." *International Development Policy* 4, no. 1: 9–30.

Fountain, Philip, Robin Bush, and R. Michael Feener, eds. 2015. *Religion and the Politics of Development*. London: Palgrave Macmillan.

Frankopan, Peter. 2015. *The Silk Roads: A New History of the World*. London: Bloomsbury.

Gardet, L. 2014. "Īmān." *Encyclopaedia of Islam*, 2nd ed. Accessed 18 May 2016. http://referenceworks.brillonline.com/entries/encyclopaedia-of-islam-2/iman-COM_0370.

Garver, John W. 1981. "The Sino-Soviet Territorial Dispute in the Pamir Mountains Region." *The China Quarterly* 85: 107–18.

Geisler, Johanna Conterio. 2014. *The Soviet Sanatorium: Medicine, Nature and Mass Culture in Sochi, 1917–1991*. PhD diss., Harvard University.

Gell, Alfred. 1992. *The Anthropology of Time: Cultural Constructions of Temporal Maps and Images*. Oxford: Berg.

Green, Nile. 2013. "The Road to Kabul: Automobiles and Afghan Internationalism 1900–40." In *Beyond Swat: History, Society and Economy along the Afghanistan-Pakistan Frontier*, 77–91. Edited by Benjamin Hopkins and Magnus Marsden. London: Hurst & Company.

Green, Sarah F. 2005. *Notes from the Balkans: Locating Marginality and Ambiguity on the Greek-Albanian Border*. Princeton: Princeton University Press.

Greenhouse, Carol J., Elizabeth Mertz, and Kay B. Warren, eds. 2002. *Ethnography in Unstable Places: Everyday Life in Contexts of Dramatic Political Change*. Durham: Duke University Press.

Gross, Jo-Ann. 2013. "Foundational Legends, Shrines, and Isma'ili Identity in Gorno-Badakhshan, Tajikistan." In *Muslims and Others in Sacred Space*, 164–92. Edited by Margaret Cormack. Oxford: Oxford University Press.

Grzymala-Busse, Anna, and Pauline Jones Luong. 2002. "Reconceptualizing the State: Lessons from Post-Communism." *Politics and Society* 30, no. 4: 529–54.

Gugler, Thomas K. 2010. "The New Religiosity of Tablīghī Jamāʿat and Daʿwat-e Islāmī and the Transformation of Islam in Europe." *Anthropos* 105: 121–36.

Guldi, Jo. 2012. *Roads to Power: Britain Invents the Infrastructure State.* Cambridge: Harvard University Press.

Gullette, David. 2008. "A State of Passion: The Use of Ethnogenesis in Kyrgyzstan." *Inner Asia* 10, no. 2: 261–79.

Gullette, David. 2010. *The Genealogical Construction of the Kyrgyz Republic: Kinship, State and "Tribalism."* Folkestone: Global Oriental.

Gupta, Akhil. 1995. "Blurred Boundaries: The Discourse of Corruption, the Culture of Politics, and the Imagined State." *American Ethnologist* 22, no. 2: 375–402.

Haghayeghi, Mehrdad. 1994. "Islamic Revival in the Central Asian Republics." *Central Asian Survey* 13, no. 2: 249–66.

Hamrabaeva, Nargiz. 2009. "Tajik Clampdown on Islamic Group Could Backfire." *IWPR.* Accessed 18 May 2016. http://iwpr.net/report-news/tajik-clampdown-islamic-group-could-backfire.

Hari, Johann. 2005. "Why I Hate Little Britain." *The Independent.* Accessed 18 May 2016. http://www.independent.co.uk/opinion/commentators/johann-hari/johann-hari-why-i-hate-little-britain-516388.html.

Harms, Erik. 2011. *Saigon's Edge: On the Margins of Ho Chi Minh City.* Minneapolis and London: University of Minnesota Press.

Harris, Colette. 2004. *Control and Subversion: Gender Relations in Tajikistan.* London: Pluto Press.

Harvey, David. 2004. *The Condition of Postmodernity: An Enquiry into the Origins of Cultural Change.* Malden: Blackwell.

Harvey, Penelope. 2005. "The Materiality of State-Effects: An Ethnography of a Road in the Peruvian Andes." In *State Formation: Anthropological Perspectives,* 123–41. Edited by Christian Krohn-Hansen, Knut G. Nustad, and Bruce Kapferer. London: Pluto Press.

Harvey, Penelope. 2010. "Cementing Relations: The Materiality of Roads and Public Spaces in Provincial Peru." *Social Analysis* 54, no. 2: 28–46.

Harvey, Penelope. 2012. "The Topological Quality of Infrastructural Relation: An Ethnographic Approach." *Theory, Culture & Society* 29, nos. 4–5: 76–92.

Harvey, Penelope, and Hannah Knox. 2008. "'Otherwise Engaged': Culture, Deviance and the Quest for Connectivity Through Road Construction." *Journal of Cultural Economy* 1, no. 1: 79–92.

Harvey, Penny, and Hannah Knox. 2012. "The Enchantments of Infrastructure." *Mobilities* 7, no. 4: 512–36.

Harvey, Penny, and Hannah Knox. 2015. *Roads: An Anthropology of Infrastructure and Expertise.* Ithaca: Cornell University Press.

Hatto. Arthur T., ed. 1990. *The Manas of Wilhelm Radloff: Re-edited, Newly Translated and with Commentary by Arthur T. Hatto.* Wiesbaden: Harrassowitz.

Hayano, David M. 1990. *Road Through the Rain Forest: Living Anthropology in Highland Papua New Guinea.* Prospect Heights: Waveland Press.

Heathershaw, John. 2009. *Post-Conflict Tajikistan: The Politics of Peacebuilding and the Emergence of a Legitimate Order.* London and New York: Routledge.

Heathershaw, John. 2011. "Tajikistan Amidst Globalization: State Failure or State Transformation?" *Central Asian Survey* 30, no. 1: 147–68.

Heathershaw, John, and Nick Megoran. 2011. "Contesting Danger: A New Agenda for Policy and Scholarship on Central Asia." *International Affairs* 87, no. 3: 589–612.

Heathershaw, John, and Alexander Cooley. 2015. "Offshore Central Asia: An Introduction." *Central Asian Survey* 34, no. 1: 1–10.

Heathershaw, John, and Sophie Roche. 2011. "Islam and Political Violence in Tajikistan: An Ethnographic Perspective on the Causes and Consequences of the 2010 Armed Conflict in the Kamarob Gorge." *Ethnopolitics Papers* 8: 1–21.

Heinlein, Michael, Cordula Kropp, Judith Neumer, Angelika Poferl, and Regina Römhild, eds. 2012. *Futures of Modernity: Challenges for Cosmopolitical Thought and Practice.* Bielefeld: transcript Verlag.

Herzfeld, Michael. 2005. *Cultural Intimacy: Social Poetics in the Nation-State.* London and New York: Routledge.

Heyman, Josiah, ed. 1999. *States and Illegal Practices.* Oxford: Berg.

Hill, John E. 2009. *Through the Jade Gate to Rome: A Study of the Silk Routes During the Later Han Dynasty 1st to 2nd Centuries CE.* North Charleston: BookSurge.

Hirsch, Francine. 2005. *Empire of Nations: Ethnographic Knowledge and the Making of the Soviet Union.* Ithaca: Cornell University Press.

Hofman, Irna. 2015. *Opening Up Markets or Fostering a New Satellite State? Detangling the Impetuses of Chinese Land Investments in Tajikistan.* BRICS Initiatives in Critical Agrarian Studies (BICAS) Working Paper Series, no. 4.

Hofman, Irna. 2016. "More Foreign Than Other Foreigners: On Discourse and Adoption—The Contradiction of Astonishment and Fear for Chinese Farm Practices in Tajikistan." In *Agricultural Knowledge and Knowledge Systems in Post-Soviet Societies*, 201–21. Edited by Anna-Katharina Hornidge, Anastasiya Shtaltovna, and Conrad Schetter. Bern: Peter Lang.

Hofman, Irna, and Peter Ho. 2012. "China's 'Developmental Outsourcing': A Critical Examination of Chinese Global 'Land Grabs' Discourse." *Journal of Peasant Studies* 39, no. 1: 1–48.

Hopkirk, Peter. 1980. *Foreign Devils on the Silk Road: The Search for the Lost Cities and Treasures of Chinese Central Asia*. Oxford: Oxford University Press.

Hopkirk, Peter. 1992. *The Great Game: Struggle for Empire in Central Asia*. New York: Kodansha.

Hopkirk, Peter. 1995. *Setting the East Ablaze: Lenin's Dream of an Empire in Asia*. New York: Kodansha.

Houben, Vincent, and Mona Schrempf. 2008. "Introduction: Figurations and Representations of Modernity." In *Figurations of Modernity: Global and Local Representations in Comparative Perspective*, 7–20. Edited by Vincent Houben and Mona Schrempf. Frankfurt am Main: Campus Verlag.

Humphrey, Caroline. 1999. "Russian Protection Rackets and the Appropriation of Law and Order." In *States and Illegal Practices*, 199–232. Edited by Josiah Heyman. Oxford: Berg.

Humphrey, Caroline. 2005. "Ideology in Infrastructure: Architecture and Soviet Imagination." *Journal of the Royal Anthropological Institute* 11: 39–58.

Ibañez-Tirado, Diana. 2013. *Temporality and Subjectivity in Kulob, Southern Tajikistan: An Ethnography of Ordinary People and Their Everyday Lives*. PhD diss., University of London, School of Oriental and African Studies.

Ibañez-Tirado, Diana. 2015a. "'How can I be post-Soviet if I was never Soviet?' Rethinking Categories of Time and Social Change, a Perspective from Kulob, Southern Tajikistan." *Central Asian Survey* 34, no. 2: 190–203.

Ibañez-Tirado, Diana. 2015b. "Everyday Disasters, Stagnation, and the Normalcy of Non-Development: Roghun Dam, a Flood, and Campaigns of Forced Taxation in Southern Tajikistan." *Central Asian Survey* 34, no. 4: 549–63.

Iloliev, Abdulmamad. 2008. *The Ismai'ili-Sufi Sage of Pamir: Mubarak-i Wakhani and the Esoteric Tradition of the Pamiri Muslims.* Amherst: Cambria.

"Imami A'zam." 2009. *Asia Plus*, May 27, 9.

Ingold, Tim. 2009. "Against Space: Place, Movement, Knowledge." In *Boundless Worlds: An Anthropological Approach to Movement*, 29–44. Edited by Peter Wynn Kyrby. New York: Berghahn.

International Crisis Group. 2010. "Central Asia: Migrants and the Economic Crisis." *Asia Report*, no. 183. Accessed 18 May 2016. http://www.crisisgroup.org/en/regions/asia/central-asia/183-central-asia-migrants-and-the-economic-crisis.aspx.

Ismailbekova, Aksana, and Emil Nasritdinov. 2012. "Transnational Religious Networks in Central Asia: Structure, Travel, and Culture of Kyrgyz Tablighi Jama'at." *Transnational Social Review: A Social Work Journal* 2, no. 2: 177–95.

Ismoilov, Ahmadjon. 1962. *Naqliyoti Tojikiston.* Dushanbe: Nashriyoti Davlatii Tojikiston.

Ismoilov, A. I., and A. B. Suptsepin. 1974. *Naqliyot va rohhoi kishvari kūhī.* Dushanbe: Irfon.

Jacquesson, Svetlana. 2008. "The Sore Zones of Identity: Past and Present Debates on Funerals in Kyrgyzstan." *Inner Asia* 10: 281–303.

Jansen, Stef. 2015. *Yearnings in the Meantime: "Normal Lives" and the State in a Sarajevo Apartment Complex.* New York: Berghahn.

Janson, Marloes. 2005. "Roaming About for God's Sake: The Upsurge of the Tablīghī Jamāʿat in the Gambia." *Journal of Religion Africa* 35, no. 4: 450–81.

Johnson, Robert. 2006. *Spying for Empire: The Great Game in Central and South Asia, 1757–1947.* London: Greenhill Books.

Jones Luong, Pauline, ed. 2004. *The Transformation of Central Asia: States and Societies from Soviet Rule to Independence.* Ithaca: Cornell University Press.

Joniak-Lüthi, Agnieszka. 2016. "Roads in China's Borderland: Interfaces of Spatial Representations, Perceptions, Practices, and Knowledges." *Modern Asian Studies* 50, no. 1: 118–40.

Jonsson, Hjorleifur. 2010. "Above and Beyond: Zomia and the Ethnographic Challenge of/for Regional History." *History and Anthropology* 21, no. 2: 191–212.

Jumabaev, Mitalip, and Sultan Parmanov. 2002. *Sarykol kairyktary.* Osh: printed by author.

Kalandarov, T. C. 2004. *Shugnantsy: Istoriko-etnograficheskoe issledovanie*. Moskva: RAN.

Kamilov, Marat. 2014. "Clans Make Kings." *Silkroadreporters.com*. Accessed 18 May 2016. http://www.silkroadreporters.com/2014/01/26 /clans-make-kings/.

Kaminski, Bartlomiej, and Saumya Mitra. 2012. *Borderless Bazaars and Regional Integration in Central Asia: Emerging Patterns of Trade and Cross-Border Cooperation*. Washington: The World Bank.

Kandiyoti, Deniz. 2007. "The Politics of Gender and the Soviet Paradox: Neither Colonized, nor Modern?" *Central Asian Survey* 26, no. 4: 601–23.

Karabaev, Daniyar, and Elise S. Ahn. 2016. "Language-in-Education: A Look at Kyrgyz Language Schools in the Badakhshan Province of Tajikistan." In *Language Change in Central Asia*, 149–68. Edited by Elise S. Ahn and Juldyz Smagulova. Berlin: DeGruyter.

Karagiannis, Emmanuel. 2010. *Political Islam in Central Asia: The Challenge of Hizb ut-Tahrir*. London: Routledge.

Karrar, Hasan H. 2013. "Merchants, Markets, and the State: Informality, Transnationality, and Spatial Imaginaries in the Revival of Central Eurasian Trade." *Critical Asian Studies* 45, no. 3: 459–80.

Karrar, Hasan H. 2016. "The Resumption of Sino-Central Asian Trade, c. 1983–94: Confidence Building and Reform Along a Cold War Fault Line." *Central Asian Survey* 35, no. 3: 334–50.

Kassymbekova, Botakoz. 2011. "Humans as Territory: Forced Resettlement and the Making of Soviet Tajikistan, 1920–38." *Central Asian Survey* 30, nos. 3–4: 349–70.

Kassymbekova, Botakoz. 2016. *Despite Cultures: Early Soviet Rule in Tajikistan*. Pittsburgh: University of Pittsburgh Press.

Kellner-Heinkele, Barbara, and Jacob M. Landau. 2012. *Language Politics in Contemporary Central Asia: National and Ethnic Identity and the Soviet Legacy*. London and New York: I. B. Tauris.

Kerymov, Lenur, Nigina Bakhrieva, and Nargis Akdodova. 2013. *Monitoring of Observance of Human Rights with the Special Operation Conducted on 24 July in Khorog, Tajikistan*. Dushanbe: Civic Solidarity. Accessed 17 April 2016. http://civicsolidarity.org/sites/default/files /monitoring_report_en_final.pdf.

Keshavjee, Salmaan. 1998. *Medicines and Transitions: The Political Economy of Health and Social Change in Post-Soviet Badakhshan, Tajikistan*. PhD diss., Harvard University.

Keshavjee, Salmaan. 2014. *Blind Spot: How Neoliberalism Infiltrated Global Health*. Oakland: University of California Press.

Khalid, Adeeb. 2007. *Islam after Communism: Religion and Politics in Central Asia*. Berkeley: University of California Press.

Khan, Naveeda. 2006. "Flaws in the Flow: Roads and Their Modernity in Pakistan." *Social Text* 89, no. 24/4: 87–113.

Khanna, Parag. 2016. *Connectography: Mapping the Future of Global Civilization*. New York: Random House.

King, Diane E. 2008. "The Personal Is Patrilineal: Namus as Sovereignty." *Identities* 15, no. 3: 317–42.

Kirksey, S. Eben, and Kiki van Bilsen. 2002. "A Road to Freedom: Mee Articulations and the Trans-Papua Highway." *Bijdragen tot de Taal-, Land- en Volkenkunde (On the Road: The Social Impact of New Roads in Southeast Asia)* 158, no. 4: 837–54.

Kirmse, Stefan B. 2013. *Youth and Globalization in Central Asia: Everyday Life Between Religion, Media, and International Donors*. Frankfurt am Main: Campus Verlag.

Klaeger, Gabriel. 2013a. "Introduction: The Perils and Possibilities of African Roads." *Journal of the African International Institute* 83, no. 3: 359–66.

Klaeger, Gabriel. 2013b. "Dwelling on the Road: Routines, Rituals, and Roadblocks in Southern Ghana." *Journal of the African International Institute* 83, no. 3: 446–69.

Knauft, Bruce M., ed. 2002. *Critically Modern: Alternatives, Alterities, Anthropologies*. Bloomington: Indiana University Press.

Kotkin, Stephen. 1997. *Magnetic Mountain: Stalinism as a Civilization*. Berkeley: University of California Press.

Kraudzun, Tobias. 2011. "From the Pamir Frontier to International Borders: Exchange Relations of the Borderland Population." In *Subverting Borders: Doing Research on Smuggling and Small-Scale Trade*, 171–91. Edited by Bettina Bruns and Judith Miggelbrink. Wiesbaden: VS Verlag für Sozialwissenschaften.

Kraudzun, Tobias. 2012. "Livelihoods of the 'New Livestock Breeders' in the Eastern Pamirs of Tajikistan." In *Pastoral Practices in High Asia: Agency of "Development" Effected by Modernization, Resettlement and Transformation*, 89–107. Edited by Hermann Kreutzmann. Dordrecht: Springer.

Kraudzun, Tobias. 2016. "External Support and Local Agency: Uncertain Transformations of Livelihoods in the Pamirian Borderland of Tajikistan." In *Mapping Transition in the Pamirs: Changing Human-*

Environmental Landscapes, 159–79. Edited by Hermann Kreutzmann and Teiji Watanabe. Dordrecht: Springer.

Kreutzmann, Hermann. 1993. "The Karakoram Highway: The Impact of Road Construction on Mountain Societies." *Modern Asian Studies* 25: 711–36.

Kreutzmann, Hermann. 1996. *Ethnizität im Entwicklungsprozess: Die Wakhi in Hochasien*. Berlin: Reimer.

Kreutzmann, Hermann. 2003. "Ethnic Minorities and Marginality in the Pamirian Knot: Survival of Wakhi and Kirghiz in a Harsh Environment and Global Contexts." *Geographical Journal* 169, no. 3: 215–35.

Kreutzmann, Hermann. 2004. "Accessibility for High Asia: Comparative Perspectives on Northern Pakistan's Traffic Infrastructure and Linkages with Its Neighbours in the Hindukush-Karakoram-Himalaya." *Journal of Mountain Science* 1, no. 3: 193–210.

Kreutzmann, Hermann. 2009. "The Karakoram Highway as a Prime Exchange Corridor between Pakistan and China." In *Proceedings of the Regional Workshop Integrated Tourism Concepts to Contribute to Sustainable Development in Mountain Regions Gilgit/Pakistan—Kashgar/P.R.China, Oct 8–14, 2008*, 13–36. Edited by Hermann Kreutzmann, Ghulam Amin Beg, Lu Zhaohui, and Jürgen Richter. Bonn: InWEnt.

Kreutzmann, Hermann. 2012. "Kirghiz in Little Kara Köl: The Forces of Modernisation in Southern Xinjiang." In *Pastoral Practices in High Asia: Agency of "Development" Effected by Modernization, Resettlement and Transformation*, 109–25. Edited by Hermann Kreutzmann. Dordrecht: Springer.

Kreutzmann, Hermann. 2015. *Pamirian Crossroads: Kirghiz and Wakhi of High Asia*. Wiesbaden: Harrassowitz.

Kwon, Heonik. 2010. *The Other Cold War*. New York: Columbia University Press.

Landau, Jacob M., and Barbara Kellner-Heinkele. 2001. *Politics of Language in the Ex-Soviet Muslim States: Azerbaijan, Uzbekistan, Kazakhstan, Kyrgyzstan, Turkmenistan and Tajikistan*. London: Hurst.

Larkin, Brian. 2008. *Signal and Noise: Media, Infrastructure, and Urban Culture in Nigeria*. Durham: Duke University Press.

Larkin, Brian. 2013. "The Politics and Poetics of Infrastructure." *Annual Review of Anthropology* 42: 327–43.

Laruelle, Marlène, Sébastien Peyrouse, Jean-François Huchet, and Bayram Balci, eds. 2010. *China and India in Central Asia: A New "Great Game"?* New York: Palgrave.

Lashkariev, Amrisho. 2016. *The Construction of Boundaries and Identity through Ritual Performance by a Small Ismaili Community of Gorno-Badakhshan*. Bonn: Politischer Arbeitskreis Schulen e.V.

Laszczkowski, Mateusz. 2014. "State Building(s): Built Forms, Materiality, and the State in Astana." In *Ethnographies of the State in Central Asia: Performing Politics*, 149–72. Edited by Madeleine Reeves, Johan Rasanayagam, and Judith Beyer. Bloomington: Indiana University Press.

Laszczkowski, Mateusz. 2016. *"City of the Future": Built Space, Modernity and Urban Change in Astana*. New York: Berghahn.

Latour, Bruno. 2005. *Reassembling the Social: An Introduction to Actor-Network-Theory*. Oxford: Oxford University Press.

Leach, Edmund R. 1971. *Rethinking Anthropology*. London: Athlone Press. First published 1961.

Lefebvre, Henri. 1974. *The Production of Space*. English translation first published in 1991. Malden: Blackwell.

Lemon, Edward. 2014. "Mediating the Conflict in the Rasht Valley, Tajikistan: The Hegemonic Narrative and Anti-Hegemonic Challenges." *Central Asian Affairs* 1: 247–72.

Levi-Sanchez, Suzanne. 2017. *The Afghan-Central Asia Borderland: The State and Local Leaders*. London and New York: Routledge.

Levy, R., C. E. Bosworth, and G. S. P. Freeman-Greenville. 2012. "Nawrūz." *Encyclopaedia of Islam*, 2nd ed. Accessed April 14, 2016. http://referenceworks.brillonline.com/entries/encyclopaedia-of-islam-2/nawruz-COM_0858.

Li, Yuhui. 2009. "Notes on the Chinese Government's Handling of the Urumqi Riot in Xinjiang." *China and Eurasia Forum Quarterly* 7, no. 4: 11–15.

Liu, Morgan Y. 2002. *Recognizing the Khan: Authority, Space, and Political Imagination among Uzbek Men in Post-Soviet Osh, Kyrgyzstan*. PhD diss., University of Michigan–Ann Arbor.

Liu, Morgan Y. 2006. "Post-Soviet Paternalism and Personhood: Why Culture Matters to Democratization in Central Asia." In *Prospects for Democracy in Central Asia*, 225–38. Edited by Birgit N. Schlyter. Istanbul: Swedish Research Institute in Istanbul.

Liu, Morgan Y. 2011. "Central Asia in the Post–Cold War World." *Annual Review of Anthropology* 40: 115–31.

Liu, Morgan Y. 2012. *Under Solomon's Throne: Uzbek Visions of Renewal in Osh*. Pittsburgh: University of Pittsburgh Press.

Liu, Morgan Y. 2014. "Massacre Through a Kaleidoscope: Fragmented Moral Imaginaries of the State in Central Asia." In *Ethnographies of the State in Central Asia: Performing Politics*, 261–84. Edited by Madeleine Reeves, Johan Rasanayagam, and Judith Beyer. Bloomington: Indiana University Press.

Louw, Marie Elisabeth. 2007. *Everyday Islam in Post-Soviet Central Asia.* London: Routledge.

Loy, Thomas. 2005a. *Jaghnob 1970: Erinnerungen an eine Zwangsumsiedlung in der Tadschikischen SSR.* Wiesbaden: Reichert.

Loy, Thomas. 2005b. "From the Mountains to the Lowlands: The Soviet Policy of 'Inner-Tajik' Resettlement." *TRANS. Internet-Zeitschrift für Kulturwissenschaften* 16. Accessed May 18, 2016. http://www.inst.at /trans/16Nr/13_2/loy16.htm.

Luehrmann, Sonja. 2011. *Secularism Soviet Style: Teaching Atheism and Religion in a Volga Republic.* Bloomington and Indianapolis: Indiana University Press.

Luknizki, Pawel. 1972. "Die Basmatschenherrschaft geht zu Ende." In *Wer zählt die Völker . . .* , 84–103. No editor. Leipzig: Brockhaus.

Maanaev, E., and V. Ploskikh. 1983. *Na "kryshe mira": Istoricheskie ocherki o pamiro-alaiskikh kirgizakh.* Frunze: Mektep.

Mahmood, Saba. 2005. *Politics of Piety: The Islamic Revival and the Feminist Subject.* Princeton: Princeton University Press.

Mametbakiev, A., and D. Abdylda uulu. 2004. *Islam ibadattary.* Bishkek: n.p.

Manetta, Emily. 2011. "Journey into Paradise: Tajik Representations of Afghan Badakhshan." *Central Asian Survey* 30, nos. 3–4: 371–87.

Marsden, Magnus. 2005. *Living Islam: Muslim Religious Experience in Pakistan's North-West Frontier.* Cambridge: Cambridge University Press.

Marsden, Magnus. 2012. "Southwest and Central Asia: Comparison, Integration or Beyond?" In Vol. 1, *The Sage Handbook of Social Anthropology*, 340–65. Edited by Richard Fardon et al. London: Sage.

Marsden, Magnus. 2016. *Trading Worlds: Afghan Merchants Across Modern Frontiers.* Oxford: Oxford University Press.

Masquelier, Adeline. 1992. "Encounter with a Road Siren: Machines, Bodies and Commodities in the Imagination of a Mawri Healer." *Visual Anthropology Review* 8, no. 1: 56–69.

Masquelier, Adeline. 2002. "Road Mythographies: Space, Mobility, and the Historical Imagination in Postcolonial Niger." *American Ethnologist* 29, no. 4: 829–56.

Massey, Doreen. 2005. *For Space*. London: Sage.

Masud, Muhammad K., ed. 2000a. *Travellers in Faith: Studies of the Tablīghī Jamāʿat as a Transnational Islamic Movement for Faith Renewal*. Leiden: Brill.

Masud, Muhammad K. 2000b. "Ideology and Legitimacy." In *Travellers in Faith: Studies of the Tablīghī Jamāʿat as a Transnational Islamic Movement for Faith Renewal*, 79–118. Edited by Muhammad K. Masud. Leiden: Brill.

McBrien, Julie. 2008. *Fruit of Devotion: Islam and Modernity in Kyrgyzstan*. PhD diss., Martin-Luther-Universität.

McBrien, Julie. 2009. "Mukadas's Struggle: Veils and Modernity in Kyrgyzstan." *Journal of the Royal Anthropological Institute*: 127–44.

McBrien, Julie. 2012. "Watching Clone: Brazilian Soap Operas and Muslimness in Kyrgyzstan." *Material Religion* 8, no. 3: 374–96.

McBrien, Julie. 2013. "Afterword: In the Aftermath of Doubt." In *Ethnographies of Doubt: Faith and Uncertainty in Contemporary Societies*, 251–68. Edited by Mathijs Pelkmans. London and New York: I. B. Tauris.

McGee, Terry. 2002. "Jalan, Jalan: Invading, Destroying and Reconstructing the Southeast Asian City." *Bijdragen tot de Taal-, Land- en Volkenkunde (On the Road: The Social Impact of New Roads in Southeast Asia)* 158, no. 4: 637–52.

Megoran, Nick. 2013. "Shared Space, Divided Space: Narrating Ethnic Histories of Osh." *Environment and Planning A* 45: 892–907.

Mel'nikova, N. V. 2006. *Fenomen zakrytogo atomnogo goroda*. Ekaterinburg: Bank kul'turnoi informatsii.

Menga, Filippo. 2015. "Building a Nation Through a Dam: The Case of Rogun in Tajikistan." *Nationalities Papers* 43, no.3: 479–94.

Meri, J. W., W. Ende, Nelly van Dorn-Harder, Houari Touati, Abdulaziz Sachedina, Th. Zarcone, M. Gaborieau, R. Seesemann, and S. Reese. 2012. "Ziyāra." *Encyclopaedia of Islam*, 2nd ed. Accessed April 18, 2016. http://referenceworks.brillonline.com/entries/encyclopaedia -of-islam-2/ziyara-COM_1390.

Metcalf, Barbara. 1993. "Living Hadith in the Tablighi Jama'at." *Journal of Asian Studies* 52, no. 3: 584–608.

Metcalf, Barbara. 2002. *Islamic Revival in British India: Deoband, 1860–1900*. Oxford: Oxford University Press.

Michaud, Jean. 2010. "Editorial: Zomia and Beyond." *Journal of Global History* 5, no. 2: 187–214.

Middleton, Robert. 2016. "History of the Development of the Pamir Region of Tajikistan (Gorno-Badakhshan)." In *Mapping Transition in the Pamirs: Changing Human-Environmental Landscapes*, 245–65. Edited by Hermann Kreutzmann and Teiji Watanabe. Dordrecht: Springer.

Middleton, Robert, and Thomas Huw. 2012. *Tajikistan and the High Pamirs*. Hong Kong: Odyssey Books.

Millward, James A. 2009. "Introduction: Does the 2009 Urumchi Violence Mark a Turning Point?" *Central Asian Survey* 28, no. 4: 347–60.

Mitchell, Timothy, ed. 2000. *Questions of Modernity*. Minneapolis: University of Minnesota Press.

Mitchell, Timothy. 2002. *Rule of Experts: Egypt, Techno-Politics, Modernity*. Berkeley: University of California Press.

Mitsubishi. 2011. *Pajero*. Japan: Mitsubishi.

Montgomery, David. 2007. *The Transmission of Religious and Cultural Knowledge and Potentiality in Practice: An Anthropology of Social Navigation in the Kyrgyz Republic*. PhD diss., Boston University.

Montgomery, David. 2016. *Practising Islam: Knowledge, Experience, and Social Navigation in Kyrgyzstan*. Pittsburgh: University of Pittsburgh Press.

Moore, Donald S. 2005. *Suffering for Territory: Race, Place, and Power in Zimbabwe*. Durham: Duke University Press.

Mostowlansky, Till. 2007. *Islam und Kirgisen on Tour: Die Rezeption "nomadischer Religion" und ihre Wirkung*. Wiesbaden: Harrassowitz.

Mostowlansky, Till. 2011a. "Kyrgyz—Muslim—Central Asian? Recent Approaches to the Study of Kyrgyz Culture in Kyrgyzstan." In *The Heritage of Soviet Oriental Studies*, 291–305. Edited by Michael Kemper and Stephan Conermann. London: Routledge.

Mostowlansky, Till. 2011b. "Paving the Way: Isma'ili Genealogy and Mobility along Tajikistan's Pamir Highway." *Journal of Persianate Studies* 4: 171–88.

Mostowlansky, Till. 2012. "Making Kyrgyz Spaces: Local History as Spatial Practice in Murghab (Tajikistan)." *Central Asian Survey* 31, no. 3: 251–64.

Mostowlansky, Till. 2013. "'The State Starts from the Family': Peace and Harmony in Tajikistan's Eastern Pamirs." *Central Asian Survey* 32, no. 4: 462–74.

Mostowlansky, Till. 2014. "Where Empires Meet: Orientalism and Marginality at the Former Russo-British Frontier." *Études de lettres* 2–3: 179–96.

Mostowlansky, Till. 2017. "Building Bridges Across the Oxus: Language, Development, and Globalization at the Tajik-Afghan Frontier." *International Journal of the Sociology of Language* 247.

Munn, Nancy D. 1992. "The Cultural Anthropology of Time: A Critical Essay." *Annual Review of Anthropology* 21: 93–123.

Murghab. 2009. "O Programme Respubliki Tajikistan po bor'be s terrorizmom i drugimi ekstremistskimi nasiliiami na 2006–2010 godakh." Unpublished government report.

Nabijan uulu, N. 2008. *Adal soodanyn syrlary.* Karabalta: Karabalta Islam institutu.

Nader, Laura. 1990. *Harmony Ideology: Justice and Control in a Zapotec Mountain Village.* Stanford: Stanford University Press.

Nadjmabadi, Afsaneh. 1997. "The Erotic Vatan [Homeland] as Beloved and Mother: To Love, to Possess, and to Protect." *Comparative Studies in Society and History* 39, no. 3: 442–67.

Nadkarni, Maya, and Olga Shevchenko. 2004. "The Politics of Nostalgia: A Case for Comparative Analysis of Post-Socialist Practices." *Ab Imperio* 2: 487–519.

Nasritdinov, Emil. 2012. "Spiritual Nomadism and Central Asian Tablighi Travelers." *Ab Imperio* 2: 145–67.

Nasritdinov, Emil, and Kevin O'Connor. 2010. *Regional Change in Kyrgyzstan: Bazaars, Cross-Border Trade and Social Networks.* Saarbrücken: Lambert Academic.

Nauka i fakty. 2004. *Nauka i fakty svidetel'stvuiut: "Net boga krome Allakha i Mukhammad—Ego poslannik."* Bishkek: n.p.

Naumkin, Vitaly V. 2005. *Radical Islam in Central Asia: Between Pen and Rifle.* Lanham: Rowman & Littlefield.

Navaro-Yashin, Yael. 2002. *Faces of the State: Secularism and Public Life in Turkey.* Princeton: Princeton University Press.

Nazrulloev, Sadullo. 1979. *Dorozhnoe stroitel'stvo i razvitie transporta v Tadzhikistane v 1917–1941 gg.* Dushanbe: Donish.

Noor, Farish A. 2007. "Pathans to the East! The Development of the Tablighi Jama'at Movement in Northern Malaysia and Southern Thailand." *Comparative Studies of South Asia, Africa and the Middle East* 27, no. 1: 7–25.

Nourzhanov, Kirill. 2015. "Bandits, Warlords, National Heroes: Interpretations of the Basmachi Movement in Tajikistan." *Central Asian Survey* 34, no. 2: 177–89.

Nourzhanov, Kirill, and Christian Bleuer. 2013. *Tajikistan: A Social and Political History.* Canberra: ANU E Press.

Nozimova, Shahnoza, and Tim Epkenhans. 2013. "Negotiating Islam in Emerging Public Spheres in Contemporary Tajikistan." *Asiatische Studien* 67, no. 3: 665–90.

O'Hanlon, Michael, and Linda Frankland. 2003. "Co-Present Landscapes: Routes and Rootedness as Sources of Identity in Highlands New Guinea." In *Landscape, Memory and History: Anthropological Perspectives*, 166–88. Edited by Pamela J. Stewart and Andrew Strathern. London: Pluto.

Olimova, Saodat, and Farkhod Tolipov. 2011. *Islamic Revival in Central Asia: The Cases of Uzbekistan and Tajikistan*. Barcelona: CIDOB.

Olson, James S. 1998. *An Ethnohistorical Dictionary of China*. Westport: Greenwood Press.

Organization for Security and Co-operation in Europe Office for Democratic Institutions and Human Rights. 2008. "Comments on the Draft Law of the Republic of Tajikistan 'The Law of the Republic of Tajikistan About Freedom of Conscience and Religious Unions' REL-TAJ/100/2008." Legislationonline. Accessed 18 May 2016. http://www.legislationline.org/download/action/download/id/2275/file/100_REL_TAJ_100_2008.pdf.

Ostergaard, Kate. 2012. "Applying Practice-Oriented Approaches to Islamic Purification and Prayer." In *Understanding Religious Ritual: Theoretical Approaches and Innovations*, 136–53. Edited by John P. Hoffmann. London and New York: Routledge.

Owen Hughes, Diane. 1995. "Introduction." In *Time: Histories and Ethnologies*, 1–18. Edited by Diane Owen Hughes and Thomas R. Trautmann. Ann Arbor: University of Michigan Press.

"Pamir High Mountain Integrated Project." 2014. SDC. Accessed 5 March 2014. http://www.swiss-cooperation.admin.ch/centralasia/en/Home/Activities_in_Tajikistan/COMPLETED_PROJECTS/Pamir_High_Mountain_Integrated_Project.

Pannier, Bruce. 2011. "Tajikistan Agrees to Allow Chinese Farmers to Till Land." *Radio Free Europe/Radio Liberty*. Accessed May 18, 2016. http://www.rferl.org/content/tajikistan_china/2289623.html.

Pantucci, Raffaello, Sarah Lain, and Sue Anne Tay. 2016. China in Central Asia. Accessed 11 April 2016. http://chinaincentralasia.com.

Parshin, Konstantin. 2012. "Tajikistan: Dushanbe Building Boom Blocks Out Economic Concerns." *Eurasianet*. Accessed 18 May 2016. http://www.eurasianet.org/node/65340.

Pedersen, Axel Morton, and Mikkel Bunkenborg. 2012. "Roads That Separate: Sino-Mongolian Relations in the Inner Asian Desert." *Mobilities* 7, no. 4: 555–69.

Pelkmans, Mathijs. 2007. "'Culture' as a Tool and an Obstacle: Missionary Encounters in Post-Soviet Kyrgyzstan." *Journal of the Royal Anthropological Institute* 13: 881–99.

Pelkmans, Mathijs. 2009. "Introduction: Post-Soviet Space and the Unexpected Turns of Religious Life." In *Conversion after Socialism: Disruptions, Modernisms and Technologies of Faith in the Former Soviet Union*, 1–16. Edited by Mathijs Pelkmans. Oxford: Berghahn.

Pelkmans, Mathijs. 2013. "Outline for an Ethnography of Doubt." In *Ethnographies of Doubt: Faith and Uncertainty in Contemporary Societies*, 1–42. Edited by Mathijs Pelkmans. London and New York: I. B. Tauris.

Pelkmans, Mathijs, and Julie McBrien. 2008. "Turning Marx on His Head: Missionaries, 'Extremists' and Archaic Secularists in Post-Soviet Kyrgyzstan." *Critique of Anthropology* 28, no. 1: 87–103.

Peyrouse, Sébastien. 2011. "Tajikistan's New Trade: Cross-Border Commerce and the China-Afghanistan Link." *Ponars Eurasia Policy Memo No. 169*. George Washington University. Accessed 18 May 2016. http://www.gwu.edu/~ieresgwu/assets/docs/ponars/pepm_169.pdf.

Pickering, Michael, and Emily Keightley. 2006. "The Modalities of Nostalgia." *Current Sociology* 54, no. 6: 919–41.

Pina-Cabral, João de. 1987. "Paved Roads and Enchanted Mooresses: The Perception of the Past among the Peasant Population of the Alto Minho." *Man* 22, no. 4: 715–35.

Piot, Charles. 2010. *Nostalgia for the Future: West Africa After the Cold War*. Chicago and London: University of Chicago Press.

Pirumshoev, K. H. P., and S. H. P. Iusufbekov. 2005. *Istoriia Gorno-Badakhshanskoi avtonomnoi oblasti: Noveishaia istoriia*. Dushanbe: Paivand.

Polese, Abel, and Slavomir Horak. 2015. "A Tale of Two Presidents: Personality Cult and Symbolic Nation-Building in Turkmenistan." *Nationalities Papers* 43, no. 3: 457–78.

Poliakov, Sergei. 1992. *Everyday Islam: Religion and Tradition in Rural Central Asia*. Armonk: M. E. Sharpe.

Popov, T. T. 1935. "Istoriia stroiki." In *Sbornik statei o stroitel'stve Pamirskogo i Velikogo Kirgizkogo traktov*, 17–35. Edited by M. M. Slavinskii. Frunze: Kirgosizdat.

Prezident. 2008. "Sukhanronī dar muloqot bo sokinoni viloyati Badakhshon hangomi kushodashavii varzishgohi markazii sh. Khorugh." Prezident.tj. Accessed 8 April 2016. http://www.prezident.tj /node/3086.

Prezident. 2012. "Sukhanronī hangomi muloqot bo sokinoni Viloyati Kūhistoni Badakhshon." Prezident.tj. Accessed 8 April 2016. http:// www.prezident.tj/node/3446.

Rafiyeva, Mavlouda. 2015. "Resident of Sughd Jailed for Propagation of Jamaat-ut Tabligh Ideas." *Asia Plus.* Accessed 1 April 2016. http://www .news.tj/en/news/resident-sughd-jailed-propagation-jamaat-ut-ta bligh-ideas.

Randeria, Shalini. 1999. "Jenseits von Soziologie und soziokultureller Anthropologie: Zur Verortung der nichtwestlichen Welt in einer zukünftigen Sozialtheorie." *Soziale Welt* 50, no. 4: 373–82.

Randeria, Shalini, Martin Fuchs, and Antje Linkenbach. 2004. *Konfigurationen der Moderne: Zur Einleitung.* In *Konfigurationen der Moderne: Diskurse zu Indien,* 9–34. Edited by Shalini Randeria, Martin Fuchs, and Antje Linkenbach. Baden-Baden: Nomos.

Rasanayagam, Johan. 2006a. "I'm not a Wahhabi: State Power and Muslim Orthodoxy in Uzbekistan." In *The Postsocialist Religious Question: Faith and Power in Central Asia and East-Central Europe,* 99–124. Edited by Chris Hann. Munich: Lit Verlag.

Rasanayagam, Johan. 2006b. "Introduction." *Central Asian Survey* 25, no. 3: 219–33.

Rasanayagam, Johan. 2011. *Islam in Post-Soviet Uzbekistan: The Morality of Experience.* Cambridge: Cambridge University Press.

Rasanayagam, Johan, Judith Beyer, and Madeleine Reeves. 2014. "Introduction: Performances, Possibilities, and Practices of the Political in Central Asia." In *Ethnographies of the State in Central Asia: Performing Politics,* 1–26. Edited by Madeleine Reeves, Johan Rasanayagam, and Judith Beyer. Bloomington and Indianapolis: Indiana University Press.

"Ravshan i Dzhamshut idut na pensiu: 'Nasha Russia' meniaet repertuar." 2010. *IA Regnum.* Accessed 18 May 2016. http://www.centrasia.ru /newsA.php?st=1280836440.

Reeves, Madeleine. 2005. "Locating Danger: *Konfliktologiia* and the Search for Fixity in the Ferghana Valley Borderlands." *Central Asian Survey* 24, no. 1: 67–81.

Reeves, Madeleine. 2010a. "The Ethnicisation of Violence in Southern Kyrgyzstan." *OD Russia (Post Soviet World).* Accessed 18 May 2016.

http://www.opendemocracy.net/od-russia/madeleine-reeves/ethnici
sation-of-violence-in-southern-kyrgyzstan-0.

Reeves, Madeleine. 2010b. "A Weekend in Osh." *London Review of Books.* Accessed 18 May 2016. http://www.lrb.co.uk/v32/n13/madeleine -reeves/a-weekend-in-osh.

Reeves, Madeleine. 2011a. "Introduction: Contested Trajectories and a Dynamic Approach to Place." *Central Asian Survey* 30, nos. 3–4: 307–30.

Reeves, Madeleine. 2011b. "Staying Put? Towards a Relational Politics of Mobility at a Time of Migration." *Central Asian Survey* 30, nos. 3–4: 555–76.

Reeves, Madeleine. 2013. "Clean Fake: Authenticating Documents and Persons in Migrant Moscow." *American Ethnologist* 40, no. 3: 508–24.

Reeves, Madeleine. 2014a. "'We're with the people!' Place, Nation, and Political Community in Kyrgyzstan's 2010 'April Events.'" *Anthropology of East Europe Review* 32, no. 2: 68–88.

Reeves, Madeleine. 2014b. "Roads of Hope and Dislocation: Infrastructure and the Remaking of Territory at a Central Asian Border." *Ab Imperio* 2: 235–57.

Reeves, Madeleine. 2014c. *Border Work: Spatial Lives of the State in Rural Central Asia.* Ithaca: Cornell University Press.

Reeves, Madeleine. 2016. "Infrastructural Hope: Anticipating 'Independent Roads' and Territorial Integrity in Southern Kyrgyzstan." *Ethnos.* DOI: 10.1080/00141844.2015.1119176.

Reid, Patryk. 2017. "'Tajikistan's Turksib': Infrastructure and Improvisation in Economic Growth of the Vakhsh River Valley." *Central Asian Survey* 36, no. 1: 19–36.

Remtilla, Aliaa. 2011. "Potentially an 'Art Object': Tajik Isma'ilis' *Bāteni* and *Zāheri* Engagement with Their Imam's Image." *Journal of Persianate Studies* 4, no. 2: 189–207.

Remtilla, Aliaa. 2012. *Re-Producing Social Relations: Political and Economic Change and Islam in Post-Soviet Tajik Ishkashim.* PhD diss., University of Manchester.

Ricci, Aldo. 1931. *The Travels of Marco Polo.* Translated into English from the text of L. F. Benedetto in 2001. New Delhi: Asian Educational Services.

Rickmer Rickmers, Willi. 1930. *Alai! Alai! Arbeiten und Erlebnisse der deutsch-russischen Alai-Pamir-Expedition.* Leipzig: Brockhaus.

Rippa, Alessandro. 2015. *Across the Khunjerab Pass: A Rhizomatic Ethnography Along the Karakoram Highway, Between Xinjiang (China) and Pakistan.* PhD diss., University of Aberdeen.

Roche, Sophie. 2013. "Continuities and Disruption in Islamic Practice: Biographies of *Shogirds* from Tajikistan." *Anthropology of the Contemporary Middle East and Central Asia* 1, no. 1: 23–53.

Roche, Sophie, and John Heathershaw. 2011. "A Recipe for Radicalisation: The Campaign against Islam in Tajikistan." *Open Democracy*. Accessed 18 May 2016. http://www.opendemocracy.ne t/od-russia/sophie-roche-john-heathershaw/recipe-for-radicalisa tion-campaign-against-islam-in-tajikist.

Roche, Sophie, and Sophie Hohmann. 2011. "Wedding Rituals and the Struggle over National Identities." *Central Asian Survey* 30, no. 1: 113–28.

Rofel, Lisa B. 1994. "'Yearnings': Televisual Love and Melodramatic Politics in Contemporary China." *American Ethnologist* 21, no. 4: 700–722.

Roseman, Sharon R. 1996. "'How We Built the Road': The Politics of Memory in Rural Galicia." *American Ethnologist* 23, no. 4: 836–60.

Rowe, William C. 2010. "The Wakhan Corridor: Endgame of the Great Game." In *Borderlines and Borderlands: Political Oddities at the Edge of the Nation-State*, 53–68. Edited by Alexander C. Diener and Joshua Hagen. Lanham: Rowman & Littlefield.

Ruthven, Malise. 2011. "The Aga Khan Development Network and Institutions." In *A Modern History of the Ismailis: Continuity and Change in a Muslim Community*, 189–220. Edited by Farhad Daftary. London and New York: I. B. Tauris.

Ryono, Angel, and Matthew Galway. 2015. "Xinjiang under China: Reflections on the Multiple Dimensions of the 2009 Urumqi Uprising." *Asian Ethnicity* 16, no. 2: 235–55.

Sahadeo, Jeff. 2012. "Soviet 'Blacks' and Place Making in Leningrad and Moscow." *Slavic Review* 71, no. 2: 331–58.

Said, Edward W. 1979. *Orientalism*. New York: Vintage.

Saparbaev, A., and K. Temirkulov. 2003. *Pamir kyrgyzdary*. Osh: printed by author.

Savvaitova, Ksenia, and Tomi Petr. 1999. "Fish and Fisheries in Lake Issyk-Kul (Tien Shan), River Chu and Pamir Lakes." In *Fish and Fisheries at Higher Altitudes: Asia*, 168–86. Edited by Tomi Petr. Rome: FAO.

Saxer, Martin. 2016. "Pathways: A Concept, Field Site, and Methodological Approach to Study Remoteness and Connectivity." *Himalaya* 36, no. 2: 104–19.

Schelkle, Waltraud, ed. 2000. *Paradigms of Social Change: Modernization, Development, Transformation, Evolution*. Frankfurt am Main: Campus Verlag.

Schoeberlein, John S. 2000. "Shifting Ground: How the Soviet Regime Used Resettlement to Transform Central Asian Society and the Consequences of This Policy Today." *JCAS Symposium Series* 9: 41–64.

Scott, James C. 1990. *Domination and the Art of Resistance: Hidden Transcripts*. New Haven: Yale University Press.

Scott, James C. 1998. *Seeing Like a State: How Certain Schemes to Improve the Human Condition Have Failed*. New Haven: Yale University Press.

Scott, James C. 2009. *The Art of Not Being Governed: An Anarchist History of Upland Southeast Asia*. Stanford: Stanford University Press.

Shahrani, Nazif M. 2002. *The Kirghiz and Wakhi of Afghanistan: Adaptation to Closed Frontiers and War*. Washington: University of Washington Press.

Shaw, Charles. 2011. "Friendship Under Lock and Key: The Soviet Central Asian Border, 1918–34." *Central Asian Survey* 30, nos. 3–4: 331–48.

Sidaway, James D. 2013. "Geography, Globalization, and the Problematic of Area Studies." *Annals of the Association of American Geographers* 103, no. 4: 984–1002.

Siegelbaum, Lewis H. 2008a. *Cars for Comrades: The Life of the Soviet Automobile*. Ithaca: Cornell University Press.

Siegelbaum, Lewis H. 2008b. "Roadlessness and the 'Path to Communism': Building Roads and Highways in Stalinist Russia." *Journal of Transport History* 29: 277–94.

Siegelbaum, Lewis, and Leslie Page Moch. 2014. *Broad Is My Native Land: Repertoires and Regimes of Migration in Russia's Twentieth Century*. Ithaca: Cornell University Press.

Slavinskii, M. M., ed. 1935. *Sbornik statei o stroitel'stve Pamirskogo i Velikogo Kirgizkogo traktov*. Frunze: Kirgosizdat.

Smith, Virginia. 2007. *Clean: A History of Personal Hygiene and Purity*. Oxford: Oxford University Press.

Snead, James E., Clark L. Erickson, and J. Andrew Darling. 2009. *Landscapes of Movement: Trails, Paths, and Roads in Anthropological Perspective*. Philadelphia: University of Pennsylvania Press.

Sneath, David. 2009. "Reading the Signs by Lenin's Light: Development, Divination and Metonymic Fields in Mongolia." *Ethnos* 74, no. 1: 72–90.

Sökefeld, Martin. 1999. "Debating Self, Identity, and Culture in Anthropology." *Current Anthropology* 40, no. 4: 417–47.

Sökefeld, Martin. 2001. "Reconsidering Identity." *Anthropos* 96: 527–44.

Sökefeld, Martin. 2010. "Selves and Others: Representing Multiplicities of Difference in Gilgit and the Northern Areas of Pakistan." In *Islam and*

Society in Pakistan: Anthropological Perspectives, 235–58. Edited by Magnus Marsden. Oxford: Oxford University Press.

Spector, Regine Amy. 2009. *Protecting Property: The Politics of Bazaars in Kyrgyzstan*. PhD diss., University of California, Berkeley.

Spitulnik, Debra A. 2002. "Accessing 'Local' Modernities: Reflections on the Place of Linguistic Evidence in Ethnography." In *Critically Modern: Alternatives, Alterities, Anthropologies*, 194–219. Edited by Bruce M. Knauft. Bloomington: Indiana University Press.

Ssorin-Chaikov, Nikolai V. 2003. *The Social Life of the State in Subarctic Siberia*. Stanford: Stanford University Press.

Starks, Tricia. 2008. *The Body Soviet: Propaganda, Hygiene, and the Revolutionary State*. Madison: University of Wisconsin Press.

Steinberg, Jonah. 2006. *The Anatomy of the Transnation: The Globalization of the Isma'ili Muslim Community*. PhD diss., University of Pennsylvania.

Steinberg, Jonah. 2011. *Isma'ili Modern: Globalization and Identity in a Muslim Community*. Chapel Hill: North Carolina Press.

Stephan, Manja. 2010a. *Das Bedürfnis nach Ausgewogenheit: Moralerziehung, Islam und Muslimsein in Tadschikistan zwischen Säkularisierung und religiöser Rückbesinnung*. Würzburg: Ergon.

Stephan, Manja. 2010b. "Education, Youth and Islam: The Growing Popularity of Private Religious Lessons in Dushanbe, Tajikistan." *Central Asian Survey* 29, no. 4: 469–83.

Stephan, Manja, and Abdullah Mirzoev. 2016. "The Manufacturing of Islamic Lifestyles in Tajikistan through the Prism of Dushanbe's Bazaars." *Central Asian Survey* 35, no. 2: 157–77.

Straub, David. 2013. *The Ismailis and Kirghiz of the Upper Amu Darya and Pamirs in Afghanistan: A Micro-History of Delineating Onternational Borders*. Master's thesis, Indiana University.

Straub, David. 2014. "Deconstructing Communal Violence During the Civil War in Tajikistan: The Case of the Pamiris." In *Social and Cultural Change in Central Asia: The Soviet Legacy*, 174–87. Edited by Sevket Akyildiz and Richard Carlson. London and New York: Routledge.

Street, Alice. 2012. "Affective Infrastructure: Hospital Landscapes of Hope and Failure." *Space and Culture* 15, no. 1: 44–56.

Suyarkulova, Mohira. 2014. "Between National Idea and International Conflict: The Roghun HHP as an Anti-Colonial Endeavor, Body of the Nation, and National Wealth." *Water History* 6: 367–83.

Swerdlow, Steve. 2016. "Tajikistan's Fight Against Political Islam: How Fears of Terrorism Stifle Free Speech." *Foreign Affairs*. Accessed 1 April 2016. https://www.foreignaffairs.com/articles/tajikistan/2016–03–14/tajikistans-fight-against-political-islam.

Taarnby, Michael. 2012. *Islamist Radicalization in Tajikistan: An Assessment of Current Trends*. Dushanbe: Korshinos.

Tadzhidinov, S., and S. Parmanov. 2007. *Legendy Sarykola*. Murgab: Kagaz Resurstary.

Taipov, Bekjol. 2002. *Sary Kol tarykhynyn kyskacha ocherkteri*. Murgab: printed by author.

Tajddin Sadik Ali, Mumtaz Ali. 2016. "Voyage of Pir Sabzali in Central Asia." *Ismaili.net*. Accessed 5 April 2016. http://www.ismaili.net/heritage/node/1627.

Therborn, Göran. 2003. "Entangled Modernities." *European Journal of Social Theory* 6, no. 3: 293–305.

Thibault, Hélène. 2014. *Religious Revival in Tajikistan: The Soviet Legacy Revisited*. PhD diss., University of Ottawa.

Thomas, Philip. 2002. "The River, the Road, and the Rural-Urban Divide: A Postcolonial Moral Geography from Southeast Madagascar." *American Ethnologist* 29, no. 2: 366–91.

Thompson, Chad D. 2008. *Epistemologies of Independence: Technology and Empire in the Post-Soviet Borderlands*. PhD diss., York University.

Thompson, Chad D., and John Heathershaw. 2005. "Introduction: Discourses of Danger in Central Asia." *Central Asian Survey* 24, no. 1: 1–4.

Tillett, Lowell R. 1968. *The Great Friendship: Soviet Historians on the Non-Russian Nationalities*. Chapel Hill: University of North Carolina Press.

Todorova, Maria, and Zsuzsa Gille, eds. 2010. *Post-Communist Nostalgia*. New York: Berghahn.

"Tojikon Galustianro ta'qib mekunand." 2009. *Minbari khalk*. December 17, 4.

Tokhiri, Tamaris. 2009. "Tajikistan Convicts Five Tablighi Activists." *Central Asia Online*. Accessed 5 March 2014. http://centralasiaonline.com/en_GB/articles/caii/features/2009/08/19/feature-08.

Toktogulova, Mukaram. 2007. "Le rôle de la *da'wa* dans la réislamisation au Kirghizistan." *Cahiers d'Asie Centrale* 15–16: 83–102.

Tolstikov, V. C. 2012. "Sotsiokul'turnaia sreda zakrytykh gorodov Urala." *Vestnik IuUrGU* 10, no. 269: 119–23.

Townsend, Jacob. 2006. "The Logistics of Opiate Trafficking in Tajikistan, Kyrgyzstan and Kazakhstan." *China and Eurasia Forum Quarterly* 4, no. 1: 69–91.

Tsentraziia. 2010. "Dvizhenie 'Tadzhikskie trudovye migranty' trebuet zapret 'Nashu Rashu' (obrashchenie)." Accessed 5 March 2014. http://www.centrasia.ru/newsA.php?st=1266149520.

Tsing, Anna Lowenhaupt. 1993. *In the Realm of the Diamond Queen: Marginality in an Out-of-the-Way Place.* Princeton: Princeton University Press.

Tsing, Anna Lowenhaupt. 1994. "From the Margins." *Cultural Anthropology* 9, no. 3: 279–97.

Tsing, Anna Lowenhaupt. 2000. "The Global Situation." *Cultural Anthropology* 15, no. 3: 327–60.

Tsing, Anna Lowenhaupt. 2005. *Friction: An Ethnography of Global Connection.* Princeton: Princeton University Press.

United States Commission on International Religious Freedom. 2011. *Annual Report 2011.* Washington. Accessed 18 May 2016. http://www.uscirf.gov/sites/default/files/resources/book%20with%20cover%20for%20web.pdf.

U.S. Embassy cable. 2008. "Tajikistan's Hasan Asadullozoda: Man, Myth, Legend." WikiLeaks. Accessed 14 April 2016. https://wikileaks.org/plusd/cables/08DUSHANBE829_a.html.

U.S. Embassy cable. 2009. "Chinese Interest in Tajikistan Increases." WikiLeaks. Accessed 14 April 2016. https://wikileaks.org/plusd/cables/09DUSHANBE954_a.html.

Van Beek, Martijn. 2000. "Dissimulations: Representing Ladakhi Identity." In *Perplexities of Identification: Anthropological Studies in Cultural Differentiation and the Use of Resources,* 164–88. Edited by Henk Driessen and Ton Otto. Aarhus: Aarhus University Press.

Van der Heide, Nienke. 2015. *Spirited Performance: The Manas Epic and Society in Kyrgyzstan.* Bremen: EHV Academicpress.

Van der Veer, Peter. 2001. *Imperial Encounters: Religion, Nation, and Empire.* Princeton: Princeton University Press.

Van der Veer, Peter. 2013. *The Modern Spirit of Asia: The Spiritual and the Secular in China and India.* Princeton: Princeton University Press.

Van Grondelle, Marc. 2009. *The Ismailis in the Colonial Era: Modernity, Empire and Islam.* London: Hurst.

Van Schendel, Willem. 2002. "Geographies of Knowing, Geographies of Ignorance: Jumping Scale in Southeast Asia." *Environment and Planning D: Society and Space* 20: 647–68.

Van Schendel, Willem, and Itty Abraham, eds. 2005. *Illicit Flows and Criminal Things: States, Borders, and the Other Side of Globalization.* Bloomington: Indiana University Press.

Vanselow, Kim A. 2011. *The High-Mountain Pastures of the Eastern Pamirs (Tajikistan): An Evaluation of the Ecological Basis and the Pasture Potential.* PhD diss., Friedrich-Alexander Universität.

Verdery, Katherine. 1996. *What Was Socialism and What Comes Next?* Princeton: Princeton University Press.

Weber, Eugen. 1976. *Peasants into Frenchmen: The Modernization of Rural France, 1870–1914.* Stanford: Stanford University Press.

Werner, Cynthia. 2004. "Feminizing the New Silk Road: Women Traders in Rural Kazakhstan." In *Post-Soviet Women Encountering Transition: Nation-Building, Economic Survival, and Civic Activism*, 105–26. Edited by Carol Nechemias and Kathleen Kuehnast. Baltimore: Johns Hopkins University Press.

Widdis, Emma. 2003. *Visions of a New Land: Soviet Film from the Revolution to the Second World War.* New Haven: Yale University Press.

Winkelmann, Mareike Jule. 2005. *"From Behind the Curtain": A Study of a Girls' Madrasa in India.* Amsterdam: Amsterdam University Press.

Wooden, Amanda E., and Christoph E. Stefes, eds. 2009. *The Politics of Transition in Central Asia and the Caucasus: Enduring Legacies and Emerging Challenges.* London and New York: Routledge.

World Bank. 2007. *Cross-Border Trade Within the Central Asia Regional Economic Cooperation.* Accessed 18 May 2016. http://www.carecprogram.org/uploads/docs/Cross-Border-Trade-CAREC.pdf.

Yountchi, Lisa. 2011. "The Politics of Scholarship and the Scholarship of Politics: Imperial, Soviet, and Post-Soviet Scholars Studying Tajikistan." In *The Heritage of Soviet Oriental Studies*, 217–40. Edited by Michael Kemper and Stephan Conermann. London: Routledge.

Yurchak, Alexei. 2006. *Everything Was Forever, Until It Was No More: The Last Soviet Generation.* Princeton: Princeton University Press.

Zakariia, S. M. M. 2005–2008. *Fazail A'mal.* Vols. 1–7. Bishkek: n.p.

INDEX

Note: Page references in *italics* refer to figures.